Every description and every action has an emotional heft. I sometimes felt that your personality was supplanting mine, so vivid were your stories.

—Mick Stern, poet, playwright, teacher of film writing
at New York University for twenty years

Tom Bissinger describes the phenomenon of psychic freezes with heart-stopping accuracy. His encounter with a Freudian psychiatrist is funny and too typical. He cuts out on girlfriends and succumbs to an excruciating showdown with his father. Tom's experiences make the use of drugs, openness to gurus, willingness to give up control, understandable. He looks behind masks, tries them on, and gives them up with little regard for his personal safety.

—Patricia Adler,
author of *My Father Who Is Not in Heaven*

To whom much is given much shall be demanded. Tom Bissinger, this tightrope walker of a poet, playwright and storyteller, veteran and survivor of so many "trips" over the abyss, splendidly lives up to this categorical imperative here, with this expertly, courageously articulated autobiography—a truly existential errand of Total Recall.

—Philip Beitchman, PhD,
author of *The Theatre of Naturalism*

The

FUN HOUSE

Memory
Magic
and
Mayhem

*For Ron,
long life! Honey
in the heart!
Enjoy!
Tom
2/20/15*

Tom Bissinger

Library of Congress Control Number: 2013920463
ISBN: Hardcover   978-1-4931-2752-8
       Softcover   978-1-4931-2751-1
       eBook   978-1-4931-2753-5

Rev. date: 12/11/2013

To order additional copies of this book, contact:
Xlibris LLC
1-888-795-4274
www.Xlibris.com
Orders@Xlibris.com
136437

In memory of my father

This is It
And I am It
And You are It
And so is That
And He is It
And She is It
And It is It
And That is That.

O It is This
And It is Thus
And It is Them
And It is Us
And It is Now
And here It is
And here We are
So This Is It.

—James Broughton

Chapter One

Growing up in San Francisco in the 1940s, there was nothing more fun than to celebrate a birthday or a holiday at the Fun House, part of Playland at the Beach, an amusement park featuring arcades, a roller coaster, Ferris wheel, and merry-go-round.

I was lured to the Fun House by Laffing Sal and Blackie the Barber, two six-foot-ten-inch tall mechanical clowns who, from a second-story balcony, jerkily rocked and rotated, their huge heads spewing raucous laughter at me as I approached. Laffing Sal sported a bright-red wig topped by a lady's green porkpie hat; her face was flushed, her cheeks and lips bright red, framing teeth that featured a large gap in the middle. The clowns taunted me, daring me to come inside. I laughed at them but was glad they were too distant to touch me. "Nyah, nyah!" I shouted with bravado, overcoming their mockery, and squeezed between two canvas-clad spin dryers that squished me as noisy bursts of compressed air shot up my butt from the ground below. Having survived, I was permitted to cross the threshold and enter the Fun House.

Inside, I scanned a vast room filled with shrieking children, studied myself in front of mirrors that turned me into a short fatty or a spaghetti-shaped weirdo, and wondered how I would navigate the Barrel of Laughs, a huge rotating, rumbling horizontal barrel. For sure, I'd run up and down its rolling motion, happily falling and sliding. Or would I go first to the Rocking Horses, a moving platform that created a galloping sensation as I ran over it, or the Moving Bridges, connected gangplanks that went up and down and toyed with my balance? I could choose a three-story climb to the top of the "longest, bumpiest indoor slide in the world" and join three other kids seated next to each other in channels, hollering as we raced each other to the bottom on burlap bags. On to the Whip, a whirling disk that would inevitably throw you to the floor as its speed increased. And then do all of it over again and again, filled with the elation at overcoming the precariousness of being a little out of control as well as the giddy pleasure of experiencing that sensation.

One visit I discovered a new excitement: the Roto-Rooter, where kid after kid clambered down into a large vat-like structure about ten feet high and twenty feet wide and stood against its circular walls. The machine slowly started turning, and as it picked up speed, the bottom fell away, and we were pinned to the wall by centrifugal force, gravity defiers, champs of empty space, screaming our heads off!

When I was done with the Fun House, I exited into the bracing air of the Pacific Ocean, fog rolling in, the cries of Laffing Sal floating away. The sea was a vast gray-green landscape surging toward the shore. Tiny dots in the Pacific inched across the horizon, coming into focus as cargo ships bound for the Golden Gate. The sand sparkled with mica, seagulls solemnly stood at attention, drinking in the sun. The ocean breathed, silent after each exhalation before the next surge of water rolled up the shore. Seawater filled my veins, and I wanted to weep with joy.

Looking back, I see that in San Francisco, then and now, one's gaze courts the ocean and sky. In Pennsylvania, my current home, people dig in—their focus, the ground. It's where oil was first discovered, as well as thick deposits of coal and gas. We want to burrow, hydro-frack, and extract. We honor not an eagle or even a turkey, as Ben Franklin suggested, but Punxsutawney Phil, a groundhog.

For now, I'll live earthbound in the East's hardwood forest. I'll watch the sky for hawks and turkey vultures, listen for the cackling of crows. I'll exult in the sight of rabbits and foxes, raccoon and deer. I'll excavate from the soil discarded machinery rubbed raw by the seasons, gather shards of leather harnesses sprouting out of the ground. But I'll always remember the Fun House because it's what I do: I build fun houses.

* * *

My house, the house I grew up in, was a three-story mansion in Pacific Heights, one of the elite neighborhoods of San Francisco. Built in 1936, my house reflected Tudor style, a pleasing design of wooden panels accenting white stucco walls and leaded glass windows. I imagined I was living as a squire's son in an English manor house built in the time of Shakespeare, but now, I think the design was equally influenced by the German burgher style of the 1800s: solid, substantial, prosperous.

The entrance fronted Divisadero Street, just a block south of Broadway, where steep hills plunged to the Marina and you could look out over the Bay to the Golden Gate Bridge and Alcatraz. You entered the house by waiting under an arched portico until the door was opened and you were admitted to the downstairs vestibule. I can hear my father whistling as he entered in the evening. I tore out of my room, down the hallway, slid down the banister, and threw myself into his arms. His hair smelled of Vitalis, his moon face rosy with Bay Rum aftershave. I'd put his gray felt fedora on my head and strut around the hallway like the film star and tough guy Humphrey Bogart.

There were rooms for all occasions: downstairs was for entertaining, holding a large dining room and downstairs living room, both of which had French doors that opened to a manicured garden that ran the length of the Pacific Avenue side of the house. The kitchen had a cozy nook, where the help ate; a storage room at the rear of the kitchen contained dry goods and a four-door icebox whose bottom shelf was filled with ice blocks delivered by Eddie, the iceman; the ice was clamped over his broad shoulders with long black tongs. The milkman delivered as well, depositing crates full of bottled milk, cream, and eggs.

The second floor had my siblings' rooms and mine, our parents' bedroom and dressing closets, a cozy upstairs sitting room, a cedar linen closet, and a maid's utility room. At one end of the third floor were the servants' rooms. My father had a printing press in a small room next to the servants, where he printed manuscripts, leaflets, and announcements. He used beautiful fonts and taught me how to arrange the leaded letters, spacers, and decorative marks. He worked meditatively, a smock over his shirt and tie, pipe clenched in mouth, and seeing him concertedly setting type and inking rollers and imprinting paper filled me with the love of arranging words and watching them magically appear.

At the other end of the third floor was the playroom with Walt Disney—like fantasy scenes painted on the walls: harlequins, kings and queens hand in hand with frolicking Bambis and the seven dwarfs. My brother's Lionel train collection was set on a huge table where multiple trains chugged through villages, bridges, and tunnels, past a volcano that gleefully belched fire and smoke when Paul loaded it with gunpowder. The stage also served as a setting for my magic show, which I performed with encouragement from my mother and her friends. The playroom was my surrogate fun house.

My ancestors were primarily German Jews. I didn't know until I was in my forties that my mother's mother's people, named Schwartz, came from Galicia, Poland. My grandmother, Florence Walter, like so many of her generation, never spoke of her origins, so her part of the family history has vanished, untraceable. My mother's family on her father's side, the brothers Walter, had immigrated from Reckendorf, Germany, to San Francisco in the 1840s and had established a very profitable textile business, D. N. & E. Walter & Co., selling carpets and carpet linings, draperies, and upholstery fabrics.

When he was nine years old, my paternal grandfather, Newton Bissinger, traveled by himself from Ichenhausen in Germany to the United States. With the name and address of a relative pinned to his coat because he didn't speak English, he eventually made his way to the Northwest, where he was welcomed by his uncles into the family business, the Alaska Commercial Company, a fur-and-skin-trading concern. Eventually, Newton broke away and founded Bissinger and Company, buying and selling cowhides, sheepskins, and tallow. A series of warehouses where the hides were brought and skinned dotted the Western states. Cowhides were sold to the International Shoe Company and Japanese leather-goods producers. The tallow was sold to India and Pakistan.

Some of Bissinger and Company's warehouses were pulleries for sheepskins. One hundred thousand sheep died every winter in the Rocky Mountains. The ranchers would skin the sheep and throw the hides on barbed-wire fences. In the spring, they'd be sold to Bissinger and Company, where the wool was pulled from the skin and stored in other warehouses until market conditions were favorable to sell them. Until the midsixties, Bissinger and Company thrived, although one night in the midfifties, I remember Dad ominously saying, "The handwriting's on the wall. DuPont just invented a plastic for shoes called Corfam. The leather business will never be the same."

From this melting pot of German and Polish Jews, three months before Hitler invaded Poland, I was born—June 1939.

My father, Paul (whose father had unfortunately given him the middle name of Adolf—who knew in 1905?), was eager to join the war effort, even though he was thirty-seven. In 1942, he was commissioned into the navy and left for Savannah, Georgia, for officer training. My mother, Marjorie, joined him, leaving my sister, Peggy; brother, Paul; and me at Mom's mother's house on Clay Street. A huge Victorian mansion, its massive palm trees in the yard running front to rear lent the grounds a tropical, Mediterranean feel. The inside was Gothic—severely brown, with ornate woodwork on the walls and ceilings, all anchored by Biedermeier furnishings. I didn't mind living at Gaggy's, as we called our grandmother, not the least because Fong, her Chinese cook, made delicious ladyfingers, which he hid in the cupboard in tins behind plates and bowls so they wouldn't be snitched by thieves such as me.

I slept in a small bedroom next to her room. In the hallway on a bureau stood a carved wooden *Madonna and Child*, sixteenth-century French. When Gaggy died at age 87, her three daughters divvied up the estate, and my mother asked if there was anything I might want. I remembered the *Madonna*. "Oh, nobody wants that!" she replied. Now it sits in my house, and even though the child looks like Richard Nixon, I love the carving.

My mother returned to San Francisco when my father shipped overseas. He wrote a poignant account of his sailing on an LST across the Atlantic to North

Africa, and from North Africa, he served on the command ship USS *Biscayne*, invading Sicily, Salerno, Anzio, and Southern France. I believe that my father experienced PTSD, in those days known as battle fatigue, as the war continued. He returned to the United States in 1944, spent a few weeks in a naval hospital in Boston recuperating, and then was assigned to the US Amphibious Naval Training Base at Morro Bay, California. The family had been reunited. I was immensely proud that my father was the executive commander of the base, overseeing the training of those who would later invade Okinawa. Only much later, after he died, when I was in my fifties, did I realize how deeply the war affected him through documents I received from the Office of Naval Affairs. How I wish he had written further accounts of his experience.

I had awaited his homecoming for two years, and what I waited for most of all was the opening of a wooden crate, shipped home by Dad from overseas that had sat in our attic, contents unknown, for over a year. When the war ended, my father unlocked the box. The family huddled around as he dipped through the packing straw and pulled out a cornucopia of war souvenirs. Two German helmets, one Italian helmet, a Nazi rifle with a bayonet that locked onto it, a belt with swastika and *Gott mit uns* stamped on its buckle, a pistol, uniforms, flags, and knives, even a depotentiated hand grenade. Every boy should be so lucky! You may think me bloodthirsty, but we had been at war since I was born. Was this not my reward? I played with those trophies; I wore them and vanquished the enemy with them. One day—I might have been away at prep school—the weaponry vanished. It was not spoken about. Nothing regarding the war was ever spoken about.

But at Morro naval base, we ran wild while our father fulfilled his duties and our mother did ladies' teas and official dinners. My siblings raised me. Five turning six, I learned how to tie my shoes and explored the hills that surrounded our house overlooking Morro Rock. Peggy, 11, Paul, 10, and I roamed those hills. Best of all, we foraged in an abandoned shed filled with shelves of colored chemicals stored in vials, tins, bottles, and boxes, each labeled with a lethal name and a skull and crossbones. There were Bunsen burners and clamps and other apparatus, enough death in the cloudy crystal mixtures we concocted to wipe out the entire Nazi war machine. I, Jim (the name I preferred to Tommy), would personally, with gutsy stealth and cunning—from the safety of our tree fort—wipe out the Hun, or if not the Hun, the grove of eucalyptus trees and bougainvillea overlooking the snug harbor, where docked the war vessels, gray ships with their stenciled numbers and gun turrets at the ready, pointing toward the Pacific and hulking Morro Rock, a cold, bare beacon and monument to our warriors at sea.

While my father was overseas, my mother worked as a nurse's assistant at Letterman Army Hospital in San Francisco, tending returning vets. She parked me during the day at the Convent of the Sacred Heart for my kindergarten and first-grade years. Why was I, a Jew, enrolled in the convent? "I had to put you somewhere," she replied when I asked fifty years later. "Did it cause psychological problems?" she asked, laughing.

"Mom, I had to write the play *Dreams, Mothers, and Death* because I had a lot of mothers as a little kid, surrogates as well as you. Not every Jew gets to hang out in a convent. Think about it. I spent those first years of school in a palatial building belonging to the Sisters of the Sacred Heart, whose heads were stapled into starchy-white helmets, whose black skirts swished on the marbled floors beneath pale, waxy and nailed-to-the-cross Jesus prominently dripping blood!"

She interrupted my rant with a wave of her hand. "Don't blame me!"

"I'm not," I said, knowing I wouldn't get anywhere if I did. "And another thing, why did we eat fish every Friday, cooked to an inch of its life! I knew that Catholics didn't eat meat on Friday, and I figured that was because probably Jesus didn't, but what was our rationale? More peculiarly, on Easter Sunday, we always served ham. You can't get much more assimilated than ham. I'm just saying. It's puzzling."

Never did find out.

My home at 2500 Divisadero was regimented—breakfast and dinner at the exact time each day and night, sitting in the same seat, surreptitiously filling the napkin with food you wouldn't eat and toss later, and bedtimes enforced. If my father didn't have civic engagements, he'd be home around 5:30 pm, stand in the foyer, and whistle for me. After our hugs, he'd head upstairs where he'd greet my mother, pour himself a Cyrus Noble on the rocks, a second, and fall asleep on the couch until summoned to dinner at 6:45 on the dot.

My father insisted on two things: don't chew gum, and don't walk with your feet splayed out, as he said, some Jews do. I had no idea what he meant. On occasion, he flicked cigarette ashes into my hair, like I was a human ashtray. I think he found it amusing, even affectionate, like petting a dog. He always did it around his friends, who for their part called me Squirt and Shrimp, which stung, as I was both the smallest and youngest kid in my class through the eighth grade. The humiliation of being a "shrimp" was remedied by Dr. Hans Lisser, a courteous, gentle, gnome-size German who administered human growth hormones to me via a shot in the ass every month of my twelfth year. What was this hormone? How did it work? All I knew was that between the act and the evidence of the act lay a secret: I was not normal. No way I could tell any classmate about being unable to grow. I hid my shrimpy humiliation, but by god, I did grow, and I'll never know whether I would have without my booster shots.

Dad was president of both the Junior and Senior Chamber of Commerce of San Francisco and of the Naval League. He served as one of three civilian police commissioners for eight years. He loved serving in these positions, hobnobbing with the city's movers and shakers. He excelled at managing and motivating, a go-to guy for boosting San Francisco's image. I can see that he didn't want to be stereotyped as a Jew, although he certainly wasn't ashamed of being one.

In the 1940s and 1950s, our parents rarely talked to us about anything meaningful. Certainly they did not share their inner life with us. Why would they? Family was about appearance and production, a GM assembly line: workers (servants) on the floor assembling the product (the children), management (the parents) upstairs in the office.

My father had an eye for the ladies before he was married. I have photos of would-be starlets or chorus girls clinging to his arm as he strolled Atlantic City's Boardwalk, a big grin on his face. He had appeared in the 1920s on Broadway with Clifton Webb and Fred Allen and Libby Holman, stars of that time. Possibly he might have pursued a theatrical career, but upon the death of Mildred, his mother, Newton demanded that Dad return to San Francisco and take his rightful role in the family business.

I always believed the theater was his true love. His great success was to bring the director of Moscow's Habima Theatre to San Francisco in 1926 to direct the first performance in English of S. Ansky's *The Dybbuk* at Temple Emanu-El. Dad wrote and directed original musicals at the Concordia Club, which was the Jewish club in San Francisco. In the downstairs bar adjacent to our living room, he and two of his buddies would hatch ideas for the shows and then read scenes to each other. They were having fun, and that camaraderie impressed me. I couldn't wait for opening night, the band striking up, knowing my father was the man in charge of it all. I was in his fun house. Did he ever urge me to follow his footsteps? He didn't have to.

The highlight of my preteen theatrical education occurred in 1947 when Dad took the family to New York via the train the *City of San Francisco*. Three days in a moving world of sleeping births and dining cars with America cinematically rolling through her mountains, villages, prairies, rivers, and cities. Three days later, we rolled into Penn Station, our father guiding us like a Sherpa through a monstrous cavern of noise and bustle. I remember one thing only of New York: going to the theater to see *High Button Shoes*, directed by Jerome Robbins, whose sleight of hand created a tumult of leggy chorus girls and silly clowns popping out of multiple cabana doors as other disappeared into them. Attending *High Button Shoes* was an eye-popping fun house of disguise and surprise, adult, and risqué!

When Mom and Dad gave parties, 2500 Divisadero became the fun house. The house would fill with the aroma of camellias floating in bowls. The garden was covered by a tent, snugged in and illuminated by dangling

Japanese lanterns, delighting the eye. The downstairs living room became a Parisian café with small tables and graceful flower arrangements; couples danced to a live band playing popular hits and Dixieland, and the dance floor sparkled with chips of light spilled by a spinning mirror ball. Guests laughed and schmoozed, and I, big-eyed, perched on the stairs in pajamas, peering through the balustrades, took in my father with his warm, lovely smile, a little tipsy, doffing a top hat and flourishing a cane, singing *Me and My Shadow* à la Ted Lewis. Cue laughter. Cue applause.

As guests entered, maids waiting by the door in black-and-white uniforms greeted them and took their coats. In our social circle, the guests and the servants knew each other, since both the privileged and the servants were at many of the same parties. One of the maids was Elizabeth, a jolly woman with a thick Irish brogue, who once invited me to spend the night with her and her family. To my dismay, my mother concurred. What was she thinking? Was this noblesse oblige on her part? Would it have been awkward or snobbish to refuse? Maybe she wanted to let me see how the other half lived? I was eight years old. Terrified.

Mom dropped me off in a working-class neighborhood, a series of old Victorian wooden tenement houses sloping down Fell Street. I climbed up to a second floor and entered a small apartment, where Elizabeth greeted me and introduced me to her family—a boy my age and two older daughters. When the father came home, we sat around the table for a healthy meal of ham, peas, and cabbage. All I could think about was: *Where do I sleep? When can I go home?* Although everyone was kind, the conversation was awkward, both the family and I looking at the other as a stranger from a strange land.

Bedtime arrived, and the boy threw a tantrum as he was made to sleep in a large crib next to where I would be sleeping because, lucky me, I got the place of honor: in bed with the father! Elizabeth and the two girls were crammed in a bed across the room, wedged head to toe. The boy in the crib cage stared malevolently at me through the bars of the crib, complaining bitterly that he was too big to be in this thing, and guess who was to blame for him being there? I ignored his rage but not the hairy, beefy man in pajamas who had now sunk into the bed inches away from me. He yawned comfortably. I had never slept with my father, much less a stranger.

"Now, Father, don't snore," scolded Elizabeth from the other side of the room. "Tommy, are you comfortable?"

"I'm not!" shouted the son.

"Oh hush now, James Billy O'Brien!"

Mr. O'Brien proceeded to snore deeply. The son glared; I was sure he was sending spells worthy of Batman's evil adversary, the Joker. I guarded my edge of the mattress, pretending to sleep. It was all so weird. Would morning never come?

Dad preferred to escape the demands of raising children. He laid out the big picture and let my mother fill it all in. Even when I had misbehaved and my mother uttered the well-used cliché, "Wait till your father comes home!" he didn't seem to have his heart in spanking me. One more chore he didn't need. I thought of him as a great man, the good father, and until my teenage years, I was his steady companion at rodeos, football games, and theater. I see us hunched over the radio, listening to the broadcasts of the fights at Madison Square Garden. As the Gillette marching anthem came on, "To look sharp, every time you shave, to be sharp . . . ," blood surged, and hairs stiffened. This was the moment of truth, mano a mano: Joe Louis versus Billy Conn in match after match—Billy, the tough Mick, fought his heart out, but the Brown Bomber always put him away. Peerless Sugar Ray Robinson, solid Jake LaMotta, wily Willie Pep, my father and I loved the fights and followed them all.

The first rupture I can remember between my father and me occurred in 1948 in Mount Diablo, at a summer home in the country, which my parents had purchased and remodeled in the modern clean lines of contemporary California. Complete with swimming pool and barbecue area, it was our weekend and summer retreat until 1951.

Diablo was a fertile sanctuary for feral cats, as well as rattlesnakes, black-widow spiders, and coyotes. I came upon a litter of wild kittens and began to play with one until it dug its claws into me, drawing blood. In a fury, I bashed the kitten against a tree until I killed it. Where did that fury come from? That rage? After the killing of the kitten, the shame of it, I feared that I could not control my anger if I ever let myself go. I thought of how I had choked down the feelings I had toward classmates and bullies who spread their terror through the school with genial malevolence. I hated my own impotence.

Somehow, the dead kitten was discovered, and my father asked me about the incident. I told him I had no idea what had happened. He didn't seem to believe me and kept grilling me until finally he accused me of lying to him. I continued to deny it until he said, "If you loved me, you wouldn't lie to me." It was true that I had lied, but was it also true that I didn't love him because of that lie? What did killing the kitten have to do with loving my father? Was love a condition that came and went? I had never really thought about it. Some part of how it is to be in the world was shaken by this thought. I shrank, and he grew larger.

My relationship with my mother was more complex. I loved to perform for my mother, and my mother—temperamental, competitive, and playful—nursed my ambitions. She was clever; she wanted that for me. She was weary of child-rearing. It was unglamorous and demanding, and she felt the competition from her elder sister, Nell, who lived next door with her own family. It was particularly rough on my sister, Peggy, who was sweet and not at all competitive, a major failing in our extended family. Sweet didn't cut it. You had to be caustic, sarcastic, and clever, or you were chopped liver. No, I was my mother's best shot.

My mother—sexy, beautiful, with masses of black hair piled Lana Turner—style atop her head-egged me on, delightfully teasing and playing with me, pushing, poking me, laughing with me, encouraging me to join her in songs and rhymes. Of course, I was her little darling, mimicking her, driving the energy higher and higher. We'd be playing word games, foolish gibberish, and words would pour out of my mouth. I wouldn't let go as the game continued: *"snookey-tookey-pukey-dookey-doodoo-pewdo."*

Then—without warning—I crossed a weird line that only she knew existed, and I became . . . *fresh*. Yes! *Fresh*—a monstrous Dionysian satyr-brat straight out of a fun house-warped mirror, drunk with insolence, defiant, hysterically rebellious, oh so delicious to the child but intolerable to the parent.

My mother would flip out; her dark, Kali side, the face of rattling skulls and dripping blood, scolded me, "Stop it! Stop it! You're being fresh!" But I couldn't or wouldn't stop myself, my laughing and shrieking more piercing, uncontrollable, hysterical.

Smack! Whack! Caught by surprise, I was slapped to the ground. *"Goddamn you! Never talk to me like that! I told you to stop!"* she screamed as I lay on the floor. She continued to kick and curse and rant, driven by demented power and spite until *"Don't you ever behave that way again, or I'll wash your mouth out with soap!"* (which she did), and *"Go to your room!"* ended it. Then, like Steve McQueen in *The Great Escape*, I sat down in my cell and hurled a tennis ball against my closet door for hours, enraged. My brother and sister experienced her tantrums as well.

Childhood is a game between the big guys and the small guys, the tormentor (who is also your angel) and the tormented. Though your star may shine, the result is predictable: a bashing sooner or later. Success, as I saw it, in my cunning way, was when my brother or sister took the hit instead of me.

My mother, despite her ferocity, had a sweet side and was a wonderful caregiver when I was sick. She was solicitous, full of cheer, and I was happy, listening to the radio from morning to night. Arthur Godfrey was first, I liked his nasally quirky humor. He was followed by soap operas: *Stella Dallas, Backstage Wife; Pepper Young's Family.* Mid-day, I dialed in *Queen for a Day*, the darker hue of Lamont Cranston and *The Shadow*, and was aroused by the William Tell Overture announcing the arrival of *The Lone Ranger*. As I got older, I listened to *Lucky Lager Dance Time* and *Your Hit Parade* and, when things really lined up, my beloved Brooklyn Dodgers. How many times did Campy whack a home-run bottom of the ninth, Jackie pull off a steal, and

Furillo gun the man down at home! The inevitable play-off against the Giants or Yanks. I lived and died with Dem Bums.

This mother of mine was leggy, had her hair coifed in a pompadour, swore, drank Scotch, smoked a pipe (to quit her habit), danced the Charleston, and taught it to me. In the afternoon, when I came home from school, I trotted into her bathroom, where she soaked languorously in her bathtub, covered by bubble bath, suds floating above her breasts. It was all so innocent, her asking me about my day. How could she not be the object of my desire? She was so beautiful.

My mother's allure was such that I could not resist her. Her desire became my desire. How many actors act to please their mother?

And yet until the age of thirty, I flinched every time a woman raised her hand toward me—not in anger, just raising her hand. That's how deep her "branding" went.

Survival became a matter of outperforming and out-talking the "opposition." I refused to be a scapegoat, not even for my mother, if I could help it. As small as I was, I was a smart kid, a good athlete. I could talk fast and get out of most situations by deflecting the energy with a joke or some kind of shtick. I began to observe clowns.

This was not difficult as our de facto church was the newly arrived television set, and our worship night was Tuesday evening. Dad, Mom, myself, occasionally Peggy and Paul, sat in the upstairs sitting room, raptly watching the *Texaco Star Theater*, starring the irrepressible Milton Berle. Throw in Sid Caesar, Imogene Coca (and their *Your Show of Shows*), Danny Kaye, Eddie Cantor, Lucy, Groucho, Jimmy Durante, and Red Skelton, and my life was an exploding nova of comedy, song, farce, and slapstick enacted by subversive, genius wiseacre-ing clowns.

The clown is trying to stay alive, desperate to survive an untenably ridiculous situation, and he can only do so by injecting himself totally into that moment. The result is usually a disaster or a near escape from disaster. The tragedian reflects. There is no farce, only nobility of purpose, which he embodies as a social example: Willy Loman, Oedipus, and Hamlet. They embody pain. A comedian lets you glimpse pain but turns it against himself—or you. But the great ones know better than to mock the audience. Better to mock oneself and wink at the audience.

My standard "bit," as my uncle Henry liked to remind me, was to stagger as if mortally wounded and fall down dead. I died with passionate frequency. I loved the spotlight. Whether this was due to my parents' encouragement or whether I was possessed of that daemon from birth or before, my life and art became dramatically entwined. Dance, sing, spiel, die with fervor—it was all part of my fun house.

Chapter Two

To run a fun house, you needed a staff. We had servants. As a child, the word *servant* had none of the loaded content that it has today. Some of our servants worked as launderers or gardeners; some were nurses, who tended the kids when my parents traveled. The most memorable was the British Ms. Elsie Jeeves, who had been my mother's nurse and thus had the right to address her as Marjorie. Jeevie was a spinster, a stately ocean liner of a woman who, at the dinner table, repeated "Chew and swallow" as a metronomic mantra. Jeevie was not unkind, only strict, and rules were rules. The antidote to Jeevie was Beetle Butler, a diminutive ageless Irish nanny for hire with a Mary Poppins personality, whose sole reason for living, as I experienced her, was to play with kids.

Our parents took yearly camping and fishing trips with their friends. Kids were excluded, but when Beetle came to stay with us, who cared? I was in heaven. No screaming, no yelling—only games and tales of other kids she house-sat and what they were up to. As she bounced around the house or in the park with me, she was just this side of reckless. I couldn't keep up with her inventive nature. Children were her puppies, and she'd wear us out. Laughter poured out of her with never a harsh word. Why would there be? I adored her.

Beetle's service was special but infrequent. The two who gave service to my parents for twenty years, who impacted me the most, were Lillian and Lorenzo Kennedy, an African American couple from Mississippi, two of the kindest and most gracious, loving souls I ever met—strong people, patient with our family. Lillian did the cooking, and Lorenzo, ever cheerful, cleaned, served meals, and was an all-around handyman. They were home when I was, unlike my father, who was at the office, or my mother, who was busy with her appointments. Our 2500 Divisadero house was very large, and I felt frightened being left alone. I was safe with Lillian and Lorenzo, and I don't recall a harsh word from either of them although I'm sure I exasperated them. Little boys are thoughtless, but I loved them and didn't want to be mean. The famous photo by Dorothea Lange of the Dust Bowl woman, her head resting on her knuckled hand—those were Lillian's hands; she had that same steely strength. She needed it to put up with my mother's moods, which as noted, could be volatile.

The Kennedys lived at our house during the week and, on the weekend, would drive a shiny-green Hudson Hornet to their home in Oakland, where their three children and Lillian's mother lived. I was pretty sure Lorenzo's car was the kind of smooth, curvaceous, glitzy machine only Afro Americans drove. It sure was ultra cool.

Lillian and Lorenzo were embodiments of integrity. There's no doubt Lillian was a second mother for me, the heart and hearth of our house, an antidote to my high-strung mother. She'd sit me in the kitchen cubicle and bring me a sandwich; while I chatted, she'd be murmuring, in her milky Mississippian accent, "Goodness gracious, Tommy, I declare." Her words were calming music to my ears. I marveled at her dignity, strength, and loyalty. It wasn't that these qualities were missing in my family; it's just that work— manual labor—was something manifested elsewhere, in downtown offices and factories.

Lillian carried my mother's breakfast on a tray to my mother's bed and dutifully listened while Marjorie gave her instructions for the day. Somehow it seemed strange that one person waited on another in this fashion, but I was too young to articulate my feelings. After Lillian left the room, every day, without fail, my mother received a phone call from Gaggy—"Hello, Mother"—and the day began.

Lillian and Lorenzo lived on the third floor, the upstairs to our downstairs. Lillian had a room to iron clothes and sew. Occasionally, I visited her there on the way to the playroom. Lorenzo would be sitting in an old green upholstered chair, reading the paper while Lillian ironed. I peeked in their bedroom but never went in.

On a visit to San Francisco in 1965, I mentioned to Lillian that I had been protesting in Selma for several weeks. Lillian scolded me for going. "Tommy, you could have died!" I hadn't thought much about Lillian since I left home, but standing in the kitchen looking at her, she aging, her hair gray and frizzy, holding on to my hands, I knew why I had gone to Selma, and I knew she was happy I had gone. She had rubbed some of her strength into me.

My mother, a privileged, complex, volatile woman and Lillian Kennedy, a hardworking, laboring woman from Mississippi, were bonded for twenty years. When Lorenzo lay dying at his house in Oakland, my mother received a call from Lillian. "Lorenzo's dying. Please come sit at his bedside."

One of the stories I recount in my book *Da Capo* is the time my mother drove Marian Anderson, the great singer and musical civil rights icon, over to Lillian's house in Oakland. My parents were friends with Ms. Anderson's manager, known only by the name of Joffe, and so via Joffe, they became her friends and would meet her, usually at a suite in the Mark Hopkins Hotel, where Marian would be sewing curtains as a way of relaxing before a concert. One day after she, Marian, had been to our house, Lillian asked my mother if it would be possible for Marian Anderson to visit her house in Oakland to meet Lureen, Lillian's daughter, and her friends. Marian agreed. My mother drove Marian to Lillian's, and they had tea and cakes with the ladies. I was proud of my mother for facilitating this event.

Lillian and Lorenzo kept 2500 Divisadero smoothly humming, and my day unfolded with regularity—breakfast every morning with my father then off to Town School just two blocks away.

My grammar school was located in an old refurbished Victorian mansion. The headmaster, Edwin Rich, aka Sir, was a multitalented, witty, wiry man; a Speedy Gonzales, he was everywhere at once. He administered the school, taught English by using the grammar book he had written to make sure you learned the parts of speech, wrote and directed Christmas musicals, and played a mean game of football. In early October, as television was coming of age, Sir installed a black-and-white TV in the gym so that we could watch the World Series. Not only was he a fan of the game, he used the event as a civics lesson to install pride and passion in our national pastime.

As my classmates and I began the sixth grade, I, although the smallest and youngest, was chosen to be the class reader whenever a teacher had to leave the classroom. Now I was in charge and could give voice to all the characters in the book; the kids listened, and I liked the attention.

After school, I went home and immediately collected my cousin, John Sinton, who lived next door. As we were the same age and had mothers who were sisters, we shared similar family traits and customs. Their servants might have a different accent, but we were all cut from the same cloth. Football or baseball in hand, John and I hit the streets, tossed the ball for a while, and then headed to the sites of two abandoned lots full of the detritus of bricks, broken tiles, and concrete shards and divided by the entrance to a cul-de-sac. We'd rummage among the rubble, eventually enrolling other kids in the neighborhood into teams; while hiding behind partially standing walls, war was our game. We'd lob bricks and stones at each other, thrilled and scared to feel a projectile whizz by or to see yours crash into the wall, sending clumps of debris in all directions. It seemed that if there was a stick or a brick, we were aroused and ready to rumble.

On the days I had a dental appointment or to see my growth doctor, the gentle gnome, Hans Lisser, I'd take the cable car downtown. My parents weren't concerned about sending a nine-year-old boy off by himself—not in the 1940s. How I enjoyed taking the cable car! I was fascinated how this beautifully polished wooden trolley rolled down steep hills, held to earth by an invisible cable and a brakeman, who, with amazing skill and strength, kept us from plunging catastrophically to our death; at the same time as we were hurtling down Jackson, me delightedly standing on the trolley's outer step hanging on for dear life, the conductor clanged the bell, chanting street names commemorating San Francisco's historical figures: Van Ness, Larkin, Sutter, Kearny, and Powell. And wonder of wonders! That moment when the cable car entered the Roundhouse and was rotated on a moving platform to reverse directions! As we spun, I beheld the machinery and the giant spools that dispensed the cable that slithered and disappeared under the street as the trolley reversed direction.

It would be late afternoon when I jumped off the trolley at Washington and Scott Streets and returned home. The last of the western sun would have disappeared behind dense streams of fog rolling in from the Pacific as I walked up the hill to 2500 Divisadero.

My sister, Peggy, six years older than me, and my brother, Paul, five years older, had different friends and schedules, so we didn't play a lot together. In the family constellation, Peggy was expected to be the princess—smart, clever, beautifully dressed, and competitive, especially with all her girl cousins. Peggy was adorable, sweet, and eager to please, the antithesis of competitive. I see her in pigtails, my defender—at least she tells me she was, and I believe her. When she got to high school, her friends started coming over to hang out. They were cute and had perky breasts, and I was their mascot. They were my fantasy life, my introduction to young womanhood.

My brother, Paul, was robust, active, and brainy—a talented guy. He played a gorgeous guitar. My parents expected him both to excel and disappoint. He was continually accused of lacking common sense. I, being the youngest and wiliest, escaped the brunt of criticism, but Paul was the scapegoat of the family. He was yelled at the most, as if inevitably destined to blunder, arousing the wrath of my high-strung mother and exasperated father.

Paul Jr. had his own karma with Paul Sr., much of it revolving around the family business. Although Paul was groomed to take over Bissinger and Company, he was blocked until my grandfather Newton died at the helm. Dad inherited the business but, ill with cancer, sold it, thinking he'd better sell while he could still make a deal, rather than have faith in Paul Jr.'s ability to enter new markets and new products.

By the time I was nine, Paul was out of the house, attending Phillips Exeter Academy, and Peggy would be leaving for Sarah Lawrence in two years' time. My fun house was emptying.

Fortunately, for the first seventeen summers of my youth, my fun house moved to the High Sierras in Northern California, where my grandmother and grandfather had built Rampart, the family homestead on the banks of the Truckee River. Two miles north of Lake Tahoe, at an elevation of seven thousand feet, Rampart bordered Tahoe National Forest, endless mountains of soaring Douglas firs.

My grandfather, Gaggy's husband, John I. Walter, whom I never knew as he died young, had built the original lodge as a fishing retreat. Other lodges and cabins were added over the years. Gaggy ran Rampart regally, with her three daughters and their families and friends as consorts and courtiers. Gaggy was, of course, the Queen, birdlike with fabulous upswept gray hair. Consider Katharine Hepburn playing her. Nell, the eldest daughter, played by a caustic Ethel Merman, would be the Princess of the Realm of Art and Sarcasm; Marjorie, the middle daughter, played by Lana Turner, was Princess of the Realm of Tennis and Mockery; and Carol, the youngest, played by Imogene Coca, was Princess of the Realm of Gossip and Weaving. Their consorts were the following: Stanley Sinton, Lord of Stock Market Quotations; Paul Bissinger, Lord of Happiness; and Henry Sinton, Lord of Comedy and Jest. (Henry and Stanley were brothers. Two brothers had married two sisters.) We children were the pawns and players. Fong, the cook, and the rest of the staff were the servants and observers.

The princesses were inventive: tennis tournaments, picnics on the beaches of Lake Tahoe, driving the wood-paneled Ford station wagon to explore the mostly abandoned Nevada towns of Virginia and Carson City, whose sagging Victorian houses were a cornucopia of remnants of the Gold Rush: old medicine bottles, yellowed newspapers, a spoon, and calendars.

Our fathers worked in the city and drove up to Tahoe on the weekends.

At night, we made our own entertainment. No radio, no TV in those days—just a remarkable assemblage of talented, eccentric, neurotic relatives and our friends who loved as best we could while Gaggy overviewed the scene, rocking benignly in her chair, silently knitting. Competition was fierce at charades and twenty questions. It was a good stage to hone your act and as argumentative as it could get about who was cheating at twenty questions or whether the actor was mouthing the word in charades, and despite a few "God damn it! I'm not going to play if you cheat!" we played on. Kids love it when adults lose their temper with each other as long as it doesn't go too far. And when the competitive games were over, we played show tunes, cowboy songs, and golden oldies: "Ballin' the Jack," "Doodlee-doo," "Margie," "Camptown Races," "Charleston."

Every day we hiked through meadows of Indian paintbrush and lupine, picked thimbleberries, or we'd set out on our own, climbing a mountain stacked to the sky with giant boulders, unsure whether rattlesnakes were lurking beneath them. Then we'd head to the pungent, fish-filled rapids of the Truckee, where roiling waves swept you downstream. In the later afternoon, we crouched on rocks at streamside and dangled bacon bits on a string to catch crawfish, patiently waiting until they clamped on with their pincers, and we netted them and proudly brought a bucketful to Fong, who cooked them in spicy broth, and still in bathing suits, we'd feast.

Every morning, we younger kids would check an area of the thimbleberry grove, where Rosebud the Fairy had hidden letters under thimbleberry leaves. We eagerly searched for and unwrapped her letters bound with moss fiber and glued onto bark, letters actually written by my aunt, Carol, and eldest cousin, Margot. Rosebud was a long-running act, up on all the latest gossip from her village as well as ours. Carol and Margot kept the secrets of Rosebud for a long time. I was happy to resurrect her on camping trips I took with my kids.

Rampart was a summer camp for children and adults alike, a kibbutz with servants, a hedonistic celebration of the California good life. In 1960, Gaggy died, and Rampart emptied out. No one wanted to take it on; it went into limbo, was sold, was not . . .

Many years later, my mother and I decided to see what had happened to Rampart. A sign said Crazy Woman Lodge, and we found a squatter living in the only building standing, with his horse grazing outside. Who could the Crazy Woman sign be referring to but my grandmother? To our shock, Rampart had burnt to the ground. In its ruins, there were a few mementos: a stone chimney starkly stood near Gaggy's white claw-footed porcelain bathtub. Cabins had caved in, the tennis court cracked and weedy. Had our clan hexed the land, or was Rampart only a blip in nature's time, slowly being swallowed by the national forest?

For three summers, age 9 through 11, I took time off from Rampart to attend a boy's camp in the Trinity Alps of Northern California, an eight-hour train trip from San Francisco to Redding, and then to Weaverville, where Grover Gates, a cattle rancher from Fresno who ran Camp Trinity, would meet us.

Impeccably dressed in a Pendleton plaid shirt, a pair of Levi's with the cuffs worn high over cowboy boots, and his trademark Stetson hat, Mr. Gates was schoolteacher, rancher, ombudsman, counselor, guide, and preacher. Every year he read to us *A Message from Garcia;* what he wanted us to know was to take his or the counselors' instructions and carry out the chore without argument or complaint. This, Mr. Gates preached, was integrity. This was personal responsibility.

As we campers at Camp Trinity were kids free of parental pressure, it took a while for his message to sink in. He deepened its importance by sending us out on horseback on camping trips into the wilderness for three or four days. We had provisions; it wasn't a vision quest, but six of us would need to cooperate and share the chores, tend the horses, and cook for the group, which meant we had to catch our daily meal. To be in the heart of the mountains, sun sparkling off tumbling waters and still pools, to navigate by oneself over boulders and streams, encountering songbirds and butterflies, hawks, eagles, and tracks of bears and then being able to hook a rainbow trout—wow! That was about as good as it could get.

Mr. Gates raised his own chickens, pigs, horses, and cows. Like a high priest, he assembled the entire camp to witness the ritual slaughter of a cow, killing the cow with a rifle shot to the forehead or the throat-cutting of a pig. We were allowed to behead chickens and then delightedly watch them run around the barnyard, blood spurting from their necks, until they keeled over. It was not blood for the sake of blood. We were required to pluck those chickens and scrape the hides of pigs. Everything we killed we ate. We witnessed the births of calves and foals. What an intense experience for a city boy to see a foal exit from his mother's womb, a thing raw and bloody, pink and red and black, all wobbly and wet, placed unsteadily on his feet, taking his first step, suckling at his mother's teat. I was both queasy and awed.

And to celebrate the end of camp was the primal theater of a pig roast! Near a river with plenty of river stones, we dug a deep five-foot long and two-foot wide hole in which we built a fire and laid stones: a cooking grave for the pig. Hours later, when a deep bed of coals remained, the pig was laid on them with red-hot stones placed in its belly; layers of corn were heaped on top of the pig, covered then by more stones and dirt. The pig was left buried for eight hours. When it was uncovered and served, the meat tenderly dissolved into mouthwatering bites, and although the food was great, the time put into preparing the experience was just as satisfying.

When I was sixteen and had a driver's license, I was employed as a grocery boy at the village store in Tahoe City—my first real job. I relearned a huge lesson from Grover Gates that I had forgotten. My first day on the job, I was told to unload a tractor trailer and carry the contents into the basement. Cans of food stacked a mile high! Man, how I bitched and moaned, railing at my boss, feeling sorry for myself, but by the end of the summer, I had learned to take it one box at a time, no complaining—just another message from Garcia. One of the best things I've ever learned.

During the school year, I went to Golden Gate Park with five classmates from Town School under the supervision of Roger Sobel, a twenty-five year-old Seabee freshly discharged from the war—a handsome, funny guy—a combination of Frank Sinatra, Gene Kelly, and Donald O'Connor in *On the Town* and the antidote to our conservative older fathers who would not dream of carousing with a group of fifth-graders. Possessed of unlimited animal energy, weekly he took us to the park in his World War II jeep. We played hide-and-seek, mostly hiding from Roger, concealing ourselves in underbrush, hoping to be the last one found. Absolute silence and stealth was required and then sudden shrieking as this giant of a Roger—curly red hair, cocky grin—flashed through the woods scaring the wits out of us as he captured and tossed us into a bush.

Roger cut through the bullshit of well-behaved demeanor proscribed by our class and social position. He was wild, not afraid to say the crude things a twenty-five-year-old man or an older brother might. He was ahead of time, anticipating the moment before the moment occurred. He'd regale us with stories about his war life, his loves, and when he met our parents, for it was they who hired him to take us to the park, he smiled slyly, as if he knew we had done or heard things our parents wouldn't have approved of.

Forty-five years since I had last seen Roger, I was visiting my mother and read in the newspaper that a Roger Sobel had found a meteorite on a San Francisco beach and insisted the beach patrol bring a bulldozer and remove the meteorite for safekeeping. Could it be him? I found a Sobel mortgage company in the phone book, but for whatever reason, I needed to surprise him, if it was he.

The next day I climbed the stairs to a house and rang the bell. A ruddy-faced, blue-eyed man in baggy sweats and a T-shirt opened the door. "Hi, Roger. Tom Bissinger." I loved the expression that followed: a slow, growing shock rose from his breath up through the jaw into the eyes and bingo! "Tommy Bissinger! Son of a gun! Come on in." We spent the next hour reminiscing. He was compiling his scrapbooks and opened one to the 1940s where I found myself among my classmates in little brownie snapshots. As we were glancing through the books, Roger turned to me. "You're the first person who's ever looked me up from that era."

The next morning, my family and Roger piled into a local diner and shared more stories. He was delightful but did not wish to dwell in nostalgia for its own sake. He always was a moment before the moment.

One of my classmates on Roger Sobel's park expeditions was Hunt Barclay, whose mother, Wendy Howell, was unlike any of the mothers I knew growing up. A socialite from Boston, she was now divorced and lived next to the Palace of Fine Arts, a grand old sandstone temple built for a 1915 exposition. What made Wendy truly exceptional in my eyes, beyond being able to fly an airplane, was that she owned a houseboat, the *Squarehead*, a barge containing two bedrooms, an open galley, and a deck that went around the cabins. On this motorized houseboat, Hunt, myself, our buddy, John Register, and Wendy would navigate the sloughs of the Sacramento River, those backwaters that make up the Sacramento delta.

Wendy had an easy smile, drank like a man, and didn't give a fig for much of anything except, as far as I could tell, her dogs. She raised and bred whippets, an obnoxious brand of skittery, wiry race hounds. Wendy had about twenty of these animals, which shit and peed all around the house, claimed all the sofas, and obeyed no one but Wendy. Boy, was she angry when we reviled the dogs!

On the houseboat, we experienced the easygoing life of the delta: shacks on the banks, the moon rising over the waters as we gently floated through the slough, Mexican songs drifting over the waters, our creepy little minds, especially when we became teenagers, fantasizing whether one of us might sleep with Wendy. It seemed to our hormone-driven minds almost possible, but Wendy only had affection for her dogs. Boys Wendy tolerated, amused by our antics until we imperiled the boat by almost steering into a bank or were found tormenting the dogs. We were useless at fixing an engine, but she didn't mind getting dirty and greasy, climbing into the hold and shouting at us to bring her a tool.

Wendy was the first liberated woman I'd encountered. My mother called her a character. I found her independence from my parent's world intriguing. Her mannish ways of dressing and running the boat, her drunken laughter, her being the alpha dog—in my mind, she was the African queen before Bogie and Kate ever set foot in the jungle. Hunt and I bonded on these adventures; we continued to reappear in each other's lives after we left San Francisco.

As I neared adolescence, I attended Reform Temple Emanu-El's religious school, not on Friday or Saturday but on Sunday! (the exact time and day that my Christian classmates were going to their church). I slunk down Jackson Street, hoping to avoid being seen by any of them, not exactly ashamed but embarrassed that I had to go in the first place, since my parents rarely went to any religious service except Yom Kippur. We celebrated neither Passover nor Hanukkah nor Purim nor anything, not once, yet I was singled out to go to Sunday school! I had to be different when all I wanted to do was fit in.

Emanu-El was and is an impressively grand stone creation, topped with a massive dome, guarded by gates (and concrete blocks following 9/11), which conceal a lovely courtyard and fountain, much as I imagine the Temple of Jerusalem might look had it been set on Arguello and Lake Streets. Its inner sanctum reverberated with the booming deep sermons of Rabbi Alvin Fine.

My bar mitzvah teacher was Cantor Reuben Rinder, who sang like an angel. Cantor Rinder's bright, sparkly eyes and warm smile welcomed me into his study, books and stacks of sheet music piled high atop a piano, signed photographs of Yehudi Menuhin and Jascha Heifetz on the wall. He'd wink and give me a mint before we settled down to the books. Cantor Rinder made my bar mitzvah instruction go down easy. I loved the man, and could he belt a song!

On September 27, 1952, I peered over the lectern, accompanied by Rabbis Fine and Heller and Cantor Rinder, prodded with nods and smiles, and guided by a long pointer toward the squiggly Hebraic letters printed on huge vellum pages. I recited for a few dozen people, gave a solid performance—too nervous to be boffo—and went home with a Parker pen and a modest lunch with my parents and grandparents. Who knew then that disco-dancing-bunny-hopping-lox-and-bagels spectaculars awaited the future youth of American Jewry? If you've got it, flaunt it, right?

My parents, in order to prepare me for San Francisco's social set teenage dances, *La Jeunesse* and *Assemblies*, themselves preparation for the debutante cotillion, sent me to Mr. Kitchen's dancing school on Clay Street. I arrived every Friday at five, slicked out in coat and tie, shined shoes, hair combed, along with thirty-five other eighth-graders. I met this new situation with a mixture of anticipation and dread. I was still the shrimp. Most of the girls were taller than me; I only came up to their sweaty armpits or had my nose pointing into their budding breasts. The girls were properly dressed in puffy crinoline dresses and black patent pumps, their hands demurely covered in white gloves. Clearasil was liberally pasted on both boys' and girls' raging acne. Mr. Kitchens, a smoothly unctuous Liberace look-alike, would sweep his dance partner, Ms. Lewis, on to the dance floor and show us the moves for the day, accompanied on the piano by Mrs. Funtangle. We would practice our parts, clumping in square and circle formations, boys laughing, goofing off, shoving each other, while on the other side of the room, girls tittered and gossiped; only after this scrum did we meet in the middle to choose a partner. Through repetition and reprimand, we learned to foxtrot, waltz, jitterbug, rumba, and cha-cha, with some bunny hop thrown in for good behavior. After our hour of exertions of grab and clutch, glide and spin, and a few stepped-on toes, we trooped out to Mrs. Funtangle's gentle rendition of "Tenderly." How sweet that song was and still is. As we got older, the exit song at the citywide dances was "Good Night, Sweetheart." The music was romantically dreamy, keeping our hormones from awakening too rapidly. We teenagers belonging to high society were on the cusp of rock 'n' roll and rhythm and blues, but those old ballads, they still grab me.

I was sure the happiest our family could ever be occurred when Broadway musicals came to San Francisco. In his twenties, Dad had acted on Broadway in *The Little Show* and then had produced a big-time professional revue in San Francisco. Musicals gave his heart a lift like nothing else. Going to theater was ritualized: we went to the Clift Hotel for dinner and then walked across the street to either the Geary or Orpheum to see Mary Martin sudsing her hair in *South Pacific* or Ethel Merman blasting her pipes in *Annie Get Your Gun*. Best of all was Danny Kaye's vaudeville revue. He tapped, he sang, he joked, he rattled off the names of thirty Russians in triple time—Tchaikovsky, Stravinsky, Stanislavski, Berezovsky, Mussorgsky, Koussevitisky—making up names, spewing them out, faster and faster, until exhaustion (ours) set in, and he ended the evening sitting at the edge of the stage crooning to us, we in the palm of his hand. Cheeky Danny, Dopey Danny, Charming Danny, Dazzling Danny—he was everything in a performer I wanted to be.

At home we played the LPs and knew the words to all the Broadway songs, but the music didn't stop there. My mother loved opera and classical. Both parents loved Dixieland and frequented the clubs where Turk Murphy and Lu Watters's Yerba Buena Jazz Band wailed. Black music? Louis Armstrong, Cab Calloway, Lionel Hampton, the Duke. Pop hits? Learned them on the piano: "Wheel of Fortune," "That Lucky Old Sun," "Slow Boat to China," "PS I Love You," "Dear Hearts and Gentle People."

Peggy had gone to Sarah Lawrence in 1951, and Paul went to Phillips Exeter Academy in 1952. I didn't realize how much I was going to miss my protectors and allies or that I would feel so abandoned, especially when my parents went on their frequent trips. The house was too grand, and I was too small. I was scared when I was alone, yet I never had a friend for a sleepover. Something was missing for me; I craved love, but didn't I have it? I had possessions, but these did not bring warmth. To accuse my parents of not loving me was unthinkable, not true, but the converse—my story that I was unloving because I lied to my father—haunted me, made me undeserving of love. When I performed, then I was loved, but it meant I had to keep performing, smiling, being cute when inwardly I was feeling a little lost, even abandoned. I didn't fit in.

My parents had plans for me after graduating from Town School in June 1952. Take a year at a public high school (I had just turned thirteen), and then repeat freshman year at an Eastern prep school.

I enrolled in Lick-Wilmerding High, located in the Potrero, a working-class industrial district far from Pacific Heights. My memories of Lick are few. I saw a classmate having an epileptic fit. I heard the word *schwantz*, as in a football coach looking at a naked player walking out of the shower. "Wow! Look at the size of his *schwantz*!" I found out that hardball was not my game, algebra was boring, and Ms. Teterin looked great in her tight fuzzy sweater. I chose to sit on the fire escape and watch freeway traffic during class. What did I care? I had been accepted to Phillips Academy.

Chapter Three

I didn't know why I was going to Phillips Academy in Andover, Massachusetts, except that my parents thought I should and sold it to me as a good idea. That they possibly didn't want me around as a teenager hadn't yet occurred to me. My brother had attended Phillips Exeter Academy, so why shouldn't I attend prestigious Phillips Andover Academy, founded in 1778 by Samuel Phillips, a friend of George Washington? Its motto, "Non Sibi: Not for Self Alone," and its mission, "To prepare youth from every quarter," were stamped on envelopes, walls, and plaques. My quarter, my San Francisco by the Bay, was a long way from the Hill, as it was known by Andover locals.

On September 1953, I boarded a plane with my brother for Boston. I was thrilled that Paul was accompanying me to Andover to help me through this critical time of leaving home. I had heard there was hazing of freshmen by seniors, and I felt secure with my nineteen-year-old brother walking beside me as my protector. In fact, a couple of seniors tried to get him to carry furniture into their dorms. He blew them off. I dreaded his leaving. He told me it would be tough at first but I could handle it, and then he was gone, and I was in my dorm in my tiny room sitting on my bed, overwhelmed with loneliness and fear. How was this ever going to work out? We boys had been told through letters and brochures that we were the elite, the best of the best, but to me, as I walked to the dining hall that first night with my fellow freshmen, hoping we wouldn't be spotted by a senior who would use us for his heavy lifting and not even sure where the damn Commons (dining hall) was, all I saw was a bunch of gangly boys like myself, dressed in khakis, white bucks or penny loafers, sport coat, and rep tie, pimply, acned, putting on a show of bravado, and some of us couldn't even do that.

I missed my parents, I missed Lillian and her cooking, and I missed the boys I had known my entire life. I was three thousand miles from home. I had never gone to a school with a student body over 150 kids. This place had eight-hundred-plus students. I felt not small, for I had grown to six feet tall, but lost. I had been sent here to make a mark for myself, become part of a tradition that had spawned world leaders, yet I was just trying to find out where classes were being held and if I had the right books and, most of all, if I would make a friend or two.

Andover was modeled on the preparatory school system in England. Arrogant, bawdy, vindictive, brilliant masters saw their job as molding bewildered adolescents into useful gentlemen. Most graduates went on to Yale and Harvard. Underneath their tweed jackets, New England WASP was the blood that ran through our masters' veins.

Andover's headmaster was John Kemper, a former army colonel, an austere figure who ran a tight ship: plenty of rules and regulations. No radios, no smoking, no lateness to classes, no skipping classes, coat and tie, compulsory chapel, faculty checkers with clipboards at each and every venue to make sure you were where you were supposed to be.

Here's how my housemasters saw me through the years in letters to my parents.

> Freshman: "Young Tom has passed all his work successfully for the year. I am sure you will be happy to see his report card, and now that the first year of adjustment is over with, we will all hope that he will go on to an even better record in future years."
>
> Lower middle (sophomore): "Since last term, Tom has settled into his work more, but he has had an increased number of demerits. He is by no means in the clear scholastically but has pulled his failures up to passing. In an effort to blow off steam, he gets into trouble in the house and elsewhere on campus. It is too bad that he has to be threatened with failure or disciplinary action to get him to work. He really has a good mind and a pleasing disposition—when he wants to use them."
>
> Upper middle (junior): "Tom is a fine citizen, a harried scholar whose attainment of grades is secondary to his interest in content."
>
> Senior: "Tom still finds it difficult to tie his attention to the routine of daily life. He needs constant needling to keep his room neat. It is this general dislike of the routine of reality that has interfered with his academic success in the past. I see signs of distinct improvement, which makes me confident that Tom's college experience will be more spectacular than that at Andover."

Wrong, but more about that later.

In fact, there were classes I liked, especially history and English, but I chafed under Andover's rigid order. I began to make friends with Tom Weisbuch, a charismatic, athletic, brainy Jew from Great Neck, New York. At the end of freshman year, we decided to room together and did so for three years. We liked each other's sense of humor. I was captivated by Tom's photographic memory and his passion for throwing himself into whatever he was doing: writing poetry, varsity wrestling, and painting. When he lost interest, he procrastinated to the last moment, folded up, and went to bed. I had to get Tom up in the morning if he was going to make chapel. It was possible to skip breakfast, but woe if you missed chapel. If you weren't in your seat—Bergeron, Bethel, Bissinger—it was a demerit, and it only took two or three demerits before you were headed to the dean and put on the shit list, which meant losing the few privileges you had. In my senior year, one of my classmates who sat next to me in chapel and assembly broke all the rules and was discovered to be having an affair with a faculty wife. He was expelled nine days before graduation, but the affair was all we could talk about. Envy? I dreamt of girls, but this was off the charts, an astonishing, even heroic thing. *Tea and Sympathy* redux.

Each year Tom and I lived in a different dorm or house. There was a lottery to choose your living space, so it was luck where you landed and who your housemaster would be. The housemasters didn't share their family life with boys, but Tom and I lucked out our senior year and lived in a dorm run by Karl Roehrig, the school psychologist and English teacher, and his beautiful wife, Ruth, and their two children. Karl and Ruth had warmth and a tremendous sense of humor, which was needed when dealing with forty testosterone-fueled lads. They readily saw how needy we were for parental loving.

Chapel brightened considerably when William Sloane Coffin, who later became a leader in the civil rights and peace movements, became our chaplain and religion teacher my senior year. Charismatic, dark-haired, and bespectacled, Bill Coffin was married to Eva Rubinstein, daughter of the famed pianist Arthur Rubinstein, and Andover was his first pulpit, the beginning of a career of dynamic oratory. He dispensed with the usual theological bromides. Only a few years older than us, he spoke enthusiastically from his own experience. There was one word he used over and over: "Boys, cultivate a sense of *wonder!*"

What touched my heart about Coffin and my favorite teachers was that they showed their own feelings and vulnerabilities and acknowledged ours. I never liked math, yet John McClement, my algebra teacher, ran his classroom like a mini-fun house. He hurled erasers at us, ran the eraser through the chalk, and then whacked us on the head and let you know it was a game: he was the coach, and we, the players. I loved that you could play and still learn, and when after chewing me out for something, he said, "You're really pissed off, aren't you, Biss?" He had me. I had to laugh. No teacher had ever talked to me like that, not even the English teacher who confided to me at a party—Tom and I squeezed into a few faculty parties given by the art and drama teachers, mostly on Tom's chutzpah—("Bissinger, reading rots your mind. You believe that?"). And off we went on a wild and, I suspect, slightly drunken discussion from his side (we weren't served liquor) on the merits of the question. Whether he was pulling my leg or not, it didn't matter. It was fun to finally be part of the adult world, even for a few hours.

The darker side was encountering my first taste of anti-Semitism. As an assimilated Jew from California, Jewishness was not really in the forefront of my mind, yet at a football game when Tuck McClintock yelled at someone in the bleachers, "You fucking kike!" and sniggered, my hair stood on end.

It wasn't just prejudices but the affected manner of contempt, ridicule, and snobbery that seemed to be so much a part of Andover's culture. The Cold War was definitely cold. When the short-lived Hungarian Revolution occurred in 1956, my friends and I yearned to do something for the freedom fighters, while others could have cared less. It wasn't our fight, they said, but what was freedom all about if you didn't stand up for it? The Hungarians' cause was our cause, and when they were crushed, we were devastated.

So I affected a war-weary, Bogie tough-guy stance. I was cold, indifferent, known as a supreme cynic and smart-ass, always ready with a clever and dismissive put-down, a mocking phrase that kept the enemy—that is, other boys—at a distance. Anything to hide my heart. Thankfully, I could open up with Tom and others with whom we shared literary pursuits and bull sessions.

In the fall of 1956, I returned to Andover for my senior year. It was the first time in four years that we seniors felt free of the faculty's boot on our necks. We had gained respect from them and, with it, easing of rules. Our hours when we could be off campus or not in our dorm rooms expanded. Tom, myself, and Bob Darnton were editors of *The Mirror*, Andover's literary magazine, and had great fun publishing our stories and poetry. My literary heroes were E. E. Cummings and Hemingway, whose writings permitted me to live a parallel life, one that vaulted me over my walled-in prep school confines and allowed me, at least in my imagination, to find common ground with my fellow human beings. Tom and I spouted Cummings's: "Buffalo Bill's defunct and used to ride a water-smooth silver stallion and break onetwothreefourfive pigeons justlikethat. Jesus, he was a handsome man, and what I want to know is how you like your blue-eyed boy, Mr. Death!" We had discovered the fountain of cool.

A busload of us seniors went on a field trip to Danvers State Insane Asylum. The best description is from a letter I wrote to my parents:

When we got there, a nurse showed us all through the women's dormitories. There were the oddest women I've ever seen, standing around or lying all curled up or with their heads in their hands, and they had no idea what they were doing there. Some mumbled to us, and others shouted, and some just stared. Then we went into a part of the asylum where the physically sick plus mentally ill were kept—ancient women with arms no bigger than toothpicks.

The nurse said that most of the patients except those that come in very recently are incurable and that some are incapable of feeding themselves or doing anything to take care of themselves. We went into the second-most violent wards, where there were big groups of people yelling and some were hitting each other. There was a girl about ten who came up to us and, pointing to a woman, said, "There's my daddy." She looked at us with a smiling face and a crazy look in her eyes.

The head nurse talked and then interviewed some patients. The first two were schizophrenic paranoiacs, and they talked freely and told us stories about how they owned the hospital, were wives of Mayor Yamaguchi of Boston, wife of Truman—and one also told us how the Salk treatment was a lot of propaganda and no good at all. It was amazing what stories they made up, and the funny thing is, they never said the same name twice. Then we saw some manic depressives, some of whom didn't say a word. But there was one old man who seemed the sanest of the insane. I think he actually knew where he was and would tell us stories intermingled with truths and untruths. He wrote poetry, which was very good. The whole trip really opened my eyes to some of the problems that confront the mental institutions.

I had never seen anything so raw—mental illness on display. It wasn't a bad thing that our school exposed us to the mentally ill, but it was callous to visit as tourists. How were we to perceive insanity? As a warning? A cautionary tale? How do you empathize with something so foreign to your experience? On the way home in the bus, we diverted the suffering we had witnessed into laughter. Our definition of normalcy had been breached, and we did not know how to interpret what we saw or allow ourselves to be moved, yet the shock of the asylum lingered.

In the spring of 1957, I fell in love at the senior prom, not with my date but somebody else's. Ada and I danced; something clicked. We exchanged addresses, and two weeks later, Ada came up to Andover for another dance. As soon as possible, we ducked out and went behind the Andover Inn, teenagers sneaking into the Garden of Eden. We kissed and kissed behind a curtain of magnolia trees and lilac bushes, and as we slid our tongues into each other's mouth, our tongues touching and curling and probing each other, I sucked and drank in kisses until my heart seemed to explode with warmth, melting years of rigid rules of prep schools and parents, and when that night ended and Ada returned home, I never saw Ada again. How could I? I yearned for her, but more, I needed to get out of Andover's orbit and discover a new life for myself. A hundred kisses wouldn't hold me back.

At last we would be going on to college. Following my father and my brother, I had chosen Stanford and was accepted. Why Stanford? Because it answered my immediate needs: the weather would be warm, and the classes, coeducational.

Graduation occurred, and just that quickly, I returned to San Francisco, ready to rock 'n' roll. I was a preppy, for sure, but Stanford lay on the horizon. My grandfather had given me a Chevy Bel Air, and I was eager for Tom Weisbuch and Bob Darnton to come West for some summer adventure.

Bob, who became a highly respected historian and head of the Harvard Library, my roommate, Tom, and I decided to pick peaches in the Sacramento Valley. As editors of the poetry magazine, we had probably over-inhaled Steinbeck or Jack Kerouac. We were drawn to express ourselves in a quintessential American way: work the land, exchange four years of book learning for the realities of farm labor. We thought picking peaches was a grand idea.

It was the summer of 1957. Tom, Bob, and I bunked into the tired, decaying Frontier Hotel next to the firehouse in Yuba City. A man named Clarence sat behind the desk, green eyeshade over runny eyes, unlit cigar in his mouth, playing solitaire. For $4.50, he slid us the key to the second floor front: one double bed, one single, peeling wallpaper, washstand, and toilet down the hall. Ninety-eight degrees outside, maybe ninety inside.

At dawn, we reported for work in the peach orchard—endless rows of trees, lots of Mexicans families, and us. Boss Man said, "You boys think you can do this?"

"Yes, sir!"

"All right then. Take those lug boxes, and fill 'em. Twelve cents a box."

"How many in a lug box?"

"Fill 'em. You'll find out. And don't pick 'em too small." He pulled out an iron ring. "They better not slip through this ring!"

Mexican families were already moving through the orchard. Bigger kids climbed high in the peach trees, along with their fathers on ladders; the women and smaller children picked the bottom branches and strays on the ground.

They vacuumed the trees! Bob, Tom, and I plucked, pulled, and tugged. It was harder than it looked, the peaches unyielding and out of reach. My mind was swirling: *Gotta keep moving the ladder, that takes time. Now I'm stuck in the branches. Hope this peach isn't too small. Yep, the Boss Man's cursing us for picking too small.* By nine o'clock, it was ninety degrees, on its way to 105 degrees in the shade. A lug box held a hundred or so peaches. Big urns of water were available, and we hit them every couple of minutes, drinking and pouring it on our heads while the Mexicans were laughing, singing, and chatting away. We were grunting, dying, no match for the locals. Maybe they weren't so happy, but compared to us, they were.

At the end of the day, our few boxes sat forlornly against the piles of Mexican ones. We took our meager earnings and dragged ourselves to the hotel, exhausted. During the night, the firehouse siren next door went off with depressing regularity, shattering our sweat-soaked sleep.

We staggered to work the next morning. Same deal. At the end of the day, we got our wages. Five bucks and change. It cost us more to sleep and eat. So ended the grand Kerouac/Steinbeck reality show.

Stanford started in late September. I drove to the campus with mixed feelings. I wanted to have fun and get laid, but beyond that, I really didn't know what I wanted. It would be strange going to school with girls; I hadn't done that since attending the Convent of the Sacred Heart. I had worked hard at Andover. What would I become, and how would I measure up? Did I really have to answer that now? I was confident I could intellectually hack it but was uneasy about the social aspects of campus life, especially about meeting girls and reentering dorm life. No matter what, I wanted to play.

I entered Wilbur Hall, my freshman dorm. My roommate was waiting, a lanky guy with an easy grin. Bouncing a basketball, he told me he was from Kansas, loved basketball, and wanted to be an FBI agent. Oi vey! *Don't judge, Tom. Who knows what "FBI" looks like?*

But I would judge him and quickly found out we were opposites. He was socially and politically conservative, was not interested in literature or theater, and quickly became aligned with the jocks, who did not interest me at all. Consequently, we had little to say to each other, and I threw myself into reading, filling notebooks for my creative writing class, and attending mixers where men met the female frosh. The mixers were heavily chaperoned and reminded me of dancing school: an awkward tribal affair—alpha males beating their chests, swarming to the pretty girls, who coyly flirted, while I, adopting the isolated, sensitive poetic mien, looked about for a sensitive poetic girl. I stumbled into conversation, teetered between profane and inane, hoping I might get a read on how far she might be willing to go with me once she figured out what a cool guy I was and the dawning realization that neither of us were cool and had nothing much to say to each other. I found myself driving to San Francisco for entertainment.

Before I could hit the jazz joints, such as the Blackhawk, where Thelonious Monk and Erroll Garner played, or go down Broadway to hear Cal Tjader, J. J. Johnson, and Kai Winding at El Matador, my buddies and I needed fake IDs.

I found a check-cashing store where they made IDs, no questions asked. I gave myself the name Frank L. Mineo, after the actor Sal Mineo. The green laminated document said I was twenty-one. Many of the joints looked the other way. (San Francisco wasn't called the Barbary Coast, a port town, loose, and easy for nothing.) Nursing a beer or a whiskey sour, real grown-up, my buddies and I listened to lions of jazz, exceptional men. Or we'd head to the Hungry i, where we'd catch the comics, my gurus.

Mort Sahl wryly commented on the events in the newspaper, dripping irony, ripping the whole hypocritical, pompous Eisenhower era. Shelley Berman went for neurotic phone conversations, Irwin Corey once goofed for forty-five minutes on Shakespeare, the whole thing metrically mangled, mocking and melodious. Lenny Bruce, whom I also caught at Ann's 440, was wicked, sexy, and savage. He busted on all the shibboleths. Oh, yes, sometimes I saw the Kingston Trio, why not? These were good times for Frank L. Mineo.

I made friends with John from my freshman dorm. He had graduated from San Bernardino High, a sexual epicenter, as he described it. As I got to trust John, I let it be known that I was a virgin. He suggested we drive to Vallejo, across the Bay, and find a brothel. *OK*, I thought, *if that's how you do it. Good. Let's get it over with. It's not like men haven't been going to brothels forever*. I was nervous on the drive, scared actually, but it had to be done. I needed to get laid. We arrived, found a taxi driver who took us to an ordinary apartment house, climbed the stairs, and met the madam. I was escorted into a room by the hooker, and the whole thing was over in five minutes. I was initiated. Barely.

In late fall, John and I drove to Tijuana to take in the bullfights and possibly have a second go at "it." In my notebook, I wrote in my best pulp fiction Hemingwayese:

> Five in the afternoon, dusty, shadowed arena, the crowd pitched forward, screaming for blood, brilliant on the black sweating skin of the huge animal, a bull worthy of the caves of Lascaux, face-to-face with the coifed, arrogant balletic toreador, standing on the sand-baked floor of the ring, twirling his trim body, driven by the rhythmic *ole*s and snort of blood pulsing out of the bull's neck and nose, he aims the sword just right, swift and deft and clean and him up against the massive writhing beast as it rears in midair, towering like a wave about to crush him, and then the animal's legs desert

him, start to wobble, buckle, and splay out. The bull collapses and heaves over to the ground, and the toreador triumphantly accepts the cheers and roses that fall from the sky like a Madonna's blessing.

Flushed with the excitement of witnessing this ritual machismo and murder, John and I headed to a cantina where we drank cervezas, and then John was out the door, and before I could catch up with him, he disappeared with a prostitute up a flight of stairs into a room. I stood there feeling lost. A taxi driver spotted me and said he would take me to a brothel. OK. Good idea.

Twenty minutes later, we were driving into a pitch-black evening far into the bush—no cars, nothing—and I was thinking, *This may not be such a good idea.* Then a darker idea. *John doesn't know where I went. I'm fucked! What if . . .* I repressed the thoughts of my premature death. Eventually the taxi slowed and parked in front of a pink adobe bungalow. The driver beeped, a mangy dog limped off, and a corpulent senora appeared out of the darkness. Whoa! My head had been imagining a movie, something between *The Treasure of the Sierra Madre* and *Viva Zapata!*, but this was no romance. I was one lost gringo.

The madam assembled eight sleepy, sad-looking, unattractive women in negligees. I hesitated, stalled for time, asked to see the rooms. She ushered me down a hallway. On either side were thin sheets of empty plywood stalls with beds on skimpy mattresses covered by a skimpy sheet. What *was* I thinking?

I mustered all my actor's sincerity and lied to the madam and the taxi driver that, hey! I wanted to retrieve my friend in town and we'd come back. Really! I must have been convincing enough because we left without much argument. As the taxi headed back to Tijuana, my curiosity for brothels had been sated. I learned you lose or claim innocence only once; after that, watch out! I had avoided an experience I thought I needed and was once again left with how confused I was about this whole sex business.

Chapter Four

Back at the Farm, as Stanford was known, and because of my having attended Andover, I was allowed to take some advanced courses in history and English. Perhaps the best course I ever took at Stanford was modern Irish literature, taught by the great short story writer, Frank O'Connor. He used class time to read aloud short stories by James Joyce and A. E. Coppard, who was known as a master of the form. The class listened as O'Connor's magnificent voice wrung emotion out of each character and filled the room with laughter and not-infrequently tears. I eventually majored in modern European literature, which allowed me to read Russian, German, English, Italian, and French classics. Books were my escape, my inspiration when depressed, and my companions when lonely.

Avoiding the growing hostility between my roommate and myself, I ventured to the theater department, where auditions were being held for the Gaieties, a musical comedy revue written, acted, and produced by students. The theater bug had been dormant during the Andover years, but now, I had the itch and was ready to find a congenial social scene where there would not only be girls, but I'd be able to give vent to who I was or I thought I was. Was I a moody, confused Tony Perkins type? Or was I a clone of my father? Whatever was hidden or concealed, I wanted to find out. The Gaieties reignited my love of theater.

One of the Gaieties's sketches concerned a bartender, whom I played, and a barfly, played by a very funny Ken Kesey, who was in the graduate writing program at the time. He also was beginning to experiment at the Palo Alto VA Hospital with LSD, which I knew nothing about and wouldn't for another seven years. I had read about marijuana, whose use I associated with black musicians in Harlem, but LSD was still hidden from the American public.

The only time outside the theater that I associated with Kesey was at one of his infamous parties on Perry Lane, where Kesey and his gang were dressed in togas to celebrate the Olympics and a band was rocking away. It was a swirl of manic energy, and I stayed aloof, watching cautiously, drinking nothing stronger than beer. I was still a self-conscious prep-school boy.

My life irrevocably changed when, at the drama department, I met a fellow student, Peter Kump, who told me about Comedia Repertory Company, a fledgling theater group he was starting off-campus and whose mission was to bring professional theater to Palo Alto. Less than a year later, I joined Comedia, moved off-campus, and effectively ended my association with the university, other than attending classes.

In the fifties, Palo Alto was a far cry from a cultural hotspot. There was a progressive bookstore, Kepler's, and St. Michael's Alley, a dark little coffee shop where Jerry Garcia hung out, playing his banjo. Comedia Repertory Company became my salvation. Since I had no idea of who I was or what role I was to play in life, better to play many roles.

To develop his theater, Peter brought in New York professionals to teach us. Vera Soloviova, an elderly lady with a thick Russian accent, formerly one of Stanislavsky's actresses at the famed Moscow Art Theatre, which made her practically a deity, taught a variation of method acting then in vogue in New York. "Tom, vere is your truth?" she scolded. "Don't do fakey-fakey! Create reality, and bring to life. Do not show, but be!"

"Yes, Madame," we meekly answered. There was Sy Syna, a swarthy bully from Brooklyn, who snarled, screamed, ridiculed, and physically threatened us. "I oughta fucking belt you. You think you could take it, you stupid putz?" As disagreeable and insulting as his method of directing was—and boy! did we hate him—his production of Brecht's *The Measures Taken* was first class. The sly beauty of Brecht's writing was that you could reject the Marxist premise that the ends justified the mean (if you cared to) and come to an opposite conclusion. It awakened in me an interest in political theater. I rejected Syna's bullying as a way to stimulate the actor, but I appreciated how the use of mask and gesture enhanced performance and freed the actor. I grasped how you could find an inner reality in a non-naturalistic setting. Reality was vital for there had to be something at stake for the actor at every performance.

The director of musical comedies, Les Abbot, was a local gem and the first upfront, unapologetic gay man I ever got to know well in the theater. He was all pep and pizzazz, had a great sense of humor, and put all that on stage on a most modest budget. He cast me as Jack, the straight roommate of the nutty Charlie in *Where's Charlie?* It fell to me, with my wobbly baritone, to sing a ballad—and not only a ballad but a lyrically stupid one ("My darling, my darling, I fluttered and fled like a starling") with my stage darling, Barbara Lingonfelter, a trained opera singer. What I didn't know was that Barbara was as nervous as I about singing. Yes, her blowtorch soprano voice easily evaporated my thin baritone, but as I held her quaking hands in mine while gazing lovingly into her eyes, Barbara squeezed the holy shit out of my fingers, crushing my bones as she hit each impossibly high note and making mine impossible. With a smile on my lips, I dreaded that song.

I was willing to risk exposure to an audience within the confines of the role, to mask my identity in order to imbue a character with integrity and vitality. I had a "wish" and the ego to drive it. Learn the tricks and the techniques: when to pause for effect, when to speed up, to emphasize, and most of all, how to share the stage and listen. Really listen. Take it in and respond, all the while singing "My darling, my darling," as if it were the most natural thing in the world.

Comedia was not the only life-changing event for me while I was at Stanford. In 1960, I turned twenty-one, which meant I could vote for the first time. I went to work for John Kennedy. Like many of my age, I couldn't get enough of him. After the paternalism of the Eisenhower years, here was Mr. Charisma—witty, handsome, and a Pulitzer Prize—winning author. He awakened my interest in politics. I had been fascinated by the McCarthy witch-hunt era and followed the arc of his rise and fall; I had mourned the crushing of the Hungarian Revolution in 1956. Now, finally, the United States had a young man ready to take the stage, bearing with him the hopes of youth. I campaigned hard for Kennedy and learned the lesson of how your vote counts. California had thirty thousand precincts; JFK was the winner by thirty thousand votes. Do the math.

I was drawn to Peter Kump. He had created a fun house. He was an innovator, as I wanted to be. He was cheerleader, taskmaster, and visionary, the one who held it all together, scrambling to come up with money or actors or dodging fire inspectors who came to check code. He was our shepherd, and I began to learn from him what it took to manage a theater and a company, how you balanced competing interests, and the art of the *schmooze*. I knew that I was not going to act forever and that I wanted to direct, and under Peter's guidance, I was able to begin my directing career.

The year of Kennedy's election, I had my first love affair. Liz acted at Comedia; was older than me by ten years or so; and had a husband, kids, and a failing marriage. She was warm, playful, kind in a way I never knew a woman to be kind, maybe because she had children and a husband and was caring in that way. The growing awareness that we really liked each other, when we began to give each other intimate looks and touches, was tremendously exciting. When she gave herself to me, it was not as an older woman but someone trembling, nervous as I.

Liz didn't ask for much. I couldn't give her a fully developed relationship, though I don't know how much that mattered to her or to me. I craved sex, and I craved it—if not sweetly, then ignorantly and persistently. I lived in a cabin in the woods not far from campus, and we would meet there, illicit lovers eager to rip the clothes off each other and explore our bodies. We dove into each other and thrashed about, bouncing up and down on the bed, my dozing cat bouncing with us. Liz met me halfway, and we had a glorious time until I graduated in 1961. I decided the affair was over and that summer went to Paris to study French.

One day Liz showed up at my dinky room on Rue de L'Hirondelle. What was she thinking, showing up unannounced? What was I feeling? I was terrified, trapped, happy one moment to make love, upset the next that she was here. Any integrity or commitment I had toward Liz collapsed. I ran out on her. She left the next day.

I didn't know how to say good-bye to her.

Although classified 1-A by the Selective Service, I was not yet called to duty, and so I arrived in Paris at the end of June 1961. My future with Comedia was secure; whether I left or not, I'd be welcomed back. I had pictured myself going to New York and entering the theater world, but that seemed premature if I was going to have to serve in the army, and at twenty-two, my number would sooner than later be called. I hatched a new idea. I'd go to film school and put off military service. France's Nouvelle Vague had redefined filmmaking, led by a group of young filmmakers: Jean-Luc Godard, François Truffaut, and Claude Chabrol, along with the Swedish master, Ingmar Bergman. Bergman's *Wild Strawberries* and *The Seventh Seal*, Goddard's *Breathless*, and Truffaut's *Shoot the Piano Player* were masterpieces, and their mostly brooding, existential themes resonated strongly with me. Who wouldn't want to be Jean-Paul Belmondo romancing Jean Seberg through Paris or be Charles Aznavour playing his heart out in a Parisian piano bar?

I decided to enroll that September in the Institut des Hautes Études Cinématographiques, the premier film school in France, although first, I would spend the summer studying French at the Alliance Francaise. I saw lots of films, yet it turned out that theater most profoundly affected me. My father had blessed my going to Paris, yet the theater that I witnessed in Paris would draw me to radical theater, very much the opposite of what Dad so loved.

The French designers and directors created theatrical fun houses that I hadn't imagined. The great actor, director, and mime Jean-Louis Barrault staged Rabelais's *Gargantua and Pantagruel* in a boxing ring in Montmartre. Jean Vilar starred in Brecht's satire of Hitler and fascism, *The Resistible Rise of Arturo Ui*. Moliere's 1668 play *George Dandin* was transformed from a comedy of manners into social realist theater. I was dizzied at so many new insights of what was possible in theater, how you could enlarge a story on both a theatrical and social level.

And then there was Rudolf Nureyev, recently defected from the Soviet Union, who partnered Dame Margot Fonteyn in *Swan Lake* at the Paris Opera. He leapt into air, defying gravity. As he rose from the ground, he didn't descend, no—he floated and continued to hang beyond what you imagined was humanly possible. His animal magnetism took Fonteyn's *Swan* to exquisite fulfillment. The audience was on its feet, the rafters shook with *Bravos!*

My personal life was minimal, a few pickups that led nowhere. There was the debacle with Liz. Fortunately, Will Kirkman, whom I knew from Comedia Repertory Company, had a nice apartment not far from me. We hung out a lot, and I relished his absurdist, jaundiced view of mankind. We were going to hell in a handbasket, he pronounced, but so gently and assuredly, with a little smile creasing his mouth, that it was hard to argue with his pessimism. And *tant pis*, he was going to enjoy himself, since, logically, why wouldn't you want to, given that we were looking at the latter days of time?

One weekend, Will and I and friends drove to the Loire region in a friend's Deux Chevaux, a flimsy, inexpensive, and very popular car about the size and half the weight of a VW Beetle. You couldn't buy one in the United States because they were so far from conforming to safety standards (in 1961). We camped out in a ruined castle that had belonged to Charles VII, the dauphin whom Joan of Arc crowned king of France. On the way there, our driver, Pierre, far exceeded the speed limit, and we spun out as we took a curve at high speed and rolled over.

As we tumbled over and over, I remember thinking, *This is it. I'm gonna die. Better protect my cassette player.* I held it in my arms, wondering what song would be playing when *les flics* found us mangled against a beautiful plane tree. Would it be Piaf singing, *"Moi, je ne regrette rien?"* It was a noble song, heroic even. As I prepared to meet my Maker, I was humming a little of the tune. After rolling over three times, the Deux Chevaux gently plopped into a muddy ditch, upside down. We tumbled out, no one hurt, and my meditation on what would happen to me after I died would have to wait.

I did make a movie in Italy, through the help of my father, who was a classmate at Stanford of director Delmar Daves. The movie, *Rome Adventure*, starring Troy Donahue and Suzanne Pleshette, with Rosanno Brazzi and Angie Dickenson, was a hit and can be seen by insomniacs on late-night TV. The director's wife and two daughters and myself accompanied Troy and Suzanne around Italy, and we would sit discreetly behind them on the specially rigged tour bus and in cafés. We were the continuity shot. It was great fun to be part of a Hollywood film and bask in the shadows of the limelight that shone on Suzanne and Troy.

One nonshoot day, the camera crew and I took a speedboat out on Lake Como. In the middle of the lake, as we idled for lunch, I stripped and jumped overboard for a swim. When I returned to the boat, the men on board, scandalized, quickly bundled me up, shielding me from the costume designer, a sophisticated lady. They were quaking: "Tom! You *funcolo! Porca la miseria!*" Italian men in meltdown, they wrung their hands and rolled their eyes.

"Annalise? She's a grown woman," I protested.

"Tomasso!" they whispered. "She is the niece of a cardinal! One step from the pope!" Two years at the Convent of the Sacred Heart hadn't taught me anything.

Many years later, in 1986, my family and I were riding in a gondola on Venice's Grand Canal. I asked the accordion player if he knew "Al Di La," a classic Italian ballad and the theme song from *Rome Adventure*. We listened to the music as we made our way down the canal. It was a magical evening, and I couldn't resist telling the two young Chinese males in the gondola the narrative of the movie, hoping I would impress them.

"When was that?" they asked.

"1961," I replied.

"Oh," they laughed. "You must be very old!" They instantly reminded me of those old theater maxims: "You're only as good as your last show" and "How soon they forget."

IDHEC, the cinema school, started in the fall. My enchantment with making a movie had faded after being on the set of *Rome Adventure*, where I observed the actual making of the film, its glacial pace, and that the editor's room was where the ingredients would be mixed and the final product assembled. It was the clay of theater I needed to mold, not the stitching of film pieces. It was the *repetition*, the word for *rehearsal* in French, that I loved. Yet a week in IDHEC I learned that calculus and physics were required curricula, something to do with cameras and ratios and lenses. I freaked out, recreating an old story I had repeatedly told myself about how humiliated I had been flunking geometry at Andover; shoved into a remedial class, I eked out a passing grade and was given a note by the teacher that said that if I took math 4, we'd both be shot at sunrise. Now I had to do calculus in French? Not happening. With little effort, I left the school. Perhaps I was done with schools, afraid to tackle abstract theories and equations. Perhaps my heart was with theater. What I knew was that I had to follow my heart, although at times a few brains might have helped.

Shortly after I had made my decision, the concierge handed me an official-looking letter from the Selective Service that greeted me and told me to report to Fort Ord, California, in March 1962. My number had been called.

I didn't return to San Francisco until winter. I continued to explore Paris, haunt its quays and cafés, and look at my country and myself from the outside, an immensely valuable thing. I learned about Algeria and the liberation movement there, heard the occasional explosions of *plastiques* in the streets and metros of Paris, indulged in the food and drink, soaked up the culture, and learned French. I fell in love, not with a girl, but with Paris, my city of wonders. I was lonely—I still had no idea who I was—but my artistic eye was opened. Julio Cortazar wrote a book called *Hopscotch* about lovers in the Latin Quarter who never arrange to meet. Chance directs them to each other. Living in a foreign city, you had to trust in chance, and when it worked out, the car landed in a ditch, upside down, and you were OK. And if not, tant pis.

March 1962, the United States had advisors in Vietnam. My father and brother had both served, and I felt it was my duty. Besides, I couldn't figure out how to get out of the draft, and I had a penchant for wanting to explore new fun houses, although fun and army in the same sentence seemed to be an oxymoron. Highway 1 bisected Ford Ord, with facilities and mountains on the eastern side and the ocean and shooting ranges on the western. The fort was close to Pacific Grove, setting of many John Steinbeck stories, and not far from Carmel and Big Sur, homes to Ansel Adams, Robinson Jeffers, and Henry Miller. I was hoping the artistic aura of the area would enhance my experience. The army didn't see it that way.

I served six months active duty, what they called the branch reserve, to be followed by six years reserve, leaving as an E-1 (enlisted man, private, MOS: supply clerk).

Though there were a fair number of eighteen-year-olds, many of the enlistees were my age, college kids with whom I could converse when not in training. Tales of the Korean War told by our sergeants didn't impress us recruits. That was so yesterday. No one saw a war on the horizon.

We mustered at 5:00 am, stood in formation, ran, ate, and fired weapons. KP duty was truly one of the worst jobs in the army because you started at 3:00 am, worked all day peeling potatoes, washed masses of dishware, and served meals. Never-ending repetition. One young kid didn't want to be in the army. He wouldn't do anything, slept in his sack, missed roll call, and on and on. He was flogged with masses of KP duty, but it didn't faze him. He clunked on, oblivious to the punishments, didn't finish anything until finally the army finished with him and discharged him. I had to acknowledge his stamina for punishment, far more than I could have handled.

Endless formations, endless marches. The weather was Pacific Ocean moisture: repetitions of sun, fog, and rain—and we marched in all of them. You were assigned to squads, five squads making up a platoon. Height was the criteria. Tallest in first squad and shortest in the fifth. No longer the shrimp, thank God, I led the second squad. When we marched, the little fellers were in the rear and had to double-time to keep up.

The army was unfair that way. Woe to the man who spoke out of line or protested an injustice. "Hit it. Give me twenty pushups!" You learned to keep your mouth shut except when yelling your serial number.

Rifle training was at the beach, starting in the predawn. March to the ocean, cold and damp. After an hour, mess truck arrived with breakfast. Firing your weapon was an all-day affair. We marched to different ranges where we squatted, lay down, stood up, and stood in a trench. Mostly at bull's-eye targets, but to get our certificate of marksmanship, we had to hit pop-up human-shaped targets that came and went—at all distances and heights. That was fun.

During rifle practice, we had our evening meal at the rifle range. The mess brought dinner, and after everyone had gone through the line and was eating, the mess sergeant announced there were seconds on pie—not enough for everyone, but some. I was sitting on a hill, watching. It was like throwing meat to a pack of hyenas as a hundred men rolled together in a cloud of sand, fighting, clawing, shoving, and punching to get a piece of pie. "You fucking idiots," I yelled. It just fucking pie!" How quickly the organized army descended into madness.

After two months of basic training, I rented a two-room cabin in Pacific Grove, forty bucks a month, just down the road from Fort Ord. As long as I was back at the base by five, no questions were asked. It was enough to get off the base after chow, go "home," and sack out by eight thirty. I had a bunk in the barracks but never used it. And on the weekends, I could entertain the fairer sex, at least from sundown Saturday to sundown Sunday.

Eros smiled on me, and I struck up an affair with a former Stanford grad, a six-foot blonde bass player a few years older than me who lived near the beach. We had a good month until she moved to Las Vegas to earn money as a hostess in one of the casinos. I eagerly awaited a weekend furlough and flew to Vegas where she met me, gave me a map of the city, handed me some money and chits, said she had a boyfriend, and drove off, leaving me feeling like Giulietta Masina's prostitute in Fellini's *Nights of Cabiria*, a cheap whore, abandoned by her lover. I looked at the twenty dollars in my hand. Was this what I was worth, thinking not of the sum of money but that I had been dismissed so casually and crudely, much as I had done to lovers in my life? I took the next plane out.

Routine was the order of the base: nothing out of step, keep time, do what you're told. As a supply clerk, my job was to issue clothing, blankets, rifle, and helmet to each incoming basic trainee. It didn't require much of anything: show up at 5:00 am and move through the day avoiding, when possible, my lumbering and canny supply sergeant, who had absolute mastery over us clerks. He had two characterizations for me: "Bissinger, you're so slow you couldn't catch a cold!" and "You're as useless as tits on a boar hog!" He had to put up with us because we were assigned to him, but he didn't have to like us. I was reminded of the comic strip *Pogo*: "The enemy is us." On the other hand, I learned how Sarge kept his platoon well supplied. He'd take a couple of privates with him when he sought to replenish or upgrade equipment. Our cook would give us cans of Sanborn coffee, and we'd drive to a storehouse and trade another sergeant the coffee in exchange for new blankets for the basic trainees. I also hauled supplies and troops in a truck, which I liked since I was alone, unobserved, able to be in my headspace as long as I remembered there were troops in the back who didn't appreciate being tossed off their benches as I sped around the base.

My army experience had added muscle and the ability to hit pop-up targets with an M1 rifle. I could fall asleep in my bunk while soldiers yapped and snapped towels, screaming at each other from one steaming, noisy end of the barracks to the other. I had Céline's *Journey to the End of the Night* and Blake's *Proverbs of Hell* inserted in my field-jacket pockets. Those authors kept my spirits burning bright. On September 30, 1962, a blessed day, I mustered out.

Cousins' House   My House

Mom's family: Aunt Nell on left. Their brother John and their father John Sr next to him. Both died before I was born. Florence (Gaggy), Mom on right, Aunt Carol in her father's lap.

My favorite portrait of Marjorie.

Mom, on the left in the back row, clowning around.

Soon after the birth of Peggy.

Stylin' on Sutter Street.

Dad's family: Millie, Newton, Paul, and Helen.

Dad worshiping the sun. As a 24 year old, escorting chorines on the Boardwalk during a pre-Broadway tryout of The Little Show-a musical revue. Dad in the Navy 1943.

Isadore Bissinger, Portland , OR 1888

BISSINGER & CO. FRONT & SALMON STR. PORTLAND, OR. DURING 1894 FLOOD

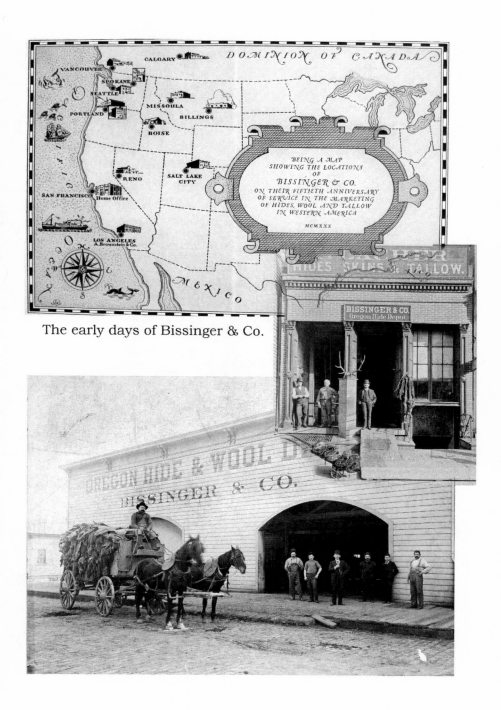

The early days of Bissinger & Co.

Manifestations of war:

Morro Rock.

USS. Biscayne, Dad's ship in the campaigns in Italy and Southern France.

Dad enjoying time off from the war.

Roger Sobel's jeep at Golden Gate Park:
Tom sitting
Hunt Barclclay
Carlos Maas
John Heinz
Charles Page
Doug Moore

Tommy playing with lead soldiers,forshadowing Fort Ord.

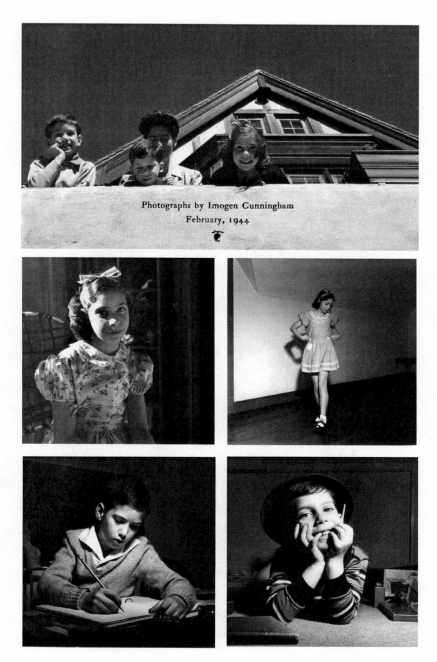

Photographs by Imogen Cunningham
February, 1944

Portraits by the famous photographer Imogen Cunningham
of Mom, Peggy, Paul, and me.

Convent of the Sacred Heart
Town School 3rd grade musical bunnies
Town School 4th Grade

Laffin' Sal and the costume kid in many disguises. My cousins John, Pat, and Peter and I were actors in skits written by my aunts to spoof Gaggy, her dotty friends, and obliging servants.

Family portrait taken in the grove at Rampart by Ann Rosener circa early 1950's. Back row from left: Dad, Mom, Stanley and Nell Sinton, Carol and Henry Sinton, my brother Paul. Against tree on right: cousin Margot (Nell and Stanley's daughter and the eldest of the grandchildren) and her husband Perry Biestman. Front row: John Sinton (Nell and Stanley's son), Tom, Pat, Peter, (Carol and Henry's children) Gaggy, sister Peggy. Missing: Joan Sinton, Nell and Stanley's daughter.

SWIMMING HOLE, TRUCKEE RIVER

Christmas at Gaggy's was a formal banquet. Dad is being served
on the right.Cousin John is pranking me behind my back.

Gaggy always looked elegant.Her elegance extended to her craft
of bookbinding. She bound first editions, many of them of famous
artists' diaries and sketchbooks. She was honored as one of three
Americans whose work was exhibited at the Brussels World Fair
in 1957.

IDENTIFICATION CARD

THIS CARD IDENTIFIES

FRANK L. MINEO
FULL NAME

1245 Filbert St.
ADDRESS

San Francisco, Cal.
CITY

EMPLOYED BY

Frank L. Mineo
SIGNATURE

| SEX | Male | AGE | 21 | HEIGHT | 6' | | WEIGHT | 150 |
| HAIR | Brown | EYES | Blue | RACE | White | DATE OF BIRTH | 4/3/35 |

RIGHT THUMB PRINT

SOCIAL SECURITY No.

SECTION 529 OF THE PENAL CODE OF THE STATE OF CALIFORNIA PROHIBITS THE USE OF AN IDENTIFICATION CARD BY ANY PERSON OTHER THAN THE ONE WHOSE PHOTOGRAPH, NAME AND FINGERPRINT APPEARS THEREON.

REB-SF

This I.D. card got Frank L. Mineo into a lot of jazz clubs. All you had to do was go into the I.D. shop, fill out a form, and voila! You became legal-ish.

Graduation from
Phillips Academy:
I'm top row, third from left.
Tom Weisbuch to my left.

Bob Darnton and Tom Weisbuch,
Upper Middle year (Junior)

KNIGHT IN ARMS
SPRING 1961

Campus 'Knight' Errant

BY STANLEY EICHELBAUM

TWO STUDENTS at Stanford — Douglas Johnson and _____ Guittard _____ in a mus_____ _____ on a _____ sion _____ Ondine _____ why _____ Ar_____ ficu_____ m_____

Here attempt_____ that the production worked against them so completely.

Thomas Bissinger's staging was pathetically unimaginative and Mary Alyce's choreography was embarrassing. Except for three performances, the cast was uniformly untalented. As for May Delafield's settings, they could not have been executed with a heavier hand. The costumes by Georgia Ryther were far more successful.

T.e Ondine story — whether by Giraudoux or anyone else — is too fanciful for slapstick humor. It should have an unreal quality, like the one a fragility. Sight gags should never have been included, like the one in which a performer backs into another player.

I cannot blame you for all the show's faults since you must have had your hands full just moving the cast around the stage. I was invited to review the show and I saw no value in a kind criticism. It would have seemed a disservice to all of you.

If theater people have no faults, how can they improve.

Sincerely,
Stanley Eichelbaum

San Francisco Examiner

MARKET AND THIRD STREETS SAN FRANCISCO
TELEPHONE SUTTER 1-2424

Mr. Tom Bissinger
Box 7481
Stanford, Calif.

May 17

Dear Mr. Bissinger:

Please excuse the delay in writing you. As you _____pected, my schedule is sometimes crushing and this week was particularly _____

I am pleased to know that you are dedicated enough to _____ to take criticism so seriously and thank you for not being _____ about my review.

Believe me, I am fully aware of the difficulties and _____ of staging a full-scale musical, especially when the cast is _____ _____ed.

I never intended, in my review of "Knight in Arms," to _____ with such finality. My time is limited and my space is _____ It is often impossible to expand on any remarks.

Anyway, I admired the flair with which you approached _____ I am certain that your future productions will _____

_____ough I cannot hope to qualify as a _____ _____ments are always based on a _____ _____ maintain that there _____ _____was handled.

_____ts, how can they improve.

Sincerely,
Stanley Eichelbaum

Ouch! I received my first review as a director during my senior year at Stanford. The show: _Knight In Arms_, was written by Horace Guittard, an undergraduate who became a well-known light opera and musical comedy star. The review stung; I wrote Stanley Eichelbaum and he replied.

Top: Stanford comedy revue, The Gaieties. Satyrs and their girls.

Middle: Comedia Repertory Co. Brecht's *The Measures Taken.* The comrades enforcing the party line: "Sink in the mire, embrace the butcher, but change the world. It needs it!"

Right: Comedia's *Men Without Shadows* by Jean-Paul Sartre. Philip Schultz and myself portray captured members of the French Resistance. Note the handcuffs.

Left: Suzanne Pleshette and me on location for *Rome Adventure*.

Middle left:The quintessential Italian gesture as in "Tom, why you taka your clothes off in front of the Cardinal's niece?"

Middle right: Suzanne and Troy Donahue wait for filming to begin.

My platoon: Fort Ord, Calif. I'm on left, third row

Chapter Five

I returned to San Francisco as the fall of 1962 began. The context of family life had changed. My sister, brother, and I hadn't sat at the same table together with our parents for years. My relations with my parents were formal. I had withdrawn from them more than they from me. I was willing to take from them even though I wasn't giving much back.

Finished with my six months of military service and facing six years' reserve duty, I felt like I was ready to step into my future, to follow my heart, which was telling me to go to New York, center of the theater world. My parents didn't stand in my way. If anything, they were encouraging. My sister was now living in New York, so I had an ally in her and with Hunt Barclay, my childhood friend, who was enrolled in the Art Students League.

I could visualize a future for myself, although I didn't know how to achieve it. I only knew that I had to be where the action was, and San Francisco, despite its sensual beauty, was too full of relatives and social obligations. I was too well known, and I wanted the freedom to be unobserved by prying eyes that knew my history. As I looked at myself, I saw that the army had tested my manhood, but what had I really accomplished that a million other men hadn't? I was undoubtedly clever, but would I ever be able to sustain a love affair? What was I afraid of, that I couldn't maintain intimacy? And would raw ambition be enough? Had I overestimated my abilities? So many questions that I needed to find answers to.

I packed a couple of bags and arrived in Manhattan on October 3, 1962, found a residential hotel on Madison and Thirty-Third and started to read *Show Business* and *Backstage*, looking for work as an "anything." It took me a few confusing weeks to orient myself to Manhattan's grid—was I walking up or downtown, east or west? No matter. I walked everywhere, inspecting the city, inhaling its air and bustle, trying on the masks of confidence and looking good that would assure my success, tens of thousands like me gathered under the show biz tent with one purpose: to make it.

Make what? Be what? Why, successful, of course. But what was success?

A job, yes. Recognition, sure, but first and foremost, I needed to honor that bitch goddess Ambition that drove my focus and determination. Such wooing of the goddess eventually crystallized into my law of elevation: if you keep at what you're doing for seven years, you will achieve "it." I eventually discovered the correction to the law—that by the time you achieve "it," you'll no longer want "it" because you've already been doing "it." Time to move on.

The sixties was a singularly creative era in New York. Whether among the old masters of dance—Balanchine, Martha Graham, Alvin Ailey—or the young Turks of theater—Judson Dance Theater, Café Cino, Café La MaMa, Bread and Puppet Theater, the Living Theatre—artists were exploding with new ideas. Kennedy's election had released a feeling that youth was ascendant—we could do anything. Simply push the old aside. Not even push, just ignore them. There were daring productions such as Genet's *The Blacks* at St. Marks Playhouse with James Earl Jones, Maya Angelou, Roscoe Lee Browne, Louis Gossett Jr., Godfrey Cambridge, and Cicely Tyson and Dylan Thomas's *Under Milk Wood* and Genet's *The Balcony* at Circle in the Square. Jose Quintero was staging epic productions of Eugene O'Neill and Peter Brook's *The Persecution and Assassination of Jean-Paul Marat as Performed by the Inmates of the Asylum of Charenton under the Direction of the Marquis de Sade*—usually known as *Marat/Sade*—made a huge impact in 1965. The theater world blazed with imagination. I was seated at the banquet, and the meals were exquisite, the conversation endless. I soaked it up.

I reconstituted my friendship with Hunt Barclay, who lived on the corner of Broome and Mulberry Streets in the heart of Little Italy. He had an artist's loft above the Café Roma, where mafiosi sat at little tables in the back, sipping espresso. Hunt was friendly with the mobsters, and one of them, who owned Angelo's Restaurant on Mulberry, commissioned him to paint a replica of Venice's Piazza San Marco on a thirty-five-foot wall. I posed as a man feeding pigeons. Meals were exchanged for the artwork, so we occasionally dined in an upscale fashion, Hunt discreetly pointing out "made" men who habituated the Café Roma.

In November 1962, as I was crossing Forty-Second Street, I bumped into a friend from Stanford who told me that a producer was looking for a production assistant. J. I. Rodale, the publisher of *Organic Farming*, had written a play warning of the dangers of sugar in our diet and how this caused juvenile delinquency. Kind of a crude message, but hey! Twenty-eight bucks a week and all the vitamin C you could eat, courtesy of JI. My first job! Foot in the door.

Fortunately for me, my sister, Peggy, was living on the Upper East Side with two attractive roommates. I adored all three: Peggy, Kathy, and Ginny.

It was like *Sex in the City* without sex. Ginny was pretty but had boyfriends. Kathy was blonde, willowy, tall, and available, though not to me, as much as I tried. She fended me off with gentle humor. Mostly, these gals provided me with good food and company, family and friendship.

I was taking classes at Circle in the Square, studying directing with Alan Schneider and William Ball. I studied Shakespeare with Fanny Bradshaw, who was a master at deconstructing Shakespeare's verse. She crammed a lifetime of juicy information about how to read and recite the Bard into ninety minutes of class time, exciting the student how to proclaim:

> What a rogue and peasant slave am I,
> I am pigeon-livered,
> A rascal,
> What an ass am I,
> Like a whore, unpack my heart with words
> And fall a-cursing, like a very drab
> A scullion.

"Mr. Bissinger," she'd say, "the comma is visual. Articulate consonants, pronounce every word, stay within the rhythm of the line. If the actor is alone on stage, he is really thinking out loud."

I even took acting classes with my old Comedia mentor, Vera Soloviova. Despite wanting to direct more than act, it was good to learn more about Stanislavsky's method for almost every actor in New York was employing some form of it. My head was swirling with the information I was absorbing, and I couldn't wait to put it to use.

I was slowly making friends, going to lots of theater and dance performances by myself and then returning home to my newly rented fifth-floor, one-room cell with bedroom alcove in a dreary gray building on Perry Street in the West Village. The saving grace of my "nest" was that my two windows faced south and revealed a neglected garden below, a murmur of life amid the concrete. But my tenement cried with tininess—tiny rooms, tiny lives whose stories slowly emerged (such as Royal and Vi, a NY transit cop and his wife who lived across the hall). Royal loved to fuck women he met while working. He said they couldn't resist the uniform. They'd come up to him on one pretext or another and want to engage or submit to the authority of the badge. Rather easily, so he said, he got their names and later went to their apartments and scored. He'd come over to my room and cry, asking me whether he was abnormal because he had such a sexual appetite, and Vi was a perfectly good, better-than-good woman—and why did he keep on doing things like this? But he kept on doing things like that, and maybe it was because of his uniform. I mean for him as well as for them.

And then there was Jeannette downstairs to whom I used to read Shakespeare sonnets. She was legally blind although she could see some, enough to stumble around her room and cook simple things out of cans. She had scraggly brown hair and wore a housecoat over a slip. Her lips were painted fire-engine red and were smeared, reminding me of a circus clown. I would analyze her situation, enraging her to the point where she was screaming at me and crying and raging, saying what I was saying wasn't true, I was mean, I was horrid. I looked at her, gesticulating wildly. I was telling her that she refused to heal herself; she refused to do anything to alleviate the miserable circumstances of her life. Instead, she chose to live as a bag lady, her room a trash heap of stale groceries, garbage bags filled with clothes and mementos of an earlier sighted life. "You're faking," I cried. "You can see well enough to get around. Get a dog, get—"

"Leave me alone," she yelled back. "How do you know what I'm like?"

I didn't know what she was like or who she was. I only knew I had sat on her bed and read an hour's worth of poetry to her, which we both loved. While we read, we were filled with the noblest, saddest, most beautiful thoughts. We were voyagers on the same ship—lonely voyagers, as were Vi and Royal. We confronted our aloneness by clinging to our various "blindnesses" in the name of love.

Other than these encounters, Perry Street was for sleeping and an occasional romantic fling, less than an affair, more like a one-night stand. Today or tonight didn't really count—it was what tomorrow was going to bring.

I had met Victor Wolfson via his sister, Tess, whom I met at a party in San Francisco. I had his phone number and called him when I first arrived in Manhattan, and he graciously invited me over to his house on East Eighty-Sixth Street, just around the corner from Gracie Mansion, the mayor's house. He greeted me at the door, a cigar in his mouth and a drink in his hand. He scrutinized me. He was grinning, a handsome, barrel-chested man with a bristly mustache and piercing eyes, dressed in floppy trousers, a striped Italian boater shirt and a Russian peasant hat covering a thick mass of hair. "You must be Mr. Bissinger." He laughed. "My sister raved about you. Come in. I'm cooking. Stay for dinner."

I hadn't expected this. We went down to the basement where the kitchen was located. "I love to cook. Do you? You should learn. Just don't get hung up about it. I'm loose with recipes. Feel your way through it. And use plenty of wine or whatever's available. Tell me about yourself."

I didn't have much to say, kind of overwhelmed by the energy of the man as he nonchalantly carried on as if I was just another member of his family, who, as they trickled downstairs, he introduced me to: his three young sons and his wife, Alice.

Over dinner, Vic filled me in about himself. He was proud of his parents, Jewish radicals who had emigrated from Russia in 1894 (about the same time my grandfather Newton emigrated from Germany) to escape anti-Semitism and tsarist political persecution. He adored his sister, Tess, and mentioned that his brother, Martin, an actor, was appearing in the *Threepenny Opera*, which was playing off-Broadway to great acclaim. Victor had had his plays produced on Broadway and had just won an Emmy Award for the episodes he wrote of *Winston Churchill: The Valiant Years*.

The man seemed to know everyone, yet here he was, befriending me, a nobody. He wanted to know what made me tick and assured me that I was on the right track in taking classes and that if I got anything, I could let him know and he would see whom he knew that might help me. He combined glamour and sophistication with a shrewd, even cutting manner, all the more so as he continued to drink. His tongue loosened; he became abusive to his eldest son, who told him to go fuck himself and left the table. He turned his attention to his wife. "Look at you, a proper Bostonian, holier than thou."

"Victor, be quiet. Don't go on!"

"Look how you dress!"

"Not in front of Tom, Victor." (Their youngest son was also named Tom).

"You disgust me."

"Why'd you marry me then?"

"Fuck if I know. Bitch!"

"Victor, that's enough," she'd respond.

"No, you with your fancy upbringing, you sit there like a lump. I don't know how I've put up with you all these years. Bitch!"

Alice, close to tears, left the room.

Alice was a prim Bostonian; she couldn't have dressed more dowdily. How the two got together, I couldn't figure out and never did, and they eventually did divorce. I sat in the kitchen, both thrilled and horrified by their exchange. My father never, ever, talked to my mother like this. Vic then turned his attention to me, as if nothing had happened, and full of charm, told me tales of his life and asked me about mine.

My tongue was also loosened by wine; I talked up my résumé, but as the evening wore on and it was just him and me, he started probing, and as he had been open about his family, I talked about mine. "You have problems with your father?" That started it. I decided I could talk to him about anything, thrilled as I was at the attention given me and the way he seemed to know my psychological makeup better than I did. "And what about your love affairs?" he asked. I confided that I "loved them and left them," kind of like Sammy Glick in *What Makes Sammy Run* by Budd Schulberg, always looking to see how I could move up and better myself. Consequently, my interior life was a shambles, at the least, confused. "Yeah, I get that," Victor said. "You have to be in control." *Shit, this guy knows me,* I thought. Victor gave me the name of a psychiatrist. "Maybe you ought to see him. This guy's the top psychiatrist in New York. He sees theater people. I went to him. Be a good kid, and try him out."

He called me later in the week to see if I had called the shrink. I told him I had an appointment scheduled for the following week. "Good boy. Call me after you see him, and we'll get together. I have a house in Warwick, Suffern County, New York. We'll go out for a weekend."

On the following Tuesday, I made my way to the office of Dr. Ernst Hammerschlag, a Viennese psychiatrist on New York's exclusive Upper East Side. He asked about Victor without saying much and proudly told me that his former home in Vienna backed up on Freud's and the two families were friends. I was in the presence of royalty.

Dr. Hammerschlag sounded like Henry Kissinger, a low rumble to his accented voice, his cryptic remarks falling like occasional rain in the desert. He was elegant, courtly, and reserved, and once more, it seemed I was back in school and the class was emotion 101 and I hadn't studied, didn't have access to the book, hadn't taken notes, and had no answers for why I was lying on his couch, passing the time, except that I felt cold as an iceberg. I wrote in my notebook: "Would someone tell me what the hell was the agreement or contract we had when we came into this brawling, miserable, fucked-up world, shining with possibility and longing and disappointment and crap? What was it I agreed to do or be when I was shot down out of my mother's womb 'cause at this point I don't know?" I showed it to him. He raised an eyebrow. "Very dramatic."

I was sure Hammerschlag was brilliant and wondered why the hell he just didn't tell me what was wrong with me, but Freudians don't fix your fixations, at least in those days. No, you have to wait for something to click in or illuminate, but I never found that "aha" moment. Thirty to forty minutes would pass. "You're not very talkative today."

"Nope." I lay there, resigned, pissed, a hopeless case.

When he cared to, he would make an observation, a little hint, and I would suck it up like candy! But as soon as the sugar high left, I went back to Albert Camus (my favorite author at the time) and existential despair, which I had hardly earned. He pointed out to me how afraid I was of "blind authority," referring to the recurring nightmares of Nazis in my dreams, ruthless, all-powerful authorities from whom I was always running through the woods, dogs barking at my heels, me silently screaming or not so silently.

I lay on Hammerschlag's couch for three years, 1963-66. I was always terrified that I would meet someone in his waiting room, exposing my evident insufficiency, although he wasn't shy about telling me that Lotte Lenya came to see him and possibly other show business folk. I carried shame—shame that I needed therapy, shame that I could afford therapy on my father's dime. After three years, I figured—OK, I'm coping. I now sat up on the couch instead of lying down. That was my greatest achievement. I bid adieu to Dr. Hammerschlag, about as emotionally constipated as when I began, and began smoking marijuana, which was a whole lot more fun and illuminating than coping.

Victor and I were in continual communication. We traveled—sometimes with family, sometimes with friends—to his house in Warwick, New York, and also to his house built in the late 1600s in Wellfleet, Cape Cod. These were fun times, much partying among his acquaintances in these two communities, a collection of agents, artists, writers, workmen, and strays he had picked up along his way. I marveled at his charisma.

To honor that charisma, I took Victor to see the movie *Zorba the Greek*, directed by Michael Cacoyannis. Like many others, Anthony Quinn's portrayal of Zorba, a peasant musician of animal energy and zest for life, dazzled me. He takes under his wing Basil, an uptight English writer played by Alan Bates, and mentors him. "Dance, boss!" Zorba demands of the Englishman who refuses. "Boss," says Zorba, "life is trouble. Only death is not. To be alive is to undo your belt and 'look' for trouble." Slowly, Zorba, this peasant with his homespun philosophical zingers, awakens the cautious Basil. I felt their relationship mirrored mine with Victor. Afterward, Vic and I went to a Greek restaurant and drank toasts to Zorba, to life, to love, to my career. "My boy," he said, "that was a great movie! Let all this shit with your parents and upbringing go. Are you getting anything out of Hammerschlag? Anything? What the fuck do I know except I love you and I want you to listen to your heart! The rest is just bullshit! We're all going to die, so you better start living! Dance!"

One day, while we were sitting in his living room, he opened a closet and pulled out several yards of a yarn quilt. "What is it, Vic?"

He held up knitting needles and grinned. "I'm knitting my shroud."

In 1965, he wanted to go to the Cape to check on repairs being made to the roof before winter struck. It was just he and I. I had known for some time that Victor was bisexual. I just knew. It may have been things he said or how he referred to other men as well as the women in his life. He seemed to have a quantity of both, someone who needed conquests more than love. And so, one night, while I was lying in bed in the upstairs bedroom, I thought, *I ought to get this over with.* I left my bed and went downstairs and got into his.

It was my only time and didn't seem to matter to either of us. No, that's not true; it was a big deal to me. I felt shame, but like other situations that arose in my life, I wanted to experience something for the sake of the experience. He may have used me, but I also was using him; nonetheless, I saw myself as the violated one, and I could hold that against him. I tried to put the experience out of my mind.

Victor wasn't my lover, but I had loved him. Now, I wasn't sure. He told me to get over it. He was a fighter; I wasn't. He never second-guessed his actions; I continually did. Ultimately, I told myself that night with Victor was like going to Vallejo to get laid. Been there, done that. I continued to see him, invite him to my productions that I was beginning to direct, and take his coaching, but I was wary of him and myself. Was I bisexual as well as he? Why didn't I know by now? The hell with it. I needed to focus on my work.

I had received an offer to work on a production of Max Frisch's *The Firebugs* at the Maidman Theater on Forty-Second Street for which I was paid $40 a week to hold script, assist the stage manager, move scenery, and absorb whatever director Max Gorelik, a famous theater designer and author of *New Theatres for Old*, could teach me. I watched how the actors comported themselves. Were they indulgent or professional? What frustrated them? What got them going?

I always loved rehearsals more than performances. Rehearsal was where the company invented, confronted, discovered, explored, floundered, failed, and recalibrated. It was also the time to commit and share. Only a handful of productions of mine did I fully enjoy. Mostly, I noted what didn't come off, what I couldn't figure out how an actor or I could do better.

I began to spend time with a former Stanford classmate Fanny Howe, with whom I had acted in a couple of University one-acts. Today, Fanny is a highly honored poet and novelist, but at the time, she was a starving writer. Fanny introduced me to her friends Kermit and Linda Roosevelt, who had a friend named Sandy Thompson, whom I completely flipped over. Oh, that she would have flipped over me. She did a little, and that was briefly glorious. Trouble was, she was married, albeit unhappily, to some reporter, then working in South America, named Hunter Thompson. I was a footnote.

Fanny introduced me to her parents, Mary "Molly" Manning Howe—an Irish novelist, playwright, and founder of the Poets' Theatre in Cambridge—and Mark DeWolfe Howe, a Harvard Law professor. In May of 1963, Molly Howe invited me to direct *The Offshore Island* by a friend of hers, Marghanita Laski, at the Agassiz Theatre in Cambridge. Molly was well known for her experimental work with the Poets' Theatre as well as her adaptation of James Joyce's *Finnegan's Wake* for the stage, a monumental job of translating and shrinking Joyce's compendium of world mythology and Irish history into a workable script for actors. Fanny had recommended me to Molly based on friendship and the plays I directed at Comedia, plus a musical version of Anouilh's *Ondine*, which I had staged at Stanford. Having lost her first director,

Molly was willing to take a flyer on an unknown. This was my first break as a director. *The Offshore Island* was an antinuke polemic and received deservedly mixed reviews, but I didn't care. I was able to hone my director's chops.

Molly was a witty, opinionated, warmhearted drama queen, and you would not expect less from one who, in her younger days, had played the Abbey Theatre and reputedly had been the mistress of Samuel Beckett. She would throw her arms in the air at moments of despair about the cast, the play, the publicity, or money and say in her lovely, light Irish brogue, shaking her head, her eyes aglitter with terror, "Oh, Tom, dear god, what are we going to do? The whole thing's an absolute, complete disaster!" A momentary pause. "Ah, then, we'll do what we can." And she'd snort with laughter. "You'll have to deal with the filthy buggers. I'm completely undone." And we'd hug, laugh, and pour ourselves a glass of sherry.

The Howes and the Wolfsons had welcomed me into their two families. I liked that very much. I was communicating with my parents by letter and seeing them on their occasional trips East or mine to San Francisco, but they were West Coast, and I was moving on, a man on a mission, and was going to follow every lead, knock on as many doors, take as many classes as possible, and be seen as often as possible. I was gaining confidence.

Chapter Six

I was in New York on the morning of November 22, 1963, eating at a diner on Hudson Street, when the radio came on with the news that JFK had been shot. I paid my bill, ran home, and watched TV, sobbing, hoping against hope. My hero had been killed. Like the rest of the country, I fixated on the news, LBJ's swearing-in, Oswald's arrest, Ruby shooting Oswald. Everything was crashing to pieces. I had followed the campaigns of civil resistance in the South, the sit-ins, the unending brutality against blacks, the ascension of Martin Luther King Jr. to prominence, and the rise of a potential rival, Malcolm X. And now the man who was leading the nation, in whom the young and disaffiliated and marginalized had placed their hopes, was dead. Everything was shattered.

I watched how the Vietnam War was beginning to grow in violence— "American as cherry pie," as Rap Brown, the militant Black Panther said.

Two acquaintances of mine, Arthur Marks and Ron Sullivan, were assembling a company for a season of plays in Monmouth, Maine, using the old turn-of-the-century Cumston Hall, long abandoned but still charming, as a theater. They hired me as a director. Ron would be the stage manager and coproduce with Arthur and their liaison in Maine, a local, Richard Sewell, who lived in nearby Augusta. Dick, rangy, excitable, honest, was running his little company on poverty plus. Few tickets had been sold, but Dick was a warrior. He would send the company around the county and beyond; we would hang posters, make costumed appearances at the local blueberry/cranberry/peach festivals, letting the greater Maine community know that the Monmouth Acting Company was your ticket for serious, hilarious, thought-provoking, fill-in-the-blank, glorious summer-stock theater.

We were put up in an abandoned 1930s-era grocery store, replete with greasy wooden floors, now emptied of everything but bread shelves and refrigerator cases that divided the store into two, with nine women sleeping on army cots on one side and eleven men on the other. The perfect summer-stock setup. What I didn't know was that inland Maine in the summer was ninety degrees of stifling humidity. Fortunately, there was a lake nearby to cool off.

Every company contains dramatic archetypes, and ours was no different. On the female side, there's the brooding actress, slightly ill, who keeps to herself and conceals herself in dark glasses and layers of clothing (Greta Garbo); a perky, bubbly ingenue whom everyone has the hots for (Debbie Reynolds); and the mature woman who mothers everyone (Meryl Streep). For the males, you have the virile swashbuckler (Johnny Depp); the old-man authority figure (James Earl Jones); the funny comedian guy (Steve Martin); the skinny kinda-gay guy (Pee-wee Herman); and the good, reliable square-jawed guy who can also play evil (Jack Nicholson).

Me? I just wanted to direct plays. I knew I could draw performances out of actors. As well as I could inspire and touch them, I'd also confront and challenge them to visit unfamiliar or possibly repressed emotions. If we clicked, they would transform the discovery into a great performance.

We led off with Anouilh's *The Lark*, followed by *Much Ado about Nothing*, Molière's *The Imaginary Invalid,* and Kaufman and Hart's *The Man Who Came to Dinner.* I directed all but the Shakespeare. We were young, ambitious, underpaid when paid at all, but we managed to put food on the table and lured audiences into the theater, sometimes packing the house, a sure elixir for any actor's ego. I was learning how to direct a company, blend personalities, soothe ruffled egos, fend off feuds, and most importantly, push beyond self-imposed limitations to the new and surprising.

My favorite show was the Moliere because we could employ the techniques of commedia dell'arte, the freewheeling, improvisatory farcical theater that I had seen in Paris in '61. Masks and gestures sprinkled with Borscht Belt humor, why not? Esther, who played the saucy maid in the show, became my girlfriend.

Because of the grocery-store-cum-army-barracks arrangements, the opportunities for making love were almost nonexistent, unless you included Lake Cochnewagan, which, in the interest of staying afloat, was dicey at best. Esther and I needed a plan. Up the hill from the theater, I had spotted a garden shed by a pond away from the road and a field away from the farmer's house. I checked it out. It was unused—dirty and cobwebbed, with scythes, shovels, and broken pots scattered about, the shed was a potentially perfect rendezvous spot, anonymous and discreet. So I thought.

Over the next few days, under cover of darkness, I cleaned the shed and installed a mattress, bedding, candles, a bottle of wine, and glasses. We were crazed, stricken lovers straight out of Moliere. The stage was set. The night arrived, and after the show, Esther and I crept into our love nest. Candles lit, we shed our clothes and spent a rapturous night in each other's arms.

We awoke in the dim mists of early morning, having heard sounds. A stray cow? The farmer walking his dog? I peeked out the window. Thirteen men were standing on the banks of the pond, talking among themselves. A fucking lynch mob! "We gotta get dressed, Esther. Quick!" Clothes thrown on, wine stashed, we waited. What to do? Whose move?

Finally, the shed door creaked open. A large man stared in. How the hell did he know we were there? Too late for that now. The words came haltingly and died pathetically. "Well, sir, the unavailability of . . . um . . . the grocery store not really . . . er, uh, um . . ."

"Best you pack up and leave now," said the farmer. Esther and I slunk into the morning glare, a gallows walk past the somber posse, a scarlet SM (for Sex Maniac) tattooed on our clothing. I'll say this for New Englanders: they're a stolid bunch, not much for expression. There are times when you appreciate that.

On the next day, Esther and I were summoned to the farmer's house to apologize and receive a dressing down from the police chief while the farmer and his wife, looking like Grant Wood's *American Gothic*, sat in judgment.

Such is the arrogance and innocence of youth that we looked on our adventure not as a crime but a lark. Dick was not happy with us, but the cast took it in stride, and the rest of the summer passed quickly, lovemaking essentially squelched other than furtive humps in the grocery store when no one was around. We packed our bags and left quickly, feeling good about the plays we had put on. We were becoming professionals. It had been a fabulous summer.

Before returning to New York, Esther and I went to Martha's Vineyard to reunite with Hunt Barclay, who had rented a small shack on Chilmark Pond with his girlfriend. The previous summer, I had stayed at a converted lighthouse just up the road, so I knew the whereabouts of the shack, and the four of us romped for a few days. We were told we could buy the shack and three acres for $10,000, but who wanted to be tied down with property so far away from New York? Victor would have snapped it up in a minute and later told me I had made a huge mistake. Today, the property would be worth millions.

Hunt's and my favorite movie at the time was *Jules and Jim*, a beautiful French love triangle whose two male characters are in love with a free-spirited woman. We even called ourselves Jules and Jim. Definitely, Hunt had eyes for my free-spirited woman, and I was, well, looking to move on.

Esther and I broke up when we returned to New York. Hunt took up with her. It didn't feel right. My best friend replaced me! So what that I initiated the breakup? It was betrayal. I rationalized that I was too busy making a career to have time for a girlfriend.

It so happened my father was in New York on business and had two tickets for the World Series: Yankees versus my favorite team, the Dodgers. We had first-game seats in the center-field bleachers and watched Sandy Koufax throw a masterpiece, striking out fifteen batters. It was like old times, seeing a ball game with Dad, shoulder to shoulder, a lifetime of ball games and plays. Side by side we were comfortable with each other—nonconfrontational.

I continued my education, taking directing classes with Edward Albee and Alan Schneider at Circle in the Square. The Off- and Off-Off-Broadway theater scene, as well as the art scene in general, was exploding. Based on what I was seeing, there was no limit to what one could do. If you could dream it, you could try it.

I attended a master class on the ninth floor of Carnegie Hall for working professionals that started at eleven o'clock at night after the Broadway theaters let out. The legendary Harold Clurman, who had founded the Group Theatre with Elia Kazan in the thirties and who had directed Clifford Odets's *Waiting for Lefty* and *Awake and Sing*, taught it. When I met Clurman, I felt I was meeting a "man," someone who had consciously developed himself and was not only of the theater but the "world." He had come of age during the Depression, and his knowledge of politics, psychology, and the arts was encyclopedic and poetically expressed. "Theater is a place to sing your sorrows," Clurman told us. That statement hinted at something. Yes, I could sing, but what was I sorrowing about? Didn't I have everything? Been given everything? Sure, in my own life, but out on the street, civil rights workers and African Americans were being murdered, Vietnamese were dying along with GIs, and a president had been assassinated. And I felt impotent about it. Only in the theater could I sing to that sorrow, express my vulnerabilities and strengths, and touch and inspire an audience. In song, speech, and movement, the stars were aligned, and I could be a lightning rod for a collective energy and turn it into gold, magic, a fun house supreme. I knew I knew how to do it! Clurman's classes further inspired me to achieve it.

I volunteered to be stage manager for John Blatchley, a director at the Royal Shakespeare Theatre, who was directing *Macbeth* at the Institute for Advanced Studies in the Theater Arts. John incorporated his psychological interpretation of what lay beneath the text so that we, as moderns, could feel the play's power for our time. After the run at IASTA, *Macbeth* was performed at the Folger Shakespeare Library at the Library of Congress. The symbolism of performing that play after the recent murder of JFK, our "King," and the resulting conspiracy theories was powerful.

Through my association with IASTA, I was hired to direct the Croton-on-Hudson Shakespeare Festival, acted entirely by teenagers. I immediately hired Ron Sullivan, my stage manager from Monmouth, to be my stage manager. He and I worked well in tandem. Fresh from my education working on *Macbeth*, I was eager to try out what I had learned on *The Tempest, Richard III,* and *The Winter's Tale.* I began my rehearsals with plenty of sound and movement exercises. It took the actor out of thinking and into responding, reacting in the moment. The kids were quick learners, and the shows, especially *The Tempest* and *Richard*, sparkled with energy and deft characterizations. The through lines of the plays were clear. I couldn't have asked for more from them. The Croton community rallied around the festival and helped with tech and design, leading me to fall into a summer romance with one of the costume designers, a woman like Comedia's Liz—older, talented, kind, generous with me, and married. We entered into the affair conscious of what we were doing, indifferent to what others might know or think. The sex was sweet, and why not? The era of free love was upon us, and suburban housewives were no different than anyone else, As the inmates sung in *Marat/Sade:*

> We want our rights,
> And we don't care how!
> We want a revolution now!

Maybe we weren't all that radical; certainly, the ending was predictable. Once out of town, I was out of sight, not knowing how to say good-bye.

Marat/Sade was playing on Broadway, and its theme—its raw violence and group dynamics as the actor-inmates marched around the stage in various degrees of lunacy and mayhem, ferociously belting out songs—echoed my sense of national turmoil. Malcolm X had been assassinated in a Harlem ballroom in February. The Vietnam War was heating up, the images from its mayhem lingering long after the television was turned off. I was scheduled to go to Camp Drum as part of an army reserve unit for two weeks' training.

Meanwhile, I jumped at the offer to direct two experimental plays at Ellen Stewart's Café La MaMa with members of Joseph Chaikin's Open Theater. I directed the *Trial of Judith Malina and Julian Beck*, the leaders of the Living Theatre who had been put on trial for anarchy, nudity, pot, tax evasion—whatever the authorities could charge them with.

When I'd go to the Open Theater's weekly workshops, there'd be two stoned hippies sitting on the stairs, working on a musical while we were improvising in the studio. They turned out to be Gerome Ragni and James Rado, the authors of *Hair*, a musical that had Vietnam directly in its sights. The Becks couldn't attend the play about them because they were in jail.

At the same time, Victor urged me to go to Saranac Lake, where a local community college was putting on *The Trials of Joseph Brodsky*. Victor had read the transcript of the trial in the *New Leader* and thought I should get the rights to it. Brodsky, later in life to be awarded the Nobel Prize in Literature, was imprisoned in Russia for being a poet. In this country, a poet practically went unnoticed! I went but was unable to obtain the rights.

Politics was unavoidable. One had to take a stand. You could feel the anger in the streets—marches, sit-ins, rallies. I had thought of going to the South to help in some manner as it seemed so much more vital than doing theater. There was a symposium called by Peter Brook at a theater on St. Mark's Place to discuss *Marat-Sade*, the war, and how the theater community could respond. The theater was packed, the audience passionate and noisy about the correct choice of action, full of self-righteousness, denouncing each other vehemently. There seemed little clarity, other than Brook's. I was both exhilarated and depressed and went home and wrote a jeremiad about what I had witnessed and read it aloud at the next Open Theater workshop. The following is an excerpt:

> Friday night revealed the simplistic nature that runs through America, that we tend to think in absolutes, that we always expect answers. As Delmore Schwartz says in a poem:
>
> > Go quickly
> > And remember: there are circumstances,
> > And he who chooses chooses what is given,
> > He who chooses is ignorant of choice.
>
> We must resist and end this either-or, black-or-white ethic to life and working in the theater. Commitment is entirely possible within the framework of contradiction—it is acceptance rather than refusal. Believe in possibilities, for it's excitement and adventure.
>
> I want to know that one dares everything and that one sees that a play is not an answer to madness or sanity—a play answers nothing. Neither does an actor—he shows us the possibilities and paths of our lives and events. We have only to dare, to shake off the indulgent inhibitions that lead us to final conclusions—I mean socially and politically, as well as emotionally, for I felt as never before the tremendous shadow of (call it) fascism, McCarthyism— all because we must find and give final answers, final solutions.

I didn't expect much response. I just needed to vent; the agitation didn't go away.

From Selma, Alabama, incendiary images on TV and articles in the *New York Times* chronicling bombings, murders, and harassment of black and white

Freedom Riders raised the stakes. At issue was our country's integrity, its lifeblood, so I thought. Let it be hijacked by ignorant mobs, or fight for justice? Each day pleas were made to join the protest in Selma. With the photographs of the unleashing of dogs and water cannons on the marchers attempting to cross the Edmund Pettus Bridge, I couldn't sit back any longer. Fuck it. I was going to Selma.

I booked a flight for Montgomery. Other newly arrived protestors and I were driven to Selma and deposited at Brown AME Church in the heart of the African American housing projects. Things were moving fast. It was bewildering—people arriving and leaving—both ends of the street on which the houses and church were located were blocked with wooden barriers and a phalanx of state-police cars. We were told we could leave the projects but not as a group.

Assigned a house and family, I dumped my bag, saying hello to a grandmother, a mother, and two daughters, one about eighteen, one eleven. While the rest of the family greeted me warmly, the grandmother coolly checked me out and didn't look happy. I was no more welcome to her than the cops at the end of the street. I took meals with my family, put money in the pot to help out. Grandma watched me like a hawk, muttering to herself, "Don't be going next to my granddaughter." The eighteen-year-old blushed; the mother said, "Mama, just be nice to the man," but Grandma knew what was going on—she had a twenty-four-year-old white man sleeping right the damn hell in her own house! The rest of the family was blessedly sweet, innocent, cautious, and a little stunned that all this was happening in their front yard.

That first evening, we reassembled at Brown's Church to hear speeches by Martin Luther King Jr., Hosea Williams, Jesse Jackson, Ralph Abernathy, and other black and white clergy. They were demanding a permit from the government to march to the courthouse in Selma. "Are you with us? Are you ready to march?" Yes! Yes! The feeling was electric, scary; we didn't know what was going to happen, but here we were, so let it happen.

We spent the days standing at the barricades singing the movement's anthems: "We Shall Overcome," "Freedom," and "We Shall Not Be Moved." We gathered in church pews listening to speeches and formed action groups for press, transport, housing, security, and first aid. We were several hundred pilgrims from around the country: students, union organizers, clergy, housewives, hippies, idealists all—more arriving daily. Assembling in the street, the police stonily watched us, took our pictures, cradled their rifles, and cracked jokes among themselves. Sure, we were confrontational, but outrage had to have an outlet, a way of standing up for ourselves. Selma was theater and beyond, a polarizing boiling intersection of race and politics, held together by King's preaching and his insistence on the theme of nonviolence. Workshops were given in how to handle provocation and outright assault as well as to look at our own violent tendencies. The elders, King and his lieutenants, most of them preachers in their thirties or forties, and the student leaders in their twenties, clashed with each other on the pace and strategy of confrontation. Into this stew white newcomers, few of whom were Southerners, were inserted into an irritated Southern town; white Selma was rubbed raw by the media attention and righteousness of the newcomers. Energy shifted, a dance of rigid lines of police and sheriffs facing what King called moral force.

On the evening of March 25, I was in the basement of the church when a sixteen-year-old black kid named Leroy Moton came in. I had seen him around; he was one of the helpers. I noticed his fingernails were red. Must be a fad. But it wasn't that. He had been in a green Oldsmobile with Michigan license plates driven by a thirty-nine-year-old white woman, Viola Liuzzo, returning from Montgomery when a carload of Klansmen overtook them and point-blank shot and killed Liuzzo, who was driving. Moton feigned death when the Klansmen came to inspect the car, which had driven off the road. As Leroy told the story, it dawned on me that it was Liuzzo's blood on his nails that he hadn't scrubbed off. He came that close to dying. It became clear what the stakes were. The FBI arrived and started buzzing around. Could we trust them? J. Edgar Hoover?

King and his advisors improvised; everyone was determined to keep the vigil alive. We headed upstairs to the church pews, and King addressed us, told us to stay calm and hold to the truth of our cause. We wept as we sang "We Shall Overcome," in reverence not only for Viola Liuzzo but as if that song would be our anchor of strength, no matter what or who lay outside. Late in the night, we trudged back to our houses, silently watched by the ever-present state police silhouetted by their cars' dome lights.

On the next day, word filtered down that the judge had lifted the injunction. We could march to the courthouse! We gathered in a group, King and his lieutenants linked arm in arm at the front. It was a bright, sunny Selma morning. We moved forward, singing ecstatically. As we entered the downtown area, whites were massed on the sidewalk, children in mothers' arms, young kids, teens, men, and women, their faces cold and hateful, mouthing "Nigger lover," "Go home, carpetbagger!" Fear was palpable on both sides. A new idea of moral force, Gandhi's nonviolence, the opening to the other was the drama being played out, but I was glad we were protected by federal marshals.

That day when King spoke was one of the most joyful days I have ever experienced. I don't remember what he said on the steps of the courthouse; surely freedom, justice, and love were the themes. We were basking in that love, proud and powerful. The air was electric, and also erotic. To be that close to death, to have witnessed the death of one who had been standing with us the day before, filled me with physical vibrations. I could feel in the air and from those around me a hunger to embrace and savor another's humanity, their "livingness." We all felt totally alive, much as it must be for those in war. I thought of my father witnessing the carnage of Salerno and Anzio Beach. Wouldn't he have had a visceral feeling for his own survival and love for those with whom he survived and grief for those who didn't? Janis's "Freedom's just another word for nothing to lose" floated through my mind. We had our lives to lose, and yet we were free because we were certain of our cause. It had been declared and shared and "Ain't no stopping us now" was our refrain. As the crowd swelled, we flowed from the courthouse steps out into the street. If we were down, King's oratory lifted us; if we were afraid, our brothers and sisters stood next to us.

We, elated, returned to Brown's AME Church and resumed our vigil.

On the weekend, I was invited by the older daughter to go to a dance club in Selma. I was nervous, unsure what reception I might receive.

The club was on the second floor of a building downtown. A couple of hundred black teens were dancing—and me, whitey. My date introduced me to a few of her friends; they mumbled a hello and looked away. I was invisible. I tried to dance, but nothing was working. I was a gangly white boy from up North with stiff legs. Broadway show tunes weren't going to cut it. Whatever music was being played, I'd never danced to it. No one was unfriendly, mind you; I just didn't exist. My only role in this setting was one I'd never experienced: invisibility.

Sunday rolled around, and four of us, three whites and a young black man, decided to go to church in the white part of town. Provocative? Yes. Foolish? Yes. It was an option that had been offered to us by one of the organizers. We had to try. We walked past the barricades, put back in place after the march, and slowly walked toward a church, any church. We didn't know where to go. After fifteen minutes, we spied a Methodist church across the street. As we started to cross, two men ran out of the church and attacked, raining blows, scattering us across the street, cursing, "You ain't never coming in this church. Git the hell back where you belong, nigger-loving sons of bitches." The parishioners had spoken. We ducked under their fists and retreated back to the projects. Although we marchers were the ones penned in, the churchgoers were the ones with their backs against the wall.

I helped coordinate the transportation of people and goods for the march to Montgomery, which meant I lined up the buses and the food trucks, manned the phones, and relayed messages. The marchers arrived unharmed in Montgomery to a huge nationally covered celebration. As the marchers, exhausted yet exhilarated, gathered for aftermath sessions, energy began to drain away. One of the white organizers for the Southern Christian Leadership Conference asked me to stay on. "Help organize, Tom."

I wrestled with the request, feeling that a better, more committed person might stay and fight the good fight, but that wasn't me. I had never felt higher, but the bottom line was I was a theater director. That's how I "saw" myself. I got on a plane for New York, my home.

Chapter Seven

I was exhilarated. Selma had been theater enacted on a national stage. I had witnessed hatred that chilled my bones. Tears of pain and joy, as well as confusion, suspicion, and fear—all so very human. What stood out for me was how committed we were to standing up for our humanity. I was no hero, yet all of us had reaffirmed, "We hold these truths to be self-evident—that all men are created equal."

My family was relieved I was back in New York. I immediately touched base with Peggy and had long conversations with my parents, who hadn't heard from me while I was in Selma. They had some bad news. Dad had skin cancer, the severe kind, and was receiving radiation treatment at Stanford University. Should I come out? I inquired. No, no, not necessary. My father was only sixty; I had to believe he was going to live for a long time.

The year1964 had been a busy one. I directed the Croton Shakespeare Festival and produced and directed *The Second Shepherds' Play,* which toured churches and YMCA's in Manhattan and Brooklyn. This medieval play concerned the shepherds' pilgrimage to Bethlehem and the encounter with Mary and the baby Jesus. The woman playing Mary, gazing at the wrapped bundle she held in her arms, reminded me of the *Madonna and Child* outside my grandmother's bedroom. I realized how attracted I was to the mother-and-child archetype, the bliss of being held in your mother's arms. That led me to thinking of my own mother, who had hired a nurse, Gertrude Ilksen, after I was born. Apocrypha has it that when Ms. Ilksen brought me to my mother's arms when I was one-year-old, I burst into tears, and the nurse was immediately fired and later attempted, unsuccessfully, to jump off the Golden Gate Bridge. I wasn't sure any of this contributed to my desire of being held in an (older?) woman's arms or not, but I found in subsequent years that this image of mother and child was one I loved to evoke and frame in plays.

At the Institute for Advanced Studies in the Theater Arts, I had directed a curious German Expressionist drama, Walter Hasenclever's *Humanity,* written in 1918. *Humanity* was fun to stage. It had forty scenes but only a few words in each scene, so it was more cinematic than play, the scenes unreeling like a silent movie—abrupt, stark, and fraught with symbolism. Sound cues were a mix of distorted instruments and voices. Lights were harsh and emphasized shadows. Actors formed exaggerated poses and uttered one word—and then black out, new scene.

I was beginning to feel like one of the cooks at the banquet of theater professionals, beginning to be entrusted with ingredients (play, actor) and then given the go-ahead to prepare a meal.

I stage-managed Off-Off-Broadway productions and directed two of the Open Theater's plays at Café La MaMa.

La MaMa, in those days, was one of the first Off-Off-Broadway theaters. Located on Second Avenue, you climbed to a second-story loft. At one end a tiny stage and at the other a row of bleachers. Ellen Stewart, La MaMa herself, a Caribbean black woman, greeted you, sold you a ticket, gave you a cup of coffee, and passionately introduced her shows. She had been and continued to be a clothing designer in order to support the theater, but she had found her vision, and one day, her theater of avant-garde productions would be world-famous. She knew which playwrights to champion, and even if there were eight people in the theater that night, nothing was going to stop her. I became a habitué to her brand of theater: magically different and new ways of writing plays, staging, and acting.

I was looking for two things: Earn an Equity card, which I did by stage-managing one summer at the Williamstown Theatre in Massachusetts. My greater goal was to be given the opportunity to direct Off-Broadway, and the only way I knew to do that was to keep working at anything that would keep me in the mix, build my network, and expand my friendships. I could almost taste how close I was getting to being recognized, but I wasn't there yet.

Somehow, people who are supposed to find each other do so. Lew Lloyd and I were part of a clique that hung out together. He introduced me to Gordon Taylor, who had had just produced a fifty-college American tour by Theatre Group London, a group of English actors, including Gordon, who had recently graduated from drama school. Gordon had traveled extensively, was wealthy, and had connections. Gordon, Lew, and I agreed to produce an international theater season and market it to college campuses. Lew, who managed the Merce Cunningham Dance Company, knew about the logistics of touring, Gordon would make connections, and I'd promote the venture. Mana Productions was born.

I think Mana had something to do with India, but maybe we just misspelled the Biblical *manna.* It could have been *manana* for all that didn't occur. Our ambitious scheme was to tour three renowned performance groups through the United States: Milan's the Teatro Studio di Palazzo Durini, internationally famous for its productions of *Commedia dell'Arte*; Athens's the Greek Art Theater's productions of Aristophanes's *The Birds* and Aeschylus's *The Persians*; and from Ahmedabad, India, the Darpana Dance Drama Company featuring *Bharata Natyam*, *Kathakali,* and *Manipuri* dances.

We went big-time and rented an office on Broadway but we had a problem. We had shows but no contracts. We couldn't secure the companies until we had forty or fifty guaranteed contracts with the colleges. In September 1965, we decided to put all our chips on the National Convention of College Performance Booking Agents. Make or break. We set up our booth along with a couple of hundred other competitors at the Americana Hotel, but the fish weren't biting. Two contracts signed. We bombed. End of Mana Productions.

Undaunted, Gordon asked me to take over Theatre Group London, who were ending their tour, and direct them for their New York debut. My first Off-Broadway show! I took over the company at the beginning of November 1965.

The repertory consisted of *A Night Out* and *The Dwarfs,* two one-acts by Harold Pinter, and *The Beggar's Opera* by John Gay, from which *The Threepenny Opera* was adapted. The actors were in their early twenties, extraordinarily talented, having trained for three years in movement technique, improvisation, and the Stanislavski method at the London School of Drama. They became my family, and I fell in love with all of them, especially Deborah. Blonde, sassy, soft-lipped, and big-eyed, she was all fun and flirtation, promise and passion. We were infatuated with each other; I was besotted by her English accent, sensual vitality, the way she whispered "darling" in my ear. I devoured every part of her, and she reciprocated.

Gordon had booked a theater in New York. We were on our way to stardom! The only hitch—and a big one at that—was that the Actors Equity union opposed giving working visas to the Brits, claiming that despite being a unique company, those very Brits were taking jobs from Americans. Just before Christmas, like a lump of coal in a stocking, despite all pleas and petitions, their visas were denied. Theatre Group London was deported, my chance for directorial acclaim blown, and my budding romance snuffed. Damned if I was going to let the romance part go. In early January 1966, I flew to London.

"It was just one of those things" is the song that came to mind. "Just one of those crazy flings/a trip to the moon on gossamer wings." Cole Porter had it right; our affair was too hot not to cool down. In one week's time, Deborah and I ran the gamut from ecstasy to agony. We hung out in Chelsea with Deb's friend, Hilly Amis, ex-wife of the author Kingsley Amis, and her eight-year-old son, Martin, who turned out to be quite a novelist himself. We couldn't get enough of the Beatles' *Rubber Soul.* Carnaby Street—the mod look, Edwardian foppery—was all so much fun. We rented a Morris Minor, and we drove to Dorset, ate clotted cream, walked on the beach, and fucked our brains out. I was trying to figure out how I could stay in Britain, and I dreaded the answer. No way. I wasn't going to be able to get a work permit in England, and I had a career to keep going despite my totally insane desire for Deborah. We were the king and queen of drama: seven days of up-and-down roller-coaster trips through Agony—and Ecstasyville. I had never been through a wringer like that; I flew back to America, devastated.

Heartbroken, I reported to Victor. He offered me an Armagnac. He was pleased that I was heartbroken. "That's progress, my boy. That's what love's all about. She's an actress, right?" (He claimed to be banging Faye Dunaway.) "You'll get over it. Now tell me about England."

Slowly putting Deborah out of my mind, I refocused on the theater and found an agent who, based on my work with La MaMa and the Open Theater, got me a job directing two Rosalyn Drexler one-acts at the Milwaukee Repertory Theater. I was happy to leave New York for six weeks, and especially to be working at an Equity theater. The plays were experimental and not well received, but I didn't care. I was working with professionals.

I directed the same two plays by Drexler that summer at Act Four Playhouse in Provincetown. One of the actors was John Cazale, one of the stars of *The Godfather* series. The actress was Adele Mailer, who had been stabbed by her ex-husband, the writer Norman Mailer, the year before. He liked the show, and I liked Norman. He was an exemplar for me of a public figure, a literary brawler whose writings provocatively examined war and sexuality, two of my favorite subjects.

I was curious to explore the new media because the definition of what was considered performance was changing rapidly. Allen Kaprow, who had created Happenings, wrote that "visitors to a Happening are now and then not sure what has taken place, when it has ended, even when things have gone 'wrong,' for when something goes 'wrong,' something far more 'right,' more revelatory, has many times emerged." Each Happening I had seen was unique; often, the interaction of the performance and the audience determined its outcome. I didn't want to let go of directorial control, but I certainly wanted to see what the emerging artists and dancers and videographers and musicians were up to. I had always gone to museums to get ideas for costumes, sets, and even staging, so why not this new wave of performance art?

John Cage was the most influential artist in articulating this new kind of performance. The technology of multi-video installations, mixers, amplifiers, speakers, and tape recorders didn't totally thrill me, but one August afternoon, I ventured to a Bowery rooftop and listened to Max Neuhaus's piece for fans in which microphones picked up the sound of whirring fans, which he mixed and massaged through giant speakers. In the audience was Mitzo Naslednikov, a striking blonde journalist, six feet tall, with a slight accent from having been raised in Paris by her Bulgarian lawyer father and her Swiss French mother. Mitzo was writing about the avant-garde scene for French journals and about to exit her romance with Max.

Soon Mitzo and I were seeing each other. She was very bright, funny, and affectionate, a spiritual explorer. Heads swiveled when she walked in the room. Finally, after only hearing about marijuana, I smoked my first joint with her; butterflies flew off the wall, harbingers of transformations to come. This was fun.

My agent hooked me up with an up-and-coming playwright, James Prideaux, who had persuaded the Amateur Comedy Club, located in the Murray Hill area of Manhattan, to produce two one-acts. The club's male membership was composed of social blue bloods and power brokers. The men performed the plays in a cozy 150-seat theater with adjoining clubhouse, drawing upon their wives and professional actresses for the female roles. In addition to the one-acts, I directed Brendan Behan's *The Hostage* the following year. The men liked to drink, have fun, and act, but they took their roles seriously, and the plays went well. Before I went to the Park Avenue apartment to coach one of the actresses in *The Hostage*—her husband was a member—another member pulled me aside: "Tom, when you see Louise, please don't even think of fooling around, if you know what I mean, because although Louise is a very luscious babe, her husband and his associates are in concrete." Armed with this enigmatic warning, I respectfully entered her apartment. Whoa! Two floors, each the size of a football field. Yep, her husband was worth a lot of concrete, none of which I wanted as shoes.

In March of 1967, a TV writer in Los Angeles named Lou Shaw was reading a political satire, *MacBird!*, in *Ramparts* magazine. *MacBird!*, which was then being performed at the Village Gate in New York, used the story of Macbeth (and parts of other Shakespeare plays) to frame Lyndon Johnson's career as a bloody ascension to power via the assassination of President Kennedy. Lou decided he wanted to produce it and later told me that he immediately flew to New York to get the rights.

Coincidentally, David Dretzin was moving the play from the Village Gate to the Garrick Theatre on Bleecker Street and had asked me to supervise the production's restaging. I wasn't going to get much credit, but I'd work with terrific actors on a show that was going to run for some time. I had moved up in rank.

After the show opened in the new theater to good re-reviews, Lou Shaw offered me the job of directing the play in Los Angeles. He put together a great team, and we rolled. It was one of the easiest productions I ever did, largely because of Lou's ability to listen to me, and I, to him. We didn't fight; we laughed, knowing we were going to knock the socks off this production. We were that confident. We opened *MacBird!* at the Players Ring Gallery in June 1967, while the play continued its run in New York, and we ran to sold-out houses for nine months. Anyone who was anyone in Hollywood came to see the show. I stuck around for a few weeks to see that the show kept its edge and then returned to New York. I received weekly royalties from the show and realized for the first time that you can make money in this business.

September of '67 found me in Boston directing *America Hurrah* at the Charles Playhouse. It had created a small sensation in New York and made the reputation of the playwright, Jean-Claude van Itallie, who had developed it at Joseph Chaikin's Open Theater. Joe was a soft-spoken man who enigmatically told me his favorite word was *yield*, but beneath his soft exterior was a man who knew exactly what he wanted. In 1968, Chaikin and I codirected *America Hurrah* at the University of Connecticut.

America Hurrah, a collection of three one-acts, was successful in Boston due to the violently wild third play on the bill, *Motel*. Two actors inside mammoth dolls caroused inside a motel room, scrawled obscenities and dirty pictures on the walls, and completely trashed the place while the motel-keeper doll watched.

Simplistic it was, but most powerful in its effect. If you said it was a parable about America's role in the world, Vietnam in particular, you wouldn't be wrong. Two of the actors in the plays just getting started on their careers were Jill Clayburgh and Al Pacino. Jill was effervescent, willing to try anything; Al was moody, a brooder, very much in the Actors Studio mold, seeking motivation for lines and actions that were clearly absurdist. Even so, you could see that this guy had magnetism.

Because I happened to be at the right place at the right time, Roger Domani, a small, wily French Belgian, hired me to direct a French version of *America Hurrah* at the Theatre de Poche, a highly respected experimental theater in Brussels. I was going to Europe! How cool was that? Mitzo came with me; I was glad to have a girlfriend, and she would help translate. Even though I had taken four years of French at Andover, I wasn't sure how fluent I would be. Tant pis! I was beginning to fulfill my dreams in ways I hadn't expected.

Roger was a bit of a scoundrel, utterly charming, surviving on wits, lies, and a knack of usually keeping one step ahead of creditors. Money was always elusive. I embraced this scoundrel. I liked the hint of criminality, that defiance of authority. By hook or crook, bare coffers and all, the Theatre de Poche had aggressively presented avant-garde theater from all over the continent. Since van Itallie was born in Belgium (his family left when he was four), there was added interest in what *America Hurrah* was all about.

When I asked to see the translation, Roger shrugged, made an "eh" gesture with his hand, which meant things were not yet quite jelled, which actually meant nothing had been done. Mitzo set to work on a translation. I met the cast, talking to them in French, all of us patient with each other. In a letter to my parents, I wrote,

> The work proceeds slowly. Basically, the Belge actors are scared of fully expressing themselves, and that doesn't help the plays, which are very extreme and physical. The actors are used to working quickly. The task is to prevent them from being superficial, which, I suspect, is their wont. Where the Americans overpsychoanalyze everything, the French ignore it. But slowly the play is being put together, and I'm sure it will be a big hit.

I was told I was the first American theater director to work in Belgium. Roger lined up radio, TV, and newspaper interviews, all conducted in French. I loved the attention, and my speaking French was received more graciously than I would have thought, both by the press and the actors. What really surprised me was that Europeans took artists seriously. Their questions were not only about theater; they were political and social. What did I think about the Vietnam War? Racial issues? Censorship? No one in the United States would give a damn what a twenty-eight-year-old director thought about anything.

Below is from another letter I wrote to my parents:

> I worked like hell the last few days as the entire theater staff seemed to crumble and no one took responsibility. I had to whip everyone into shape, which was the job of the two directors of the theater, plus help paint sets, buy props, build sets, etc. It was quite incredible, and I'd hate to go through it again. The show went excellently; everybody was terribly excited, so much so that the following night, there were five police to make sure that salacious parts of the play were eliminated, due to the order of the Minister of Internal Security, who was there for the premiere.

If that didn't guarantee sellouts, what would? The play sold out.

Belgium would not be the last time that plays I directed would be censored. Sometimes it was the script, sometimes my staging. Why should the theater lag behind the other media? Films were breaking free of the code, dance had nudity, and chastity seemed a thing of the past. Drugs and rock 'n' roll were happening, and given the landscape of war that occupied the nightly television screen, the immorality of which you couldn't argue about, why be timid about sexual expression? Provoke the audience? Yes, I wanted to.

I planned to return to the United States, but Roger had managed to include *America Hurrah* in an experimental festival of film, theater, happenings, music and political discussions at the Casino Knokke on the Belgian Coast. Shortly after New Year's Eve, 1968, Mitzo and I made our way to this seaside resort. The chief feature of the main room in the casino was a series of huge murals in a rotunda, which surrounded the viewer, painted by the surrealist René Magritte, a truly stunning display of his work at the height of his creativity. An artist about to make a name for herself was showing *Bottoms*, a film featuring a hundred nude rear ends of assorted Londoners. The artist was Yoko Ono. She spent most of the time enfolded in a black bag at the entrance to the casino hall. I never saw her out of the bag.

We returned to New York. I couldn't put my finger on it, but Mitzo and I were drifting apart. We had other lovers but kept a facade of togetherness for a while. We liked each other, maybe a lot, but we were headed in different directions. Mitzo was ambitious for her writing career; I, for theater. She was a spiritual seeker. India and yogis fascinated her. Theater was my church, and I was aiming to be a high priest of it. Ambition is not kind to lovers. Our paths were diverging.

The Vietnam War was at a boil. I had avoided almost all my reserve duty because I was in a "control group," which basically meant I didn't have to attend evening meetings because I worked in the theater at night. Due to the number of men being called to active duty, my control-group status was revoked, and I would be drafted unless I joined an active unit. I looked around and joined a gravediggers unit based in Manhattan, but mercifully, before I had to dig a grave, I was honorably discharged.

The Festival Theater at the School of Drama of the North Carolina School of the Arts in sleepy Winston-Salem hired me to direct *A Taste of Honey*. Mitzo had joined me, and she made headlines.

Below is from page 3 of the *Winston-Salem Journal*:

> At first she was just another pretty girl walking down Fourth Street in a miniskirt. But on closer inspection: A wide band of lace just below the waist revealed that she apparently didn't have anything on underneath . . . . The men whistled and yelled, and some looked as if they might just cry . . . . One man driving on the far side of the street from the girl reacted like a pro. He looked, turned the wheel and drove straight for her—across four lanes of traffic.

Mitzo was pissed and dashed off a letter to the editor. Among her points were these: "It is not in my habit to walk around naked or to show others what I don't want them to see . . . . Why do the men run away like rabbits when they try to make a pass at you, and you answer in a mild but authoritative way, 'I haven't asked for your company, so scram!' And most of all, why do the men seem so dumb and uninformed?" And on and on.

The society pages noted: "In the audience opening night was the Mystery Girl who caused quite a stir with her good looks and scant dress." She was duly identified by name as the guest of the director.

We zipped out of town in my Austin Healey, which I had bought in Brooklyn for $300 and spent a week on Ocracoke Island at Cape Hatteras, where I took LSD for the first time. It was fun floating in the literal and cosmic ocean; I spent hours drifting in the waters offshore, blissfully undifferentiated from nature. Later, in the shower, I felt myself oozing down the bathtub drain, a tiny and tinier being, losing all sense of self as the universal sound of the cosmos, the original heartbeat, vibrated me past space and time until I suddenly realized the sound was actually a panting dog on the other side of the bathroom door. Then a neighbor's knock at the front door froze me. Paranoia! The trip was bumpy after that, but despite the paranoia, LSD had removed masks and revealed a consciousness that transcended my usual way of thinking and being. Once that door was opened for me, I was curious to find what else was "out there," at the least to reexperience the transcendence I had felt floating in the ocean.

Mitzo and I separated for good in the fall of the year. As always with me, good-byes were not easy and so were never said. She had her apartment; I had mine.

Many years later, I reencountered Mitzo. My wife, Kristen, and I spent an evening with her in Paris. She spoke of time in India, where she lived in an ashram in Pune led by Bhagwan Rajneesh and was introduced to Tantric sexual practice. Again we lost touch.

In the 1990s, I found out that Mitzo had become Margot Anand, had written a bestseller, *The Art of Sexual Ecstasy*, and developed a practice called SkyDancing Tantra. She led and still leads retreats and seminars around the world, has put out books, CDs, and DVDs, and is a superstar in the realm of spiritual sexuality and the consciousness movement. Would that I could take a little credit for her success, but our relationship was more about defining who we were as we came of age in New York City.

Chapter Eight

In October of 1968, my father visited New York, and I, innocently (so I thought), brought him to meet Victor. I had had a weird experience with Dad just a year earlier in Milwaukee when I was directing at the Milwaukee Rep. He was on a business trip. I joined him and a fellow businessman at dinner. At the end of dinner, they started negotiating the price of cowhides that Dad was selling. Pencils out, they went back and forth. I had never seen him in action—this was fascinating! Too high, too low, they slowly worked their way to an agreeable number. I wasn't sure whether or not he had lost or won the negotiation. I wasn't a great negotiator, but I wanted to see it in him. He seemed satisfied, however, and uninterested in discussing the deal which made me feel he had possibly come out on the short end of it. Something bothered me and left me confused, and now, a year later, Dad was in Victor Wolfson's house.

Understand, the meeting may not have happened like this, but this is how I experienced it. Mentor versus father. For years, I had pledged my allegiance to my mentor while trying to differentiate myself from my father. Artist versus businessman. My father was a civic man whose work and companions featured business and military men, cops and boards of corporations. Even his theater buddies were drawn from these ranks. My mentor was a loner, his pen his sword. Both were Jews, both could schmooze, and both were well off. One was bisexual, the other not. The former was cynical, the latter hopeful. Both men's careers had peaked. My father had not long to live; Victor would live another twenty years.

Dad entered, jovial, friendly, dressed in a suit and tie. Victor was casually dressed. As we drank whiskey in Victor's living room, Dad chatted. Victor listened but apparently didn't need to show any respect for my father, ignoring what Dad said and changing topics. I felt like a little boy watching the drama unfold. I could be a confrontational director, the provocateur, yet in this room, I was an onlooker. I don't remember what was said, but what I heard was sarcasm and mockery from Victor and chat from my father. Maybe my father was playing his cards really well, giving nothing away. For me, the stakes were enormous. I was consumed with getting something from the father that he couldn't give and possibly wasn't interested in giving. I might have said, "Dad, why are you putting up with the way this guy's treating you? Don't you love me?" I wanted him to say to Victor, "Listen, you son of a bitch, I don't like the way you're talking to me. Who the fuck do you think you are?" Or did I just want them to fight over me, little Tommy? Who loves me the best?

Yes, I was throwing back in my father's face what he had said to me so many years earlier that had wounded me so deeply: "If you loved me, you wouldn't lie to me." I had decided, based on that one phrase that I was unlovable, a liar, and that trusting in love was dangerous. That was the story I told myself. And now I was saying to myself, *If you loved me, you'd act differently.*

My father followed an officer's code of behavior: honorable, respectful, and decent; one gave and followed orders. That was the world he came of age in and served. Victor's world was licentious, unruly, provocative. The theatrical emblem of Dad's world would be *South Pacific,* Rodgers and Hammerstein's tribute to World War II's heroism and romance; Victor's would be *The Threepenny Opera* by Brecht and Blitzstein, featuring Mack the Knife and London's underworld. In my mind, as I looked at these living emblems, Mack the Knife was slicing Emile de Becque, the hero of *South Pacific,* into ribbons.

I felt confused, helpless, and nauseous. I had asked my father to meet Victor and, in doing so, had betrayed my father—for what? Self-righteousness? Revenge? As I saw it, a father's role was to provide for his family and educate and nourish his sons and daughters. Once that was accomplished, his job was done. Why wasn't that enough? My mentor's job was to mold who I was, show me the world as he saw it, for better or worse. Who I was for Dad was not who I was for Victor. I saw how Victor treated his sons and that he was having little more success with them than Dad was having with me. Was it inevitable that fathers and sons had to battle each other? When was there reconciliation, if ever?

If I had one day I could take back in my life, it would be that day. It was my second bar mitzvah. I was now a man; my father had died to me, so I thought. I saw him only one more time.

I left Victor's depressed and disgusted with Victor for how he had behaved. The hell with fathers and mentors! Something had to change. As I walked to the subway, I was fed up with everything. What was I doing with my life? The country was angry about the war, assassinations, and civil rights. We were killing Vietnamese in rice paddies, drenching our soldiers in Agent Orange.

Broadway was tired. What about theater that addressed things that really mattered? The dean of American playwrights, Arthur Miller, had written, "I feel that a writer puts a severe limitation upon oneself when he is unable to believe in a reality that is not physical, sexual, or visceral."

Yeah, find me a play like that.

The American Place Theatre, a leading Off-Broadway theater, hired me to direct two one-acts. We opened in December 1968. One of the plays, *The Young Master Dante* by Werner Liepolt, was reviewed by the *New York Times* as

> Apparently a castration myth. Certainly it was not a castration hit. Into a Gothic circle of hell, where a warlock is an innkeeper and his wife a child-desiring wanton, a new Dante wanders. The inhabitants, sickly nighttime crones with anal dispositions, crowd around the young hero, who imagines he can pluck the flower of pleasure from the innkeeper's wife. He cannot. The warlock emasculates him, and only the wifely wanton achieves anything, with a newborn baby.

Why did I love this play? Was I working out my night with Victor? Or did I love the Hieronymus Bosch vision of warlocks, wantons, castration, magic, sex, candles, a dwarf (played by Hervé Villechaize who later became a star on TV's *Fantasy Island*)—everything you could imagine in Hell's Theater of the Grotesque? Maybe I just needed to scream, and this was my therapy. The names of the characters suggested the flavor: Sodomantis, Anticrustus, Cannilingus, Omnivicious, and so on. Into this weird world came the innocent Dante. I went for broke.

"A shadow play of sexual intercourse, very nearly as embarrassing as it was intriguing," noted one reviewer. The warlock's wife and Dante were behind a gauze curtain, illuminated by torches. They slowly, beautifully entwined one another, each orally gratifying the other. Of course they were clothed, but the shadows were suggestive, and some of the audience bolted out of their chairs, scurrying for the exit.

Near the end of the play, Dante is spread-eagled on the bed, dominated by his warlock "father." Dante is facedown, naked. There was a trapdoor under the area of his genitals. From Dante's ass, the Warlock pulled Coca-Cola bottles, sausages, hamburger, peppermint patties, pompoms, Frisbees—American icons all. It was intended to be crude, offensive, and surreal—exactly what the author called for or, more accurately, what I invented from Werner's dialogue. Was the play a Rorschach test for audiences or for those who created it? How did the bourgeoisie react to Bosch's paintings? Goya's scenes of war? Picasso's *Guernica*?

One night, the warlock was sick, and the producer implored me to play the part. I had to carry a script. I'm sure I pretty well stunk, but the show had to go on. We were drawing full houses despite—or because of—the reviews. It came time for the castration scene. The naked Dante was lying on the bed. I pushed the trapdoor and reached for the burgers and such. I found something, clamped my hand around it, and started to yank. Dante's body jerked violently, and I realized I had not burgers but testicles. My friend Andy Robinson's! I quickly released my hold. Close call! Serious damage averted, show continued, and friendship maintained.

The Young Master Dante wasn't great art, but it was visceral and imaginative. It was, to my mind, beautiful. The final scene of the warlock's wife sitting on a bed, holding Dante's child, was another in a series of *Madonna and Child* poses I so liked. A golden glow infused the darkened stage and sumptuously illuminated her red tresses, a scene worthy of a painting by a Flemish master.

As 1968 ended, Roger Domani invited me back to Brussels to direct *MacBird!* at the Theater de Poche. I told him the show would not go over in translation. You had to hear the parody of Shakespeare in English to catch the wit, and moreover, the play was full of Americanisms. Roger was undeterred, and the play went on, to mostly poor reviews. Brussels, in the early winter months, was dreary. I was alone and happy to return, not to New York but to Philadelphia.

I had been invited to stage Sam Shephard's *La Turista* at Philly's Theatre of the Living Arts. My work had been previously represented there by a touring production of *America Hurrah*. Shepherd was one of my favorite playwrights. His wildly anarchistic plays—full of jazzy rhythms, fountains of rambling, hopped-up speeches ranted, chanted, and sung by eccentric characters—were new and fresh. I was eager to direct—and more. The theater had been searching for a new artistic director since Andre Gregory had been dismissed in 1967. My name was one of five guest directors being considered for the position. *La Turista* puzzled and delighted critics and audiences; I had a shot at getting the job.

To be the artistic director of a professional repertory theater would be the fulfillment of everything I had been striving for. It would fulfill my law of elevation: that after seven years of paying the dues, I would achieve what I sought—being the head of a theater company. Yet the unfortunate correction to that law (as I had formulated in my mind) was that I would no longer be interested because I had already accomplished what I had set out to do? Was that really true? No, this was different.

I set out my aims in a position paper for the board of directors of TLA to consider. Among the ideas were the following:

> I think everybody should get together to find out why they are
> there, not just the actors, tech people, staff, and board of directors.

I am trying to get actors who are receptive to all kinds of acting, who believe in what this theater is doing and have a commitment to working in an experimental form all the time without resisting it. I don't want any separation between the actor and the man or woman.

Let's find out what happens. Not that a consensus should be reached, but an awareness of possibilities, imagination as the solution. I'd like to know if that secretary has any interest in what or why I'm doing something. I want to get rid of the barriers between the audience and the actors, change the seating configurations, put audience on the stage, and create another theater, called The Space, where there would be no chairs, only mats or shifting stages that you would move to and watch.

"The theater is clay," I wrote. "Mold it, fold it, smash it. Space to be free, not space to be contained."

This is what I was suggesting my fun house would look like. Heady stuff. Pretentious as it may sound today, in 1969, I was cocksure and arrogant. "The times," as Dylan suggested, "they are a-changing."

While waiting to hear from TLA, I directed *Scuba Duba* by Bruce Jay Friedman at the Bergen Mall Theatre in Paramus, New Jersey. *Scuba* had been running on Broadway since 1967. Warner Bros. had bought the rights for the movie. This was its first tour; after Bergen, it was headed to Philadelphia's Playhouse in the Park. The symmetry was perfect. Once again I was privileged to work with a good cast. Dick Shawn, a star in Las Vegas nightclubs and Broadway musicals, and well known for his role as the Nazi in Mel Brooks's *The Producers*, was headlining the cast. Herve Villechaize, the dwarf from *Master Dante*, was back; he was too much fun to be around, with his French accent, a dagger hidden in his boot, and a lovely, normal-size wife. Others in the cast were Morgan Freeman, Jennifer Warren, George Bartenieff, and a young actress named Judi West, whom *Playbill* described thusly: "Lovely blue-eyed, lacey-valentine blonde with delicately chiseled features, she speaks in a husky voice that is completely beguiling."

We started seeing each other, driving to the theater in my Austin Healey. Judi had played the Marilyn Monroe character in the national tour of Arthur Miller's *After the Fall*. I fell for her big-time. She had other relationships, so the situation was complex, but as long as we were rehearsing, her time was mine. And I wanted to be with her all the time.

Shawn was a sweetheart, a bouncy, ebullient fellow, an incredible improviser; he regaled me with tales of Las Vegas. "I love Vegas, Tom. A show at eleven pm, another at one am, finish at three am, go have drinks and dinner, party till dawn. Take a steam bath and play eighteen holes of golf. Go home and sleep until four pm, take it easy, eat a light dinner, rehearse, and do it again. Chorus girls, Mafiosa, Hollywood—everybody's partying. It's very nice."

The play concerned Harold, a Jewish man who thought he was a liberal but flipped out when his wife ran off with a black scuba diver. Harold (Shawn) then turned to a girl in a bikini (Judi West) for company. The play was a madcap farce, abetted by Shawn as a raving idiot, spouting obscenities and racial slurs. It was considered daring, as well as hilarious, for its send-up of white liberalism. Worked in the Bergen Mall but in starchy, proper Philadelphia?

I was in my hotel in Philadelphia when John Bos, the producer of TLA, called. "Tom, you got the job." I was thrilled. I couldn't wait to get to the theater and tell the cast. A burden had been lifted off my shoulders. My life was falling into place.

We opened *Scuba Duba* in a lovely theater in Fairmount Park, and the park's commissioner immediately closed down the play. "I definitely think the play is obscene," said the commissioner. "I don't think it's the kind of entertainment to which the citizens of Philadelphia are entitled. I think it's trash." Hand it to the censors for looking out for the rest of us. The word of our censorship was front-page news.

After hasty negotiations, the *f*-word was deleted from the script. Shawn substituted "censored," as in "You mother censored!" which got huge laughs. Like all good censors, the commissioner turned the show into standing room only. Judi and I returned to New York, she to resume her career, me to clean out my apartment for the move to Philly. Was I the flavor of the month for her, or she, for me? I promised I'd find roles for her in the upcoming season at TLA.

There was hype of a big rock 'n' roll event coming up in August 1969 in Woodstock, New York, but I had made plans to visit my parents in California and see some friends before starting my new job.

I landed in California, smoked a lot of weed with old friends, took in a Grateful Dead concert at the Avalon Ballroom, and hiked Mount Tamalpais in Marin County, where my parents had a summer home. It was at that home in Kent Woodlands that I saw my father for the last time. His life was coming to an end, although neither of us knew that. He looked OK; the lymphoma had been treated successfully. My head was full of the new job; I didn't pick up any cues he might have been offering. I was a full-blown hippie out of the cast of *Hair*. He didn't like that look. That meant nothing to me, so when we blew up at each other, the flimsy edifice that held the father-son relationship collapsed into rubble. Because of where we were coming from, what could have been my proudest moment with him (that I was artistic director of a major American repertory theater) or my most compassionate moment ("How are you doing, Dad? Anything I can do to help?") was not to be. My mother could only watch and support my father. He spat at me that the way I looked and dressed was disgusting, disgraceful, words to that effect. "If you don't like the way I look, I don't have to be here. Screw you," I said, or worse, and stormed out.

I thought I knew who he was, the civic man who hid his emotions from his family; I am sure he had no idea who I was or rather who I had become, with my Jewfro hair and drooping mustache. He was brittle, had been since the onset of his illness. The high-dosage radiation treatment had covered his entire body, and who knew in those days how much damage it might have caused to his healthy organs? It was a fact that he had tried to commit suicide one night between treatments by swallowing a lot of sleeping pills; my mother heard him heaving and retching and called 911, and they rushed him to the hospital and pumped him out. No one ever talked about it—and what could we have done anyway? So we were silent then, and I was silent now, and if, as my sister-in-law said later, he treated his children as if we were on a stage set and how we looked and could be presented to the world was the most important thing to him, then at this moment, I was not presentable—and what else could I do but exit the scene?

I didn't know how to forgive or ask for forgiveness.

Shortly before returning to Philadelphia, I was driving down Broadway about to get on the Bay Bridge when I spotted a hitchhiker and stopped to pick him up. It was an odd coincidence that he was from Philadelphia and knew about the Theatre of the Living Arts. He gave me names to look up when I got to Philly. His name was Ira Einhorn, and surprisingly, he would become a part of my life in the future.

Chapter Nine

I was thirty in June 1969. Michael O'Donoghue, my Ping-Pong playing buddy and consummate wit, later to be the first head writer for *Saturday Night Live*, gave me an art piece for my birthday, a framed blank piece of paper with *30* typed on it. I asked him what it meant. "When you've ended writing an article for the newspaper, you type thirty at the bottom, meaning it's finished." What was my friend implying? Was I finished with New York? Hell yes, I was ready to leave 98 Greenwich Avenue. There had been too many robberies in my apartment, courtesy of the heroin epidemic. It was time to make a new life and a new home.

I hadn't had a home, a real home, since I left for Andover. I was a transient on this planet, occupying ground, setting up a tent but not putting down stakes. I had been in a lot of homes, but the home I was seeking, that hearth, that heart, I hadn't found. I was on the move, "making it."

Where do all the hippies meet? South Street, Philadelphia, USA.

Fifteen minutes from city hall, five minutes from the Delaware River, in a crumbling neighborhood, among abandoned houses, ailanthus trees sprouting out of loosened brick windows and tarred roofs, stood the Theatre of the Living Arts, a movie theater reclaimed from the detritus of the neighborhood by idealistic theater lovers under the guiding vision of Andre Gregory, who had been fired two years previously. Now, elderly Jewish merchants hung on to their mom-and-pop stores, delis, and bridal shops. African Americans squeezed into small tenements and the Southwark projects. Everything moved slowly, an air of defeat and urban decay writ large. There was little traffic except on South Fourth Street, where fabric merchants, immigrants from Eastern Europe, hawked their wares. Their middle-aged children had moved to the Greater Northeast neighborhoods.

It was presumed scary, even dangerous, to venture to the Theatre of Living Arts. As you drove the deserted streets at night, TLA was a ghostly outpost, a dim beacon in the moribund streets. Nonetheless, the Theatre of the Living Arts would become my fun house, my Playland at the Beach. Here was my sandbox in which to make magic.

I reported for duty in early September, Peter Fonda riding into town in *Easy Rider*. I was wearing striped bell-bottoms, a loose-bloused paisley shirt and safari jacket, gold-rimmed glasses, beads around my neck, and sporting an Afro. John Bos, the producing director, and I had auditioned actors in New York and Philadelphia. Our resident company consisted of Judd Hirsch, fresh from the lead in *Scuba Duba* on Broadway; David Rounds; Morgan Freeman; and Larry Bloch, all with Broadway experience. Marion Killinger and three TLA veterans—Sally Kirkland, Mike Procaccino (later to become Michael Cristofer, Pulitzer Prize playwright), and Bob DeFrank. Another half-dozen nonprofessionals from Philly rounded out the cast. Eugene Lee, who had yet to make his name as a major Broadway set designer, was on board, and I brought my New York neighbor, Franne Newman, to assist on costumes. She begged me, "Please, I'll do anything." She ended up marrying Eugene Lee.

The first play was George Farquhar's 1706 Restoration comedy, *The Recruiting Officer*. Not exactly mainstream, but I had a hunch that a military play and love story, full of characters and action, had the right ingredients for something unexpected and thrilling.

Then on October 14, 1969, midafternoon, my brother called to say that Dad had died of a heart attack in London. I took in the news, returned to a rehearsal, and later that evening booked a flight to San Francisco for the funeral.

I was numb. A month earlier, my mother and father had been visiting London when Dad suffered a severe stroke in an inoperable part of the brain, leaving him unable to speak or move. He had remained in a hospital in London and my sister and brother joined my mother. The doctors said there was a possibility he could understand what was being said to him. The plan was to fly him to San Francisco and continue his care, but that opportunity never arrived. I went to the funeral, wondering if I would feel anything. As soon as the service at Temple Emanu-El was over, we drove to a family service in the cemetery chapel.

This is from my notebook in 1982:

> I was there, and I wasn't.
> Sitting in the little room at the House of Peace
> (a beautiful day as I remember).

The rabbi talked as a bird flew in, and women in black curly lamb
coats stately sat.
The bird, lyrical and alive, fluttered and fled; the rabbi persevered.
At the house, whiskey and hors d'oeuvres, dinner served to
mourners—no Kaddish, no home.
Death. Done.

I returned to Philadelphia and resumed directing the play. It took me twenty
years after his death to say the words, "I love you, Dad." It happened this way.

In 1989, I was trying out a gestalt class at Daylesford Abbey in Malvern,
Pennsylvania. My friend Ellen told me to take the "hot seat" when offered,
since I would receive hands-on therapy for free.

"What do you want to work on?" asked Mariah, the teacher.

"I've never mourned my father's death," I replied.

Forget his death—I never mourned his life. Mariah chose someone to lie
down on a couch and told him to play my father as a corpse. She selected a
song, Dan Fogelberg's "Leader of the Band." She instructed me to go to my
father and talk to him.

As Fogelberg's musical tribute to his father filled the room, I knelt by this
substitute dad, mopped his brow, touched my forehead to his, put my head on
his chest, and hesitatingly whispered that I loved him. The resistance gave way;
his inert body sang to me. Somewhere, from deep in the sea ice, I couldn't hold
back. Tears began to flow. Venom dissolved into sobs. I bawled for a long time,
telling this ersatz father what I never told my real father: He needed to hear
that I loved him. No, I needed to hear that I loved him.

Was it an ersatz performance or the real deal? I trusted my tears. I trusted
my aching heart. I was happy to accept the help; I needed help to mourn, to
atone and heal, even if it might take me a lifetime.

The great poet Robert Bly said in a workshop I attended that a father's
only obligation to his son was to clothe and feed him and that a mentor, if one
had a mentor, became the guide and, further, that the father in some way was
obligated to betray the son. Had to cut him loose. It was possible that blood
was too thick and that another man with no ties to the son was better able to
challenge and inspire. But didn't the son also betray the father?

In 1969, these thoughts hadn't concerned me. That chapter of my life
closed, I returned to Philadelphia.

Back at TLA, I hired a local folk group, *Good News*, consisting of Larry
Gold and Michael Bacon (who have both gone on to distinguished careers),
to write fourteen songs for *The Recruiting Officer*. Very young guys at the time,
they totally embraced the concept of the play. The set designer created a pit
underneath the middle of a raked stage, where they peered out at the audience,

Larry on cello, Michael on guitar. And when the cast came on at the finale to sing, the audience stood with them and sang as one.

The show was a smash hit, one of my favorites of all time. We changed performance rules. Larry Bloch, who had served in the military, wanted a bigger part, so he gave an antiwar speech in the lobby at the intermission to confused patrons who wondered why the actor was there in the first place. Was he given permission and what did this have to do with the play? It seemed spontaneous. Act 2 started in the lobby with two of the characters talking among themselves as they walked toward the stage. If you heard it, you heard it; if not, not. Crates of live chickens, borrowed from the local kosher butcher shops—yes, in 1969 you could still select a live chicken from Aaron's Butcher Shop and have it butchered on the spot—clucked away during the performance. None were butchered, at least not by us.

The cast and crew bought into the production, singing and playing as one unit, one heart. A lot of love poured from that stage and back onto the performers, and I learned one big, big lesson at the end of the run: Never, ever, close a show when it's selling out! We had a subscription season, right? Postpone, delay, but *do not close a show that is making money!*

We closed the show. Big mistake.

For the second play, I had chosen Ron Ribman's *Harry, Noon and Night,* a dark, intellectual drama, acted by most of the cast from the former show, plus Judi West, my girlfriend from *Scuba Duba.* The guest director had meltdowns with Judi, who in turn had meltdowns with the director, which put me in an awkward place. I couldn't satisfy both Judi and the director, and I couldn't fire him because I was already focusing on the next play, which was going to open in The Space, now an empty garage that needed an overhaul to get it ready for an audience. The romance with Judi was on my back burner. My "I'm in control—everything's OK" mask was slipping.

It was around this time that George Keegan, property master for TLA, invited me to a party at his house. As the former head of PR for Sunoco, George was tuned into Philadelphia and decided to invite Ira Einhorn, a self-proclaimed "planetary enzyme," one who seeded events, people, and ideas and put them into orbit with each other. "You don't know me, Ira," said George, "but I think you should meet Tom Bissinger, a radical Jewish guy from New York who is TLA's new director." At the party, Ira and I talked; I realized he was the hitchhiker I'd picked up in San Francisco. Small world. Ira had friends he wanted me to meet, which was fine with me since he seemed to have the pulse of Philadelphia, at least its young people. He came to see the plays, and we began to meet from time to time.

Things were bubbling at the theater. Under a looming deadline, in the abandoned garage behind TLA, we were creating The Space: a theater without seats, much as I had promised in my manifesto to the board of directors. We were going to stage *Gargoyle Cartoons*, a bunch of surrealistic adult fairy tales written by Michael McClure, one of San Francisco's beat poets. As a follower of the beats, I knew about McClure and had read a few of these wonderfully funny and bizarre plays in the *Drama Review* magazine. When I was in San Francisco in 1969, I met McClure, who gave me permission to choose the ones I wanted and perform them. The show opened in December of 1969.

What McClure wrote, and I staged, was in the vein of shows produced at Andy Warhol's Electric Circus and Ken Kesey's Trips Festivals at San Francisco's Fillmore Auditorium. We stretched the parameters of theater by adapting the psychedelic experience. It was theater for the adventurous, the young, and the stoned. And you didn't have to be stoned. The Space became the fun house. The combination of McClure's wicked fairy tales and an altered physical environment radically revised how you experienced theater.

In the large second floor of the former garage, the audience moved from play to play. The *Philadelphia Inquirer* wrote that in *Spider Rabbit*, the actor Bob DeFrank

> hops around like a rabbit, stuffing his mouth with carrots. "Hi, I'm Spider Rabbit," he says in a Howdy Doody intonation whose innocence—"I hate war"—is belied by six wire legs and innumerable hand grenades he keeps pulling out from his Army duffle bag. At first it all seems gentle and good-natured, until hunger so ravages him (he's out of carrots) that with his electric knife he slices off the top of a human prisoner's head, gorging himself on gray matter. It's as disgusting as it sounds, and grotesquely sums up the terrible, awful paradoxes of, for instance, American involvement in Vietnam. In light of the My Lai massacre (balanced against "pacification" programs) the spider and the rabbit in America's character are all too real.

Just as the audience reacted to the gross antics of *Spider Rabbit*, in *The Meatball*, they were treated to the spectacle of two giant padded fuzz balls, Geek and Sleek, high on pot or acid, dancing and rolling around the floor and over spectators like, well, meatballs. The music was fast; the audience clapped and stomped in time to the beat.

After these "assaults" on the audience, we settled them down with *The Cherub*. In this play, a mammoth sheet through which holes had been cut for people's heads to fit through covered the entire room and audience. Balloons dropped from above through a spray of multicolored flashing lights. Performers with painted faces seemed to sprout from all directions as they popped through holes glowing with florescent rings. The actors spoke as if in a dream, a mixture of humor and sadness. It was all deliciously disembodied.

Well, you knew it was too good to last. Reviews and word of mouth had been terrific, so much so that the Fire Department took notice and closed us down for lack of proper permits. Larry Magid, Philly's rock impresario, who had seen the show, rescued us; he invited us to perform at the Electric Factory. Larry had been repeatedly harassed by fire, police, and building inspectors due to the fact that his rock 'n' roll acts thumbed their noses, metaphorically speaking, at Philadelphia's repressive establishment. Thanks to Larry's generosity, we moved, but the shows never captured the "vibe" we had in the Space.

Christmas arrived. I was alone. *Gargoyle Cartoons* had completed its run at the Electric Factory, and the company was on holiday. Snow fell, filling the streets with ice and slush. The nights were Dickensian: bleak, wet with fog, shadowy figures sliding by murky, deserted lots, seventeenth-century brick houses sagging with exhaustion. A few blocks away lay the rotting docks and crumbling warehouses that fronted the Delaware River. I crawled into my burrow at 229 Monroe Street, feeling sorry for myself, filling notebooks with drippy prose about relationships. And then, I started an affair with Tona, a pretty street-smart Jewish girl with full red lips and lively, flirty eyes. She had seen *Gargoyle Cartoons*, introduced herself, and later came over to my house, suggested ways she could help decorate it, and without further ado, moved in with me.

The affair with Tona didn't last long, but it was memorable. To get to know the board of directors of TLA better, Tona and I held several soirees for two couples at a time. These couples were from Philadelphia's Main Line, pedigree people, very nice, enthusiastic about the theater, curious about the alternative lifestyle of Tom and his girlfriend. After dinner, when the cognac and a joint came out, Tona would coyly remark, "I'm just so hot!" and casually drop the top part of her dress, revealing a very nice pair of breasts. The men's eyes shot out of their heads, the wives were coolly amused, the temperature in the room rose, and the Beatles, the Rolling Stones, Jefferson Airplane, and Quicksilver Messenger Service kept the mood rocking. Tona carried on as if nothing could be more natural, and it was, in fact, natural. I mean, she liked putting people on, and she liked men admiring her. I was one of them.

Tona was also an antique maven. She decorated our house, a 1792 colonial brick house with eight rooms and one bathroom, with artistic vengeance. Her philosophy was that there was no corner, ledge, shelf, or floor that couldn't be improved with an antique. One room in particular, the upstairs bathroom, was a gallery unto itself. This room achieved greatness. Tona decorated as if it were a stage set from the late Victorian era—rugs, antique lamps, curtains, statuary, paintings, chairs, and marble tables—so that when you entered to take a crap, it was an easy minute of confusion, your eye so dazzled by the cornucopia of tchotchkes, before you realized: Oh! Look! There's the toilet.

If *Gargoyle Cartoons* was a glorious penultimate act, then *The Line of Least Existence* by Rosalyn Drexler was the theater's finale, in all senses of the word. Rosalyn was a New York character who figured prominently in the New York avant-garde theater scene and art world. She had wrestled professionally and was a kind of a mother figure to me. I had already directed several of her plays in Milwaukee and Provincetown and found her humor delightfully whacky and offbeat.

The plot, such as there was, concerned Pschug, a Hungarian refugee who was searching for his daughter, who was the mistress of Dr. Toloon Fraak, whose sex-starved wife was carrying on with the talking family dog, who had a talent for psychoanalysis. As Drexler wrote, "The line of least existence is preferable to going out of your way." Kind of dry, sly humor.

I wrote in my journal:

> I like the play far better than I thought I would—through all of Rosalyn's dream-crazed world emerges comic truth and a tender feeling. The characters have respect for each other—they are all rather naive, much as cartoon characters are. Although they do incredible things, no one is damaged, the world spins on, and we are touched by their craziness. A fun house!

But the show, ah, the show was wobbly. If you knew that Paul Simon song, "Slip Slidin' Away," that was what rehearsals felt like. They started OK. Judd Hirsch played the psycho doctor. He was professionally solid, came to work every day with a no-nonsense attitude. In fact, Judd was one of the few actors I had met who was businesslike. He was organized, and he was not only a hell of an actor, he was a genuinely nice guy. For the part of the dog in the show, we hired a little guy from New York, Danny DeVito—a total delight and very funny.

John Hall, a fine rock 'n' roll guitarist, was commissioned to write a score. Technically, a score should be written before you go into rehearsal. John did his best with little time. He hired two great musicians to play in the show: drummer Billy Monday and guitarist Don Preston. The fourth member of the band was rigidly uptight and objected to the guys smoking dope and insisted they stop. I stupidly agreed. The band was tense, grumpy, and divided.

Our lead actress had to be able to belt songs as well as act. Jennie could do both; the trouble was she was unreliable about showing up on time for rehearsals. Heavy drugs were rumored to be an issue. Reluctantly, we fired her, and her replacement didn't cut it.

Then there was Eugene Lee, a brilliant stage designer (totally in sync with my fun house desire to transform the shape of a theater), who rearranged it so that the audience wouldn't recognize it from previous shows. He took his time—who cared about deadlines? We waited. We never rehearsed on the actual stage until final dress rehearsal. The stage design was maddeningly complex and difficult to build. I fumed, but there was nothing I could do to speed the process. Much of the usual audience seating had been removed and covered over by Plexiglas panels and metal bleachers. The audience would be seated in these bleachers as lights played over this new environment from above and from under the Plexiglas runways. Construction was endless. Eugene attacked the foreman of the stage crew with a hammer because he suspected incorrectly that Max was messing around with his girlfriend, Franne, and absurd as it was to watch Eugene run around the stage chasing Max (much like the characters in the script!), it was trivial compared to the meltdowns by some of the actors. It was like watching the proverbial train wreck in slow motion. You knew it was coming—and O god! Don't let it be too painful!

Crisis has a way of either bringing out the best in people or making their neuroses bloom. We were in full bloom—delays, kvetching, and miscasting. The script that was funny when I first read it now came across as obvious and puerile. It had me perplexed. Danny's dog was funny. Judd's psycho psychiatrist was funny. But the show wasn't. Everybody's effort was valiant, but the love that the cast had engendered in *The Recruiting Officer* had evaporated. There was no way to stop the impending crash. I got stoned just to come to rehearsals. It didn't improve anything; it just made me realize how the play was slip-sliding away from me and I, from it. The show finally opened like a nightmare that I was glad to have awakened from, but the angst remained.

The Line of Least Existence was an overproduced, laborious wet dream. Literally. We ended act 1 with an inflated plastic penis, three feet wide and ten feet long, that ejaculated soapsuds a foot deep all over the stage, while the song "Wow Me Now" raged and the lights under the Plexiglas shimmered in multicolored patterns. Definitely the "climax" of my career at TLA.

Sometimes you run with a good idea, and sometimes the idea runs away from you. The reviews were awful. The critics outdid themselves. "Tom Bissinger has gone beyond the line of innovation and good taste and reached the line of lowest existence," "TLA gave birth last night to a spastic that soon died. It was grotesque," and "Tom, dear Tom, Mom's strung you out, and you've bombed."

I was angry, hurt, defiant, confused, and sad, in no particular order. I was exposed. My masks of *Making it, I'm in control, I'm right!* were hanging around my neck. I had received a major shock to whoever it was I thought I was.

The truth was that this wonderful theater, my Playland at the Beach fun house, wasn't fun anymore. The rides were closing down. The Fat Lady had sung her last song. I felt ready to jettison theater, not just TLA, but theater herself.

When John Bos, the producer of TLA, and I gathered the staff at the end of the season, none of us knew what was going to happen to the theater. A couple of one-man shows had brief runs, and a group of San Quentin ex-cons put on *The Cage*, a taut drama about their experiences in prison and moved it to a successful Off-Broadway run. But TLA was a hundred grand in debt, and the board no longer wanted to fund the deficit. The decision was made to close shop.

I decided to put on a Black Mass. Didn't really know much about masses, black or otherwise, but I thought we should observe the passing of TLA with a ceremony of some kind. We needed, or at least I did, some kind of collective gathering where we could share stories about our experiences at TLA. Sheets of silver Mylar were hung all over the theater to better reflect light. We set up a coffin on stage and had candles burning and bells tolling when the mass started at midnight. Staff, local actors, and neighborhood folk chanted and helped themselves to the sacrament: LSD, wine, and pot. As different musical groups jammed, offerings were burnt; cash and draft cards went up in flames. The holy smell of death and decay mingled with our own sweat and blood. We danced, prayed, wept, read poetry, told stories; music shook the walls, and by 5:00 am, we hugged and kissed each other good-bye. There was nothing more to say. A few of us trooped down to Fritz's, a deli on the corner of Second and South, had eggs and coffee, and watched the sun come up over the Delaware.

I thought I had experienced my last hurrah, but Samuel Evans, the godfather of black politics in Philadelphia, summoned John and me to his office and asked us to produce and direct *The Black Experience in Philadelphia*, starring Ossie Davis and Ruby Dee. The play showcased the inspirational evolution of black leadership in Philadelphia's churches, politics, and the arts over two and a half centuries. I'd like to think Sam didn't care that we were white guys but just wanted the best production possible. My job resembled traffic control, interweaving dance, music, and narration. That was fine with me because I was directing in the Academy of Music, one of the grandest concert halls in the world. Looking around at the soaring tiers of seats, the plush red upholstery, the crystal chandeliers, the gilded boxes, I was able to say, "I've played the Academy."

A Broadway producer offered me a Broadway show: *The Trial of Ethel and Julius Rosenberg*—great story, not well written. I turned him down. He reoffered it. Nope, didn't like it. It was eventually produced and bombed. I said no to an offer to direct at a local Shakespeare festival. I had been running like crazy, doing my "what makes Sammy run" act for seven years, and now that I had accomplished my desire to run a theater, hadn't I completed the law of elevation, silly as it was? I had always been a yes; now I was a no. Did I have to justify that? Had I achieved everything I wanted? I didn't know. I was full of questions. Was I exhausted? Unmotivated? Now that my father was dead, had I lost the desire either to compete or complete with him? Was I committed to theater at all? All that had seemed so purposeful but a few months earlier—my proclamations to the board of directors and the actors, my hopes for a new theater—had lost their meaning. I was sick of working with neurotics. Theater was a breeding ground for them, and to be honest, could I safely exclude myself from calling myself one? However it would all play out, I was saying, "Screw it!"

In the so-called real world, the Vietnam War ran on and on, a nightly news tragedy. Everything was lopsided, out of kilter. I sat in my house, wondering, *Now what?*

Ira dropped by the house, and I told him I felt clueless. He suggested I read P. D. Ouspensky's *The Psychology of Man's Possible Evolution*. I had never heard of Ouspensky or his teacher, G.I Gurdjieff, or the thought, as the book suggested, that there was a consciousness to which you could awaken, that we were not fated to sleepwalk through life, and that our habitual behavior could be transformed. That was exciting. It was life here and now, not rehearsed and memorized, that counted; in fact, it was the only thing that mattered.

I had been a telescope turned around, viewing from the wide lens into the narrow—obsessing on women, on actors' moves and motivations, my father, mother, and me. I had to turn myself around, pull back, take a wider view, open up the lens, and become part of the grand design, whatever that might be.

Was I being summoned to a new adventure, no longer rooted in theater? Given my background, was it possible to extricate the performer from whoever I thought I was being? There was an enigmatic Sufi saying, "Either be who you appear to be, or appear to be who you are." And all along, I thought life was about doing.

I inhabited the colonial house at 229 Monroe Street like a pair of old, comfortable slippers. The brickwork sagged, and the house leaned over the sinking brick sidewalk, which formed the corner of North American and Monroe, tilting the house toward the setting sun, which disappeared behind a street full of abandoned, boarded-up houses. I enjoyed living between the cracks at the edge of the empire. I had an opportunity now to reevaluate and remake myself. My only immediate neighbor was Mr. Perkins, a withered, gnarly black man who had eyes that shined glassily, pods that reflected an unworldly glow. He didn't have much to say, mostly pushed a beat-up shopping cart along the cobbled street, talking to himself, *"The Spirit don't die—it's just translated!"*

I needed to hear that.

Chapter Ten

It was May 1970. I had departed San Francisco in 1962 with a youth's desire for fame and fortune. That desire was whetted and honed by teachers, comrades, and mentors whom I encountered on my path to Philadelphia; now that I was in the City of Brotherly Love, unemployed, I was free to explore South Street, a destination about to happen. Restless youth looking to express themselves to others like themselves began drifting to the area.

As the old Jews looked on warily, almost dazed by the new energy inhabiting their neighborhood, their old culture reminded me of Isaac Bashevis Singer's folkloric shetl stories. For an assimilated Jew as myself, this Jewish way of life seemed encased in amber; it was gorgeously slow and sweet, and it wasn't going to last. It felt comfortable to walk past the delicatessens, foggy with the steam of sweet cabbage soup bubbling on stoves; the fabric, lingerie, and bridal establishments where Philadelphians had shopped for decades; and the poultry stores where chickens were butchered on the spot. For sidewalk entertainment, Bennie Kratz, all five feet of him, bewigged in a terrible toupee, talked a mile a minute, shanghaiing pedestrians into his men's clothing store. He must have done OK for he drove to and from his store in a Rolls-Royce. The other Benny was a hunched-over gnome who scuttled along the sidewalk dragging tools to his house. If you wanted a tool, he had three floors of them, packed top to bottom, tons of metal covered in black grime, lying in heaps and piles that only he could decipher. Grinning at you wickedly, he might just have the tool you had to have even though they weren't cheap or cheap enough. "Come on," he'd rasp, "what are ya waiting for? Buy it! You'll never find anything like it."

The only non-Jews I can remember, Fats and Slim, were two Oklahoma-born black cowboys who ran a clock and clock repair shop. They talked slow and hardly ever got out of their chairs, just pointed at the goods. "Take your time, boy, we got all the time in the world. That right, Fats?"

"That's right, Slim." And if it wasn't a vintage clock you wanted, you found vintage clothing across the street at the local thrift, next door to the Society Hill Pool Hall, where Minnesota Fats had played matches.

There were others merchants, but most of the stores had closed and had For Rent or Sale signs in their windows. Malls were being built in the suburbs.

We were the new immigrants, but who were we?

We arrived from Europe and around the United States, from inner cities and suburbs. Some were the grandchildren of the Jewish merchants, some were people like me who had moved here for work, and others had heard that rents were cheap and something was happening. In a few years, boardwalk would come to South Street, and buildings that once sold for $1,000 would be selling for $450,000 and up. Not now. We were urban pioneers who wanted to hang out with others of our own kind—not work too hard—deal a little dope, do some street theater, and rebuild a neighborhood building by building. I began to see that South Street itself could be a giant fun house.

Ira Einhorn, true to his word as a planetary enzyme, introduced me to Curt Kubiak, an ex-GI who had become an architect by attending Drexel night school for six years. His Polish working-class background was the antithesis of mine. His father was a plumber, and that was Curt's work until he became an architect.

Curt was also the Pennsylvania primate of the Neo-American Church, whose mission was to champion the use of psychedelics. The church listed among its directors and clergy Timothy Leary, Richard Alpert, and Allen Ginsberg. Arthur Kleps, chief Boo Hoo of the church said of his title that "we have intentionally chosen something that has absurd qualities to remind ourselves not to take ourselves too seriously. We share agreement with three principles: (1) the principle of freedom-of-consciousness expansion for everyone, (2) the principle of not identifying psychedelic substances (such as LSD) as drugs but rather as holy or divine substances, (3) the principle of not administering or giving the sacraments to people who are unprepared for them."

Curt's role as chief primate was to encourage and coordinate the activities of Boo Hoos in Pennsylvania. This was my first occasion to not only meet someone who was doing psychedelics on a regular basis but also actively disseminating information about their use in scholarly journals, such as the *Psychedelic Review*, featuring articles not only by Leary and Alpert but by René Daumal, William James, RD Laing, Henri Michaux, and other explorers of "inner space."

My brain was on fire. I loved reading about worlds I had barely imagined and now were being dangled in front of me, not only through taking a small pill or smoking a joint but by the differentiation between a real mind and a robot mind, the latter being the mind of personality, which, as the texts suggested, was an illusion. As I translated this information to my professional career, I saw that traditional theater had congealed into something slow and nonspontaneous for me. I had reached out in certain productions to replicate the psychedelic experience, but now, I was committed to finding out for myself how far I could explore consciousness. I wanted to be educated. The fun house was becoming an interior journey.

Although I wasn't taking LSD often, I was smoking a lot of weed with Curt. He had an infectious laugh and an original mind. He'd sit on the floor for hours, a heavyset man with a Laughing Buddha belly, Fu Manchu mustache and beard, and sparkling eyes, smoking joints and expounding on anything and everything. When high, he could be a loud and dominating bully with those who disagreed with him, tendencies I came to regret later in our relationship.

Curt started a synergy group based on the writings of Buckminster Fuller, who defined synergy as the whole being greater than and different from the sum of its parts. We met in an old abandoned house on Third Street that the owner of Wexler's bar lent us in exchange for fixing it up. In these meetings, open to anyone, we explored Bucky's teachings and how to apply them to South Street, which was scheduled to be demolished for a crosstown expressway. (The plan for it had been drawn up by City Planner Edmund Bacon, whose son, Michael, had written music for *The Recruiting Officer*.) Our goal was to stave off the expressway and help rehab the neighborhood by creating a People's Park on an abandoned lot on the corner of Third and South, next to Wexler's bar.

Much of my day was spent fixing up the park as well as volunteering on other restoration projects in the neighborhood. Both Curt and I were receiving unemployment benefits and liked to take off for state parks—our chance to get out of the city—have fun with his kids if they were out of school, enjoy nature, and sit at some waterfall or cliff outcrop and smoke and talk. When we'd return to Philly late in the day or at night, I liked the feeling of one or two of his sons leaning on my shoulder in the back of Curt's VW bus, sound asleep. I was becoming Tom the Uncle. Family felt good to me, and I began to think I would enjoy having kids of my own. But with whom?

Tona and I were no longer simpatico. She had slept with the lighting designer at the theater while we were still together. I wasn't greatly upset for we were pursuing two divergent paths: mine into the world of psychedelics, mysticism, and neighborhood; hers into the world of antiques and her family whom I found nowhere as interesting as my friends. The woman who exposed her breasts had no reason to do so anymore. She moved out.

I was stimulated and confronted by Curt's and Ira's machismo and their "in your face" style of confrontation. I saw it revealed in Curt's bullying tendencies toward his wife and children that I chose to overlook, much as I had done with Victor and his family. Ira's dismissive and condescending attitude toward women was not something I wanted for myself, yet my relationships with women, invariably messy, had included the condescending and dismissive. Women, in my iconography, swung between Kali and the Madonna. I feared their demands and took advantage of their weaknesses. It was easier to smoke a joint, listen to music, and flip into my headspace. Although my father was dead, it was obvious to me that I was still grappling with my uneasy relationship with my mother.

I opened the Off the Wheel Swap Shop at 428 South Street. My sympathetic landlady liked the idea and waived the first month's rent. Patrons could trade any usable giveaways for the shop's seconds, such as clothing, furniture, shoes, jewelry, paintings, balloons, and candles. An inspector from Licenses and Inspections wanted $3 for a mercantile license, but I told him no money was being exchanged, so he picked out four dresses and a pair of shoes and swapped me his fountain pen. I was never suited to be a regular shopkeeper; the routine bored the hell out of me, so the shop continually changed. One day it had a small café dispensing apple cider; another day crafts were made. It was essential that the store be a fluid, theatrical medium of exchange, be it conversation or goods. We were processing information, using the store as a fun house to highlight and spoof the consumer economy. I loved the neighborhood children, who traded their crayon drawings for candy and balloons. It was a great way to meet people, bullshit with them, and play the roles of shopkeeper, entrepreneur, visionary, and fool.

As in all things idealistic, the bloom on Off the Wheel Swap Shop faded as the swaps became more unequal—dreck in, good stuff out. I learned one thing about material goods—if you give it away, the vultures will pick you clean, which is OK if you are doing it as an experimental study in human psychology or as charity. But the swap shop was becoming a trash shop. I kept it going for a few months until the reality hit that I had to come up with $100 per month for Harriet and actually be in that store every day. By then, the synergy group had fleshed out the first South Street Festival.

Paint was secured by the South Street committee and made available to all who wanted to paint storefronts, buildings, walls, sidewalks, and streets. And on a lovely Saturday morning in October, having secured a parade permit to march the entire length of South Street, we paraded, led by a police car, followed by the Challengers, a black drum group, and the Fire Department's fire-prevention float. Then, the Synergy Strutters, a group of longhairs playing kazoos, banjos, temple bells, tablas, and flutes, Hare Krishna-ed down the street. Whoever was in our community bounced along with us—pushing baby strollers and riding bikes—while waving to an assortment of amazed curiosity-seekers who had stumbled out of their apartments or just happened to be shopping. All cheered as our pièce de résistance, Ms. Renaissance Slum Goddess, clad in a pink party dress, hard hat, and combat boots waved from a float mounted on a Ford Falcon, decorated with roses, balloons, and girls. Midway in the parade was old Mr. Fleming, a retired black junk dealer, who gave rides to children in his ancient wooden wagon, pulled by his pony, Rex. Fleming had been hauling junk in the wagon all his life; this was his first parade.

The coup de grâce was delivered later on a vacant lot adjoining South Street. The synergy group had joined forces with Al Johnson, who had a small architecture firm called Alley Friends. Al was a rebel architect and loved creating alternative structures. He found ready allies in Curt and Curt's architect school buddy, Walt Bowker, along with George Keegan, my associate from TLA. The South Street Bubble would be a twelve-foot-high inflatable, shaped like a pillow, made of four thousand square feet of clear plastic. The plastic sheets would be laid out, taped together, and blown up with a window fan. This was a stealth operation. We had no permits, and were studying how to put the darn thing together under Alan's guidance when three squad cars arrived, demanding to know what we were doing and where our permits were. (As I have mentioned, the police had an adversarial relationship with its citizens, particularly, the black and long-haired counter-culture part of that citizenry.) We eloquently bullshitted them, confidently asserting that we were appearing under the auspices of the permitting agency who had folded us into the preexisting permit so that the . . . etc. The cops pulled to the side and silently watched us with, as one reporter said, "authoritative incredulity." We began inflating.

A door was cut in the side, and a rock band climbed into the bubble with their instruments and amps. We spray-painted "Welcome" and "Blow-Up" on the sides and then gave the spray cans to the gang kids, who sprayed faces and flowers and "5 'n' South" all over the bag. Then we let the people in and we—freaks, society ladies, drunks, kids, tourists, shopkeepers—danced the afternoon away. We maintained the peace by serving as deflectors, diverters, and fools. Never underestimate a good jester! Despite the open doorway slit and numerous punctures, the bubble remained inflated, the good mood stayed infectious, and whew! No one got hurt, which was an important criteria for judging an event. We looked at each other when it was over and marveled because it was possible a thrown beer bottle or an out-of-control drunk could have destroyed a peaceful day.

A flimsy plastic bubble costing $41 sitting on hard pavement in the midst of a harder neighborhood created a fun house that altered the way a neighborhood appeared for its residents and visitors, leaving them open to imagining a neighborhood of coexistence and fun.

The neighborhood now needed what all trendy neighborhoods need: a coffee house. A couple of guys from the Netherlands rented a storefront; a bunch of us tossed in some bucks, fixed up the first floor and voila! The Crooked Mirror was born, a place of our own to hang our art and meet and greet each other. We could have gone to the delis, and still did, to nosh on cabbage soup and lox, but the Crooked Mirror was ours. It was there I met my first wife, Cathi.

Cathi had run away from her family in New Hampshire, left high school, and made her way to South Street. She had "risk" written all over her, but I didn't see that. She had been on the road; she had taken risks. I saw her beauty, her protean zest for life, for painting, photography, trying anything. She had limpid eyes that were seductive. And she was all of sixteen. I was thirty-one.

The year 1970 was the time for tearing down walls: racial, economic, social, sexual, age, or gender. Who you showed up to be was who you were until proven different.

So Cathi moved into my house on Monroe and became my consort. Cathi got an older man who had a rep in the neighborhood. I got a beautiful young girl. Together, we laughed and loved and lived in a bubble of our own, our own undersea Octopus's Garden, a make-believe regular couple who loved going out into the community and had a flair for the theatrical. It seemed like a good match.

I also began spending more time with Ira Einhorn, a relationship that gave me the shock of my life some years later. Ira called himself the Unicorn, which he took as a poetic transliteration of his German last name. Ira had almost nothing in his apartment in Powelton Village, near Drexel and the University of Pennsylvania, but a vast library, which he generously shared with his friends. His way of disseminating a book, usually concerning the exploration of consciousness, would be to give the book to me or another and inside would be written a list of names to whom the book would be passed. The same for scholarly papers that he knew about, such as those written by ethnobiologist Andrew Weil, who was reporting from the Ecuadorean jungles about the tribal use of hallucinogenic plants and healing herbs.

Ira liked to make things happen. He midwifed book deals for unknown authors and introduced new age celebrities, such as psychedelic spiritual explorers Ram Das and Ralph Metzner, to Philadelphia. At Ira's apartment, we sat while John Cage quietly and, with great humor, read from *Finnegan's Wake* and then led us in chanting "The best form of government is no government at all, and we shall have it when we are ready for it." Cage was a merry soul.

Ira had many guises and maybe could have been called an unbearable genius at role-playing: an intellectual guide, trickster, manipulator, and as far as women were concerned, a Don Juan. He cleverly trolled for women on college campuses, casting himself as a feminist, extolling the women's virtues while at the same time letting them know that monogamy was outdated and relationships—his, at least—were open-ended.

In 1971, Ira ran for mayor of Philadelphia, and I was his campaign manager. We saw this as a lark, especially as the favorite for the post was the anti-Ira, the current police chief, Frank Rizzo, a heavy-handed, charismatic cop, particularly antagonistic to hippies and African Americans and deeply beloved by the working-class white people of Philadelphia. Ira was cast into the group of second-tier candidates who weren't to be taken seriously. Ira got his few moments in front of the cameras, which he took to like a fish in the water, to speak to the electorate as a planetary enzyme before that electorate put Rizzo into office.

There were late nights when Ira and I would drive around Philly, her streets glum and eerie, slowly cruising through neighborhoods I didn't know existed or dared not venture into—forty thousand abandoned properties at the time. Toking on a joint, he would fill me in on the history of the city, and then, by extension, her possibilities, and by further extension, the possible evolution of the human race. It was pompous, pretentious, sure; as an inquiry, thought-provoking and fun. It was only when the matter of women came up that he became competitive. In an interview in the *Philadelphia Inquirer,* Ira said that the most important issues today were women's issues. When we read that, we who knew him laughed. What bullshit. Ira needed to be a dominant alpha male. I was already with a woman; it didn't matter. But then things changed with Ira.

In 1972, Holly Maddux, a thin, porcelain-skinned Grace Kelly beauty, a Bryn Mawr graduate, moved in to Ira's apartment. She was from Texas and had a little accent that could become a lot if she wanted to mess with you. She had clear-blue eyes and basically was the WASP antithesis of the Jewish—stocky dark-haired, bearded Ira. Holly both played the acolyte to Ira and pushed back against him. She was somewhat shy and gentle and very earnest, a thinker. Ira was emotionally unavailable; Holly didn't have the self-assurance to trust her emotions. Her genteel reserve was no match for Ira's bullish nature, yet Holly could be the matador at times and stick him where it got his attention. Holly tried to outdebate Ira. That wasn't going to happen. He was unyielding. He would never give in to a woman.

In 1974, Ira, Holly, my second wife-to-be, Kristen, and I vacationed together on Cape Breton Island, Nova Scotia. Holly and Ira kept to themselves. Holly, not as well known to us, didn't share the intimacy with Kristen that I had with Ira. We all got on, but theirs was a troubled partnership. To compound this painful situation, Kristen was happily eight months pregnant, while Holly had had an abortion with Ira before the trip.

Kristen thought Ira was full of himself, and he didn't try to win her over. It was all or nothing with him. Holly took to baking pies and cakes; she struck up a friendship with a woman who had a farm nearby while Ira sunned nude and wrote his journals.

The last time I saw Holly was at my wedding with Kristen in 1977. Ira was supposed to be my best man, but he never appeared. He and Holly arrived at the church at nine, although the wedding was scheduled for eleven. No one was there. He took offense and left in a huff; Holly walked the three blocks to our house and was part of the celebration. Ron Rozewski became my best man. Kristen had been the nanny for Ron and Carole Rozewski's child, Mary, and Carole was Kristen's maid of honor. I was pissed at Ira. It appeared our friendship had ended.

Shortly after the wedding, Kristen and I left on a trip around the world. When we returned in November of 1977, I reconstituted my friendship with Ira on a cooler level and visited him at his apartment once or twice. I didn't see Holly and inquired after her, but he didn't know where she was. He said she had dropped out of sight. Other friends told me they hadn't seen Holly since October of 1977. This was strange, although we all agreed Holly had a nomadic gene and maybe was finished with Ira. Maybe she really had gotten fed up with the Philadelphia scene and started over elsewhere, although word was out that even her parents didn't know her whereabouts.

New Year's Eve 1978, Kristen and I were living in the country and were hosting a housewarming party. As the party raged on, a group of men huddled in the mudroom, popping beers and smoking joints. We were all happy and high. Ron Rozewski was shocked to find Ira at the party and was determined to get an explanation as to why Ira didn't show up for my wedding. Ira was visibly uncomfortable and tried to avoid Ron's questions about not showing up and Holly's disappearance. Ron asked Ira if he realized he was the most likely suspect regarding her absence. Ira let out his signature high-pitched laugh. "What do you think?" As Ira broke away, Ron said, "If you killed her, I hope you at least did a good job." Ron later said it was his Special Forces training and contempt for Ira that prompted him to make such a remark. It turned out Ira didn't do such a good job.

Ira called me a month later and asked if I would store a trunkful of his books in my barn. I said I'd get back to him. Fuck it, I wasn't going to schlep his stuff for him. Ira's trunk would easily weigh several hundred pounds. Put it in my barn? I was trying to empty it of the last owner's trash.

I phoned him and told him. After I hung up, I wondered why Ira would want to store books in my barn. He had few possessions other than his enormous library. His books were his treasures. Why would he want to put some of them in my barn? It didn't add up, but I soon forgot about it.

In 1979, I was entering the Painted Bride Art Center to perform *Cabin Fever*, a new play I had written. Bob Ingram, editor of the local newspaper, stopped me and asked me if I'd heard the news.

"They found Holly. She's been in a trunk in Ira's apartment for months, dismembered, her parts wrapped in newspapers. Ira's arrested for murder."

All of us who knew him were stunned. His misogyny was one thing. Killing a woman? Whoa. He denied doing it, said it was a CIA-Russian plot to discredit his research. No one believed that. The headlines screamed, "Hippie Guru Murders Girlfriend." How could I and his many other acquaintances have misjudged him so completely?

Then I remembered he had asked to store the trunk in my barn.

Ira's mother, Bea, called me and asked me to speak on his behalf as a character witness for his making bail. I had been to her house for dinner on several occasions. I couldn't refuse a mother's plea, even though I didn't believe in his innocence. It was only bail, I told myself, not a trial. Arlen Spector, soon to be Senator Spector, was his lawyer. Sitting next to the judge, I testified that I knew Ira and had traveled with him. Ira was composed and confident. Fortunately, I didn't have to answer any questions as to his innocence or guilt. It was over quickly. It was the last time I saw Ira.

Ira made bail, predictably maintained his innocence, and never once expressed remorse over Holly's death. He eventually fled the country and eluded the police of several nations for many years.

While Ira was on the lam in Ireland, Barbara Bronfman, evidently a true believer, warned him that the Dublin police were closing in. Ironically, I had introduced Ira to Barbara on a trip that he and I took to Montreal. I had the names of friends of my brother's, Charles and Barbara Bronfman; Bronfman also happened to be the Seagram's whiskey family. Barbara immediately took to Ira, and Ira liked powerful, rich people. Due to the phone call from Barbara, Ira fled shortly before detectives arrived at his door.

Ironically, women were his benefactors more often than men. In 1990, a book by Steven Levy, *The Unicorn's Secret*, included excerpts from his diaries, where he confessed to strangling and beating women, almost killing them, and the excitement and delight he took in it. We knew his behavior with women to be loutish, but none of us was aware of this side of him. It was a sober awakening.

He was not captured until 1997, in the South of France, where he was living a quiet, bourgeois married life. Ira fought extradition to the United States, arguing that French law outlawed the death penalty, which he would face in Pennsylvania. Legal battles went on for four years, but he was handed over to the United States in 2001, on the proviso that he not be given the death penalty. After a brief trial, he was convicted and sentenced to life in prison, where he remains today.

Details of Holly and Ira's last days were parsed and pondered, but what we always were left with, kept coming back to, was that a beautiful, talented woman's life had been snuffed out, murdered by one of our own.

JULY 4 thru AUGUST 31

at

MONMOUTH

A LIMITED NUMBER OF
SEASON PASSES

is now available for the 1963 summer season of the new

MONMOUTH REPERTORY COMPANY

Cumston Hall, Monmouth, Maine, (Rt. 132)

Performing one of five presentations every night but Sunday.

"The Imaginary Invalid" - "Much Ado About Nothing"

"The Lark" - "As You Like It" - "How She Lied to Her Husband"

FIRST TIME IN U.S.A.

Thomas Bissinger and Mary Howe

present

The Offshore Island

by

Marghanita Laski

Agassiz Theatre

(CAMBRIDGE)

VANITY OF NOTHING

The Imaginary Invalid by the Monmouth Repertory Company. I was able to try out my commedia del'arte ideas. Esther is front row left.

The Second Shepherd's Play. Mary holding the infant Jesus as the shepherds gather round.

The house on Chilmark Pond, Martha's Vineyard. Esther in foreground.

Bottom: Hunt and my Jules and Jim moment

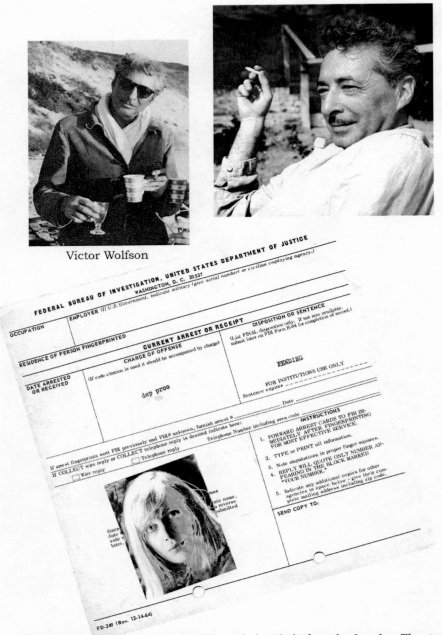

Victor Wolfson

Deborah Norton with her deportation card shortly before the London Theatre Group was denied working visas by Actors Equity and the Immigration Dept.

Mitzo

Phil Bruns as MacBird in the Los Angeles production. 1967.

"Motel," one of the plays composing America Hurrah. 1968

Producer John Bos and me at TLA.

The TLA Company 1970

Jerome Raphael   Judd Hirsch   George Keegan John Bos Billy Monday Roz Drexler
Bob Buckler Rachel Drexler
Stacey Jones   Yvonne Stafford Betsy Henn   Eugene Lee   Nancy Petersen
Ken Hornung Gretel Cummings   Ken Goldman   Max Clark   Don Earl
Joe Costa Susan Lunenfeld Danny DeVito Tom   Francine Newman   Lew Rosen
Grove Hunter Don DeWilde   John Hall

People's Park 3rd & South
Construction of People's Park: Top: Cathi .Middle: Cathi videotaping, Walt
Bowker next to her. I'm trying to figue out what I'm doing. Did that a lot.
Bottom: George Keegan starts digging. Passerby becomes interested.

South Street before gentrification
(trees growing out of building)

George Keegan, Joel Spivak and Tom discuss
while a youngster works.

Passerby now digs.

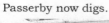

My next door neighbor Mr. Perkins:
"The spirit don't die,
it's just translated."

Mr. Flemming on his ponycart leading the parade across Broad Street

George Keegan and Tom with Sean meeting for the parade.

3rd and South

The first South Street Parade.

Not a lot of people watching, but the paraders had fun and the parade was the first step in defeating the Crosstown Expressway.

Taping the seams. Curt Kubiak, kids, Tom,
George Keegan, unknown, Bob Klein

Crowd jammin' in the Bubble to Jacob's Creek.

South Street Bubble
1970

Entrance to the Bubble.

Al Johnson, designer, cutting the seam: George Keegan,
Sean Waterman and Don Earl 'supervise.'

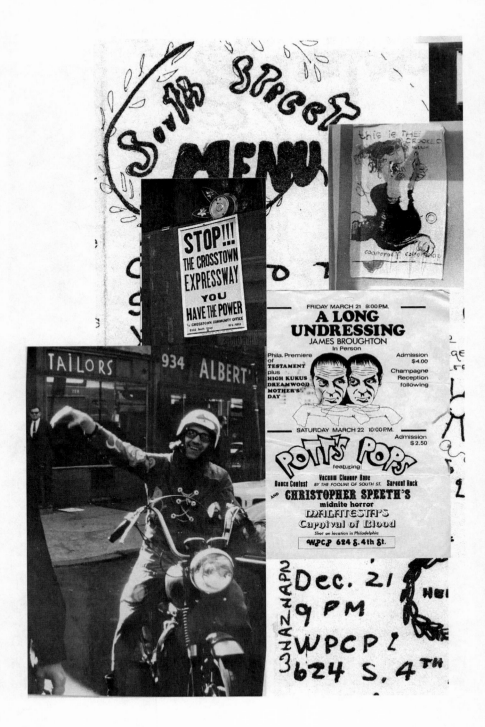

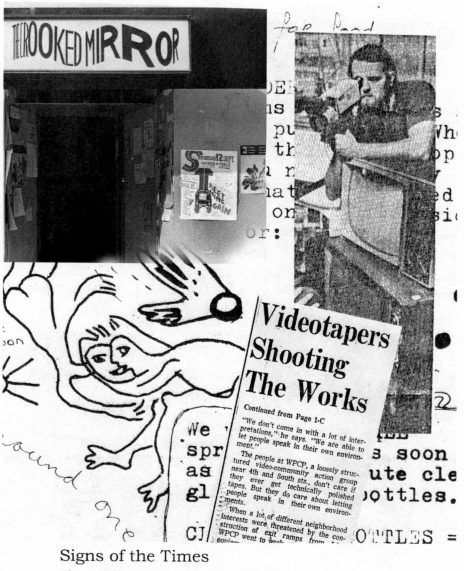

Signs of the Times

Above right: Curt Kubiak videotaping

Bottom left: Partner Walt Bowker on motorcycle

James Broughton is an esteemed avant-garde filmmaker, poet and playwright. Tom Potts is a South Street artist. Christopher Speeth is a Philadelphia filmmaker.

Ira Einhorn at an Ira for Mayor campaign stop at U. Of Penn.
Steve Waterman to his right recording. The use of movie camera
by newsmen rather than video dates the era: 1971.

Chapter Eleven

In *Cat's Cradle,* Kurt Vonnegut coined the term *kerass,* meaning a group whose consciousness is connected. It was now early 1972, and I had been smoking a lot of dope with my *kerass.* I noticed that after the high, I would experience confusion, sometimes paranoia, not so much about what I had done but about the many possibilities in front of me. My indecisiveness ran counter to my desire to be the director, to control events. The answer was to procrastinate and smoke another joint, telling myself that doing nothing was also a choice.

Yet the fact remained that I needed something to do. Unemployment insurance had expired, and I was eating into my funds, the bulk of which came from dividends from D. N. & E. Walter, my mother's side of the family business.

Our *kerass* was involved in holding and attending meetings aimed at stopping the Crosstown Expressway. South Street was beginning to glimmer on the city's radar, but whether it would be blasted into a concrete thoroughfare or reinvent itself as a thriving community was still an unanswered question. TLA was now a movie theater, and its claim to fame was the midnight showings of John Waters's movie *Pink Flamingos.* I worked for our new food co-op, broke pavement, and helped plant a hundred flowering pear trees along South and adjoining streets, but there was no central thing that occupied me like a play would have.

In one of his journals, André Gide wrote, "I was like a sailor who drops his oars and lets himself drift; at last he takes time to look at the shore; while he was rowing he saw nothing."

I had been drifting. Cathi and I had broken up and gotten together several times. Our happiest times were when we traveled.

We visited the brother of one of the members of our *kerass* living on Denman Island in the Strait of Georgia of British Columbia in the summer of 1971. A simple cabin, eating salmon bought from a local fisherman, hanging with a bunch of young people who had opted out of the mainstream—everything felt fresh and clean. Upon our return, we crawled back into our house on Monroe Street, sat at opposite ends, and regarded each other, two refugees who spoke different languages and communicated haltingly, our words pushing past the other. Occasionally we met, embraced, but tentatively, as if the house might pitch over if we came together too forcefully.

My focus was on being part of the narrative of an evolving neighborhood that we were beginning to call the South Street Renaissance. In this drama, the cast numbered in the hundreds, often playing multiple roles. There were artists freshly minted from Philadelphia's many art schools, hippies, gays, new entrepreneurs, old Jewish merchants, drifters, speculators, realtors, and those heroin addicts whom we called not-to-be-futures who debuted, dazzled, and disappeared.

The sixties were used up. Assassinations, war, and perhaps most iconically, the breakup of the Beatles in 1970, signaled that the era of innocence was over. "Nothing is real, nothing to get hung about," sang the Beatles in *Strawberry Lane*. The power of indulgence took hold in the seventies. Irreverence was replaced by cynicism. The war continued, Watergate was looming, and the use of hard drugs was on the rise.

In the spring of 1972, Curt Kubiak and I and a few others began experimenting with a new drug called PCP, phencyclidine, also called angel dust, originally developed for human surgery but whose use in humans was discontinued in 1965 because it was found that patients often became agitated or delusional while recovering from its anesthetic effects. It was said to have been used as a horse tranquilizer.

It was true that putting the kind of energy that was meant for a two-thousand-pound animal into your body was not exactly doing it a favor, but it certainly unloosened the screws holding the rational in place. Forget that—it blew those screws to smithereens and launched us into an ice-cool Karlheinz Stockhausen electronic soundscape, featuring otherworldly sounds from distant stellar confabulations. We assembled at Curt's house, sprinkled some of this substance on mint leaves, and smoked it. Soon, we would be lying on the floor, outer-spaced but together. It wasn't a party drug; we didn't want to move, anesthetized as we were—no drinking or other foolishness accompanied our eight-hour trip through the cosmos. We were drawn into people piles, and on the rare occasion when someone drove a car, preferably one who had not indulged, the effect was as if a magnet sucked the car down the street.

Zoom, we'd be at the end with no sense of traveling there. We saw ourselves as psychonauts, exploring the far reaches of consciousness.

Curt, Walt Bowker, and I decided to form a community center called WPCP, which stood for Work Peacefully Communicate Patiently, a veiled tipping of the hat to the drug. I would use my funds to pay Curt and Walt a salary so that we could bring WPCP into fruition. In our fun house, we visualized a TV studio and community center—an electronic playground with living-room content. We would be electronic monks, Dr. Feedbacks with a quarter-inch Akai video cameras. We would interview Philly's movers and shakers (according to our definition), cover the fight against the Crosstown Expressway, and capture the eccentricities of our own street people, artists, bozos, riffers, and riff-raff.

I had my eye on a store for rent on Fourth Street with 1896 MARKET carved into the third-floor stone facade. It surpassed my expectations. We rented one side of the massive ground floor, eighty feet long and twenty feet wide with sixteen-foot ceilings held up by massive wooden joists. Our side, a former sweatshop, was piled with dusty bolts of fabric and sewing machines. Near the rear of the building, a wide staircase, half of which was walled off, led to an office overlooking the entire floor. The partners were excited; we saw nothing but opportunity. Where some see trash, others see treasure, although, as one of our more dubious PCPers observed, "There's a thin line between clairvoyance and bananas."

There were two more floors, but they were filled with pigeon shit and were more space than we needed. Group Motion Dance Company eventually took over the second and third floors.

To transform the space, we took the bolts of fabric, cut swatches of random lengths, and stapled them to the wall, creating a forty-foot patchwork quilt worthy of an Amish quilting bee on speed. After the wall was finished, Curt designed a large staircase to go up the side of one wall—bolted onto a ramp that would be suspended by cables from the ceiling—that ran into a sound and light booth over the entrance. Most days found Curt and me constructing the fun house. He always reminded me to slow down and take some "admiration time" to appreciate what we had accomplished.

A year later, when Epstein's Lingerie went out of business, we took over the whole first floor. We cut a door into the middle of the dividing wall and decorated the new side with different fabric. We eliminated that part of the wall dividing the rear staircase, which now became the Schizophrenic Staircase because if you sat on the steps, you'd see two different shows. It was a comically surreal fun house.

One room might be filled with a giant inflatable bubble with cushions, Stockhausen beeps, shimmering gongs and flutes softly playing as people slowly danced in it, while the other side was a living room—easy chairs, couch, drawing tables, and video monitors showing recent footage of street happenings.

WPCP was cold and drafty. We thought to emulate Philadelphia icon Benjamin Franklin and his famous Franklin stove. We read books on the design of the Franklin stove. The difficulty was that our stove had to heat a huge volume of air and have enough draft to draw the heat up three floors—about sixty feet. It would be crazy expensive to heat WPCP with the ancient oil furnace buried in the basement, so we designed a large sheet-metal trapezoidal box, a kind of squatting Sumo wrestler of heat. When we lit it for the first time, billows of smoke filled the room. A total disaster. Design modifications—larger opening, smaller opening, electric fans, different kind of baffles—were tried, but it was we who were baffled. We never got it right and settled for small fires, which seemed to work. Ichabod, a carpenter buddy, his girlfriend, and her two kids camped next to it for the whole of one very cold winter.

Others, homeless and broke, made their home in WPCP, unbeknownst to the general public and the landlord. John and Claire made an apartment for themselves in the grimy, windowless, oil-stinking forty-by-eighty-foot basement. They laid down a carpet, installed a brass bed, bureau, and lamp. Hung their clothes from water pipes and lay in their bed while the black Muslims, to whom we had rented the upstairs space on Friday nights, excoriated the white devil during their weekly meetings. Black Muslims, in their crisp suits and red bow ties, sweet potato pies for sale, never knew they were being monitored.

We began to follow two world-renowned figures: architects Buckminster Fuller, inventor of the geodesic dome, then in residence at Penn, and Louis Kahn. We were amazed that these two world figures were taken for granted in Philadelphia, almost ignored. Maybe it was the Quaker influence, which promotes modesty and suppresses anyone who shines too brightly.

WPCP declared a people's high centennial as a response to the bicentennial coming to the birthplace of the nation in 1976. We said no to big buildings, big money, and center-city projects and yes to a diffuse, diverse celebration of neighborhoods, of which Philly had many—ethnically driven, robust, full of people who liked to party. South Street was an incubator of dreams and entrepreneurial imaginings. It was becoming a magnet, pulling young people from around the world, as if Marc Chagall had painted his circus folk into South Street and his characters danced into life.

We went around town giving multimedia slide presentations of our decentralizing-the-celebration proposal, videotaping it all with our quarter-inch Akai cameras. Occasionally, a few minutes of our footage were shown on local TV news. We asked Louis Kahn his thoughts. He offered them clearly and succinctly. "Clean the streets. The streets are an agreement among those who use them, an expression of our comings and goings, a room in which to share the spirit. Hang banners across the block in all the neighborhoods, expressing the spirit of that block. Let it be a poem, a light, the feeling of that agreement."

Kahn wanted to maintain institutions but make new agreements. He would ask, whether of a room, a window, or an institution, this simple yet difficult question: "What does it want to be?" One of our greatest architects, Kahn died in 1974 in New York's Penn Station and lay in a city morgue for two days before being identified.

Kahn and Fuller talked to us, not at us; their thinking was fresh, their designs challenging. It's no accident my two partners, Curt and Walt, were architects. I liked sketching layouts for public parks and their structures, fun houses as new theatrical possibilities; even so, the old colonial house on Monroe Street was my theater du jour.

The 229 house was a beacon for lost souls, pilgrims, wanderers, and seekers. Many people vibed the house with no connection to others or me. The wind literally blew open the door and voila! a couple of eager Portuguese sailors, fresh off a cargo ship, wandering through the neighborhood, stumbled in, speaking little or no English. No worries, Cathi was cooking lasagna, and the sailors had a bottle of Madeira. Bobby, a navy sailor, a good kid—not too bright, simpering sweet—looking to get a sex change in the worst way but not having the cash, floated in. We were his people. He'd change out of his uniform and became the happiest of cross-dressers, teetering around on his high heels, a puppy on stilts, a tight skirt confining his thick legs. Nogeeshik might be there, an American Indian who was the subject of a famous Andrew Wyeth painting in tempera, or Rahul Mahadeo, an Asian Indian who jammed on sitar to our improvised chanting.

Peggy and Steve Waterman and their four-year-old son, Sean, lived with us. Sean would be the little imp, jesting with us as much as we with him. His father, Steve, would be setting mikes, operating the dials on his Nagra, tape-recording our conversations or playing LPs. Peggy, an accomplished photographer, put out paints and paper for us to play with, and as the night wore on, the cast of characters spontaneously arrived, intuiting that the *kerass* was gathering. No invites needed, we were a salon without borders, a combination of merry pranksters, dada, and dope.

A frequent drop-in at Monroe Street was a skinny black musician, Matt Hopkins, a prodigy on the flute and vibraphones. Matt was around twenty, kind of an idiot savant, meaning he seemed to be able to access information and dispense insights in rants beyond our comprehension. He mixed church theology (I think he was a music director at a church) with galactic sightings, presences unseen in our material world. He could also be a blithering idiot who hadn't eaten or slept for days. He had a dislodged eye; you never knew at whom he was looking. He hipped me to a lot of the newer jazz musicians like Pharoah Sanders and Charles Lloyd. When the People's Park at Wexler's empty lot opened, he was the musical attraction. The park now had benches, some climbing apparatus, and a stage. Matt brought his vibraphone and began to play.

The crowd came around, especially the 5 'n' South gang, who were curious to see this black guy not only playing but addressing them directly. Matt was on a roll, verbally taunting them in an effeminate way, mocking them, laughing at them, challenging them. You knew something was going to erupt, and it did. The gang attacked Matt, the vibes flipped over, mallets flew, and Matt crumpled with a scream, unconscious as a stone. We didn't know if he had been knocked out or killed. The gang ran off, and we carried Matt, draped in our arms like Christ off the cross, to a neighbor's house.

After twenty minutes or so, he awoke and declared he had planned the whole thing; he had deliberately gone into a *samadhi* state to protect himself. How Matt-like, if true. He put on his pea jacket, threw his scarf around his neck, hoisted his vibraphone, walked downstairs, and declining a car ride, disappeared onto South Street as if nothing had happened. Matt Mysterioso.

Then there was Sly Baba. Sly was really Gil Locks, who had recently returned from living on a roof at Sai Baba's ashram in India. Sai Baba was world-renowned, able to materialize gems and a sweet powder called *vibouti* in the palm of his hands. Gil, influenced by the guru, showed up in Philly with only a toothbrush and the Word of God, which he proclaimed to one and all. How he came to my house is interesting.

In 1969, Gil, living in Mill Valley, California, visited my New York apartment, having been given my name by his wife, Renee, who in turn was a friend of the photographer and lecturer on the avant-garde Jeff Berner, whom I had met through Ira Einhorn. Gil was a nationally ranked insurance agent at the time, a smooth talker with a hypnotic intensity to him. He could have been Elmer Gantry in another lifetime. Anyway, Gil showed up at my door, and I suggested we go see the Living Theatre's *Paradise Now* at the Brooklyn Academy of Music.

Paradise Now was a full-frontal assault on his senses and mind, a ceremony of incantation, ritual, nudity, and lots of audience participation. It was mesmerizing; Gil's mind was blown, and not long after, he shucked his corporate suits for a monk's robes and headed for India. The Beatles had been in India; Ram Dass had returned and written a best seller, *Be Here Now*, which was one of my main reads. So Gil's appearance, although unusual, was part of a larger happening.

Gil was still the salesman though. He still wanted something from you, more like your soul than your bucks, although he'd take some of them too. His seductive mantra was "Just say yes! What are you resisting, my brother and my sister? You're stuck in your old habits. You want to be responsible? To whom? What for? Give it up! Love, love, love." The Charmer was tempting. Letting go—of your hang-ups, your guilt, your marriage, your possessions—was tempting, especially when the fruit dangled in front of you was the direct route to God, love, and freedom. Gil had watched Sai Baba carefully and knew how to play the guru, whether straight or high on pot and acid. He played you for the highest stakes; it was all or nothing—give your life to God, or be miserable. It was that simple; all you had to do was let go and let God—very tempting. I liked his message but was wary of the messenger. Quickly, he acquired a set of disciples, each wearing matching overalls with a toothbrush stuck in its breast pocket, including one of my actors from the TLA, Ken Goldman. Kenny was married with children and gave all that up to fall under Gil's sway. Even being arrested in a Superman cape standing on the four-lane Schuylkill Expressway at rush hour did not dampen Ken's ardor for Gil.

One night Gil was lying by the fireplace with Curt and me and told us that before he had gone to India, his father had been complaining that his life was futile, a failure. Gil told his father if that were the case, he ought to kill himself. The next week, his father killed Gil's mother and then killed himself. Whether this act tipped Gil into his current behavior or not, his was quite a confession. Not long after this confession, Gil moved to New York City and spent two years sitting in silence as a guru on a park bench in Central Park while Ken Goldman attended him and his followers. Gil gave me insight into the charisma of gurus and how an obviously "good" or "spiritual" message could be used by the guru to abuse his power for gain, be it financial, sexual, control of others' minds, or all three.

As South Street attracted the latest healers and dealers into the neighborhood, Abie Kravitz watched the flow from his fruit-and-vegetable stand. Abie was an iconic figure, an old, squat Russian Jew, whose black cap pulled down over his forehead gave him a slightly thuggish yet dapper look. He peered out from thick glasses spattered with horseradish, which he ground fresh in a homemade grinder and then pickled and bottled. A short stub of a man, he'd sit on a stool watching the parade, get up when a customer would look over his horseradish and vegetables, which as the years progressed and indifference set in, got limper and limper.

He'd drive up in the early morning and unload boxes from his old Buick onto his stand: pomegranates, bananas, pears, apples, cabbage, collards, and hunks of horseradish root. He looked like a root—stumpy, hard, browned by the sun. A black lady would come up and ask to see the greens. "How much you want?"

"Let me see 'em."

"You don't need to see them, they're good!" he'd say, flopping them on the counter.

"Hmmmpf!" the customer sniffed. "They don't look so fresh, Abie. Kind of used."

"Fresh! Not fresh! Go down the street, and pay more."

The fruit and veggies may have been Abie's job in the old days, but now his mission was to patrol the street, checking the action. "I love my 'ippies," he'd say, confiding in me that he could bring a woman to orgasm by massaging her palm.

"No shit, Abie?"

"Would I shit you, you shiddy validdy?" He'd blink through his splattered glasses. I often saw him grabbing a hand of an unsuspecting female, but I couldn't testify to his powers.

Abie told me he had escaped from Russia after the Russo-Japanese War, where he had been shot in the ass. He had arrived on South Street in the 1930s, when South Street and environs were wall-to-wall pushcarts. Although he was now the last street peddler, he had managed to buy a home in Philly's posh (compared to South Street) Mayfair neighborhood, where, he was proud to proclaim, his house looked out at the brick wall of a bank. How's that for status?

Many thought he was a dirty old man, at best an anachronism. Isaiah Zagar and myself were of a different opinion. Isaiah, today a well-known artist whose wall murals are seen throughout the neighborhood, and his wife, Julia, opened the Eyes Gallery in 1969. They were the first to pioneer South Street's revitalization. Isaiah and I thought of Abie as somewhat mystical, a saint of peddlers, and perhaps more. He had outlasted himself, and that made him attractive to us—a living relic, the godfather of South Street.

When his stand on the corner of Fourth and South was threatened by the opening of Jim's Steaks, we moved Abie to the outside of WPCP. Eight days after the birth of Kristen's and my son, Zachary, Abie blessed Zak with a brit milah, a naming ceremony. Abie held Zak while giving the Hebrew blessing, and then we toasted with honey wine—best ceremony I ever attended. WPCP felt more secure with Abie on the watch, but we knew he wasn't going to be around much longer.

The 5 'n' South gang from the Southwark projects had approached WPCP and requested that they be allowed to hold dances in our joint, much to the consternation of the businessmen in the area, who had not been thrilled that the black Muslims were holding their meetings at WPCP. Curt and Walt argued it was better to respect everybody and be inclusive. If we couldn't walk our walk as well as we talked our talk, then who were we and what were we doing?

Personally, I was afraid of some of the black teenagers who were measuring me every step of the way. We needed a power broker, a go-between, and Georgie Stewart, a pal of ours—a scrappy, cocky ex-boxer—fit the part. A trim welterweight, George was wary, like he was casing a job, looking to see what he could boost. I trusted him completely. He was profane as the day was long, peppering stories and scrapes with "I swear to God, Tom, it's all true, on my mother's grave," and he'd cross himself and give you a wicked grin. I was glad he was on my side, especially when I saw him come on a troublemaker at a dance, throw a lightning-fast combination, and toss him out of WPCP before anyone knew what happened.

George was a fixture in the South Street area for many years, hustling dope, ultimately developing a nasty heroin habit. He had a lover's heart and a thief's mentality. I spoke with him shortly before his death. He was crying, telling me he wanted to stop but he couldn't. He was found dead of an overdose in his apartment a week later.

Chapter Twelve

On a wintry December evening in the early seventies, a plane took off from Boston with a group of Broadway Show of the Month Club subscribers, a large delegation from the NAACP, and three South Streeters: Dale Shuffler, a local potter; Cathi; and myself. The booking agent, a friend of Dale's, had given him three unused all-expenses-paid tickets—freebies. We were headed for a one-week trip to Morocco.

No one seemed curious about our presence. We landed in Tangier, amazed at our good luck, and went to our four-star hotel. We dumped our bags and hit the streets. South Street redux! The casbah was jumping: a maze of twisting, labyrinthine streets; shops selling everything under the sun (vegetables, fruits and herbs, carpets, shoes and other leather goods stacked floor to ceiling); artisans beating metal pots over hot fires; men dragging on water pipes; and hustlers pulling you into their store. Spices, incenses, slaughtered and charred meat permeated the smoky streets; men squatted in hooded djellabas; and women glanced slyly with kohl-lidded eyes. Cathi's natural exuberance, youthfulness, and warm smile set the merchants at ease. I could speak French, which helped. The young gay guys hounded Dale; they were persistent before giving up. As we sipped mint tea, I asked the waiter if I could buy some hash. No problem. Five minutes later, a guy returned with a loaf of hash. Ten dollars.

On a Tangier street corner, we heard three blind musicians scatting as fine as anything by Ella or Bobby McFerrin. They bopped, hopping onto each other's lines, surfing through them, rapping the sounds while a drummer kept time. People kept walking, just three musicians doing their thing. We stood in wonderment.

For the following days, we split from the rest of the other travelers, rented a car, and explored small brown baked towns, where cloth canopies and djellabas billowed in stark relief; tethered camels cleaned their teeth with their enormous tongues; and people huddled in their robes against the mud wall of a souk, looking like rocks, waiting for a bus or nothing at all. The wind whispered mysteriously in our ears. Dogs howled, and we shivered. I was glad I was with Dale and Cathi; we worked well by consensus. One of us would have a hit where to go and what to do. We had no plan, just hippies soaking it all in, kind of like South Street.

After a week, we met the NAACP and the Show of the Month Club in Casablanca and returned home. I was happy to have had this romantic interlude with Cathi. It disguised momentarily how our fifteen-year-age difference was beginning to grate. We endlessly discussed how we could "fix" the differences, but fixing sounded like repair, and without agreement on what needed to be repaired, we went around in circles. As the older one in this relationship, I assumed it was my responsibility to figure it all out. Things were slowly building to a head.

I was thinking, *Was marriage in my future? Was there something wrong with me? Maybe I really loved Cathi; maybe I didn't. I couldn't figure out what needed fixing, so maybe . . . I ought to marry her? Maybe our relationship would be resolved by this action? Maybe this is what I wanted all along and was too scared to admit or commit to?* I was filled with "maybes."

At the same time that my head was spinning from this muddled inquiry, I noticed that speculators were starting to see South Street property as viable. Prices were rising rapidly. I figured that I'd better buy a building while the buying was good.

I didn't buy 229 Monroe Street. As it turned out, I was glad I didn't. Instead, in March of 1973, I bought an abandoned turn-of-the-century three-story tenement for ten thousand dollars at 407 Bainbridge, one block north of South Street. The front door opened onto an extra-wide two-block plaza that once featured wall-to-wall pushcarts and horses.

407 Bainbridge, my home to be, was a reclamation project. Thieves had stripped the plumbing and electric, and all that remained were a series of rooms that had previously served three or four families. The Southwark projects, where the 5 'n' South Street gang came from, were a few blocks south; somewhere, in the back of my mind, I knew the house would serve more as an outpost than a home. Random crime and coming gentrification coexisted uneasily.

Nonetheless, Curt and I put our heads together and decided to make an architectural statement. We would blow out the south-facing windows on the third floor and install a giant five-foot Plexiglas bubble, like a vertical turret on a B-29 bomber. The back half of the roof we'd tear out and install three-foot-by-fourteen-foot wooden joists we found on the street and angle them up to rest on a newly created door and windows opening on to the roof. On the second floor, we would tear out the front windows and leave an open arch and set the wall back about six feet, thus creating a veranda. We'd build a wall out of beveled glass doors that had been tossed onto the street. In those amazing early years on South Street, all kinds of building materials were discarded, waiting to be recycled by pack rats such as us.

I had never done much carpentry, other than working with Curt on WPCP. Now he would teach me the craft. I'd always loved carpentry because at the end of the day, you saw you actually accomplished something.

I had the house. Now I decided I wanted a wife. I was in a deciding frenzy. Put a window here; get a wife there! It was folly, but I was determined to make a decision. I suggested to Cathi we get married. She was suspicious. Where was this coming from? I told her fate had consigned us to each other. Wasn't it time? Everyone was married, was going to get married, or had been married. I thought of that Neil Young song: "Old man, take a look at yourself. I'm a lot like you." Was I going to be an old man, looking at the shore from Gide's drifting rowboat? No, I wanted some of that "normality" I had so far avoided. Bainbridge Street would be my home—our home. And so we decided to marry in a Quaker ceremony in June of '73. South Street accepted our announcement as yet another "groovy" happening.

Curt, Ira, and Walt looked at me curiously. There was nothing to say. They were incredulous, but who cared what anyone thought? I didn't need permission from anyone! I was thirty-three; Cathi was eighteen. Was there a problem? I was numb as a nail and performing as if nothing was the matter—the supreme actor, Humphrey Bogart cool.

In the Quaker ceremony, we pronounced the vows to each other, witnessed by a bunch of friends sitting in a circle in our living room on Monroe Street. We signed a certificate saying we were husband and wife. Never had that word "wife" resounded with such awesome finality—a nail in the coffin.

There's a poem by Dylan Thomas: "The hand that signed the paper felled the city." As soon as I signed that paper and the wedding reception began, I disappeared. I stepped out the door of my old, worn-out fun house to clear my thoughts. It was dusk. The sky was a Maxfield Parrish blue. All this beauty and my heart felt so hard and confused, and I saw that change was coming, not just to me but to the house across the street, which was getting rehabbed, and my next door neighbor Mr. Perkins, who was gone. I had noticed some weeks ago that I hadn't seen the old man for some time, so I called the police, and they showed up, knocked a bunch of times then broke in to a dark, musty, cold house, and the young cop insisted I go in first. He turned on his flashlight and spun it around the room, but there was nothing, and he told me, "Go on up," lighting the stairs, and I climbed the same kind of spiral staircase that was in my house. As I gained the landing, I saw a pair of boots and then legs, and there was old Mr. Perkins—dead, stiff as a board—and I remembered him saying, "The spirit don't die—it's just translated," but now I wasn't so sure. I knew in my heart the marriage was a huge mistake, but it was too late for all that.

Cathi and I flew out to San Francisco. Cathi was a hit, and together, we performed our roles beautifully. Everyone was rightfully charmed by her youthful beauty while I was numbly floating on the ceiling, disembodied. We returned home to drive to Manchester, New Hampshire, to meet her parents. I was dreading this. Her father, Paul, same name as my father, was not that much older than me. It was going to be awkward at best.

The parents were polite and edgy; they were not enjoying this marriage any more than I was. They insisted we sleep in their bed. Creepy. The mother prepared enough food for six bridegrooms, and I didn't know if she was trying to please me or kill me. I thought the latter but shoveled it in, knowing not to insult your Italian mother-in-law who was watching you with the "eye" and who could barely conceal her "What the fuck did you do to my runaway daughter!" disdain. Paul took me to a local baseball game. He was a decent guy—I liked him—but it was physically impossible for him to introduce me or mention our marriage to his friends, who were saying hi to Cathi. Yep, I was on another planet and couldn't wait to get the hell out of town.

Weirder shit happened. Cathi and I went canoeing in the local river but never got to it because of violent stabbing pains in my appendix area, so severe I collapsed on the ground. It wasn't my appendix because I had had that out at sixteen. I was in psychosomatic reaction, riven by negative emotions stabbing me in the gut. All I kept hearing was "You fucked up!" That thought froze me.

We drove home in silence. Cathi opened wedding presents, I went back to WPCP, and life assumed a patina of normalcy. I was out of whack. Sex life was shot; it was like I wasn't even a participant.

Curt and I resumed working on the house at 407 Bainbridge. More South Street parades and events were planned. We did a Foolerie show, replete with crafts, food, and kids' games in Rittenhouse Square. On the way home, I gave a ride to a young puppeteer named Kristen and her puppet stage. I admired how she made all her own puppets and played all the parts.

Chapter Thirteen

I was at home by myself in the fall of 1973 when I heard a knock at the door that changed my life.

When I opened the door, I was looking at a young woman whose two long braids hung down to her waist; she had a sunny, sturdy appearance and an open face with beautiful green-gold eyes that took me in with no guile or nervous nonsense. I didn't remember her name, but I knew it was the puppeteer. "I'm Kristen Cutler. I'm looking for Ichabod. Do you know where he lives?" We went upstairs to my Rolodex to find the information. As she wasn't in a hurry to leave, we talked, and the more we talked, the more I wanted to keep talking because whoever she was, I was buzzing as if twenty thousand volts were flowing through my body.

When Kristen left, I leaned back in my chair, thinking, *What the fuck just happened?* For the well-being of my marriage, I had to put Kristen out of my mind. I tried not to think of her, resigning myself to my failing marriage with Cathi, who was hectoring me about my friends taking too much of my time and not treating her with respect. We had mutual grievances, and I was in no mood to settle disputes that carried no resolution. Whatever Curt, Walt, Ira, and others were accused of, I was undoubtedly guilty of as well. The end game was near, although I didn't know it. Yet.

A month later, Cathi came home and announced that she had run into Kristen Cutler at the co-op. They had talked about puppetry and shared South Street gossip, and the upshot was that Cathi had invited Kristen to dinner. *God, are you listening? I had nothing to do with this!*

Kristen arrived and *bing*! The voltage meter started clicking.

After dinner, I put on Sly and the Family Stone. Kristen and I started dancing, moving like a pair of dolphins frolicking in the ocean, exploring, twisting, turning, and sliding by each other smooth as silk. I hadn't had this much fun in months, if not years. Cathi exploded. "I can see you're both getting along better with each other than you are with me!" And she stormed out the door. Kristen rightly looked concerned. There was no way I wanted to stop what was happening. The music blared, "I'm gonna take you higher," and around the room we swirled, as if we knew the moves before we even made them, and then at midnight, she had to go home. We gently hugged, and I watched her disappear down American Street.

Now it was the question of how much longer I could hold on to my marriage when I couldn't get Kristen out of my mind. She consumed my thoughts. Weeks passed; I hadn't seen her. The weather turned colder.

Cathi and I were invited to a Thanksgiving party.

I was shaving in the bathroom; Cathi was combing her hair. As offhandedly as I could, I mentioned that I had run into Kristen and invited her to the party. Within seconds, Cathi leapt on me, beating me with her fists, cursing the living shit out of me.

"You mother-fucking kike bastard, you Jew prick, goddamn you! I hate you!" I had never heard any anti-Semitic remarks from her, and I flipped. My razor clattered into the sink, and we started brawling, both of us blinded by rage. Neither of us was holding back; we were way too immersed in our hatred for that. We battered each other until I pinned her to the floor and started slugging her. Killing the kitten in Mount Diablo flashed through my mind. I stopped abruptly, got up, and left the room. I had completely lost it. What was going to happen now?

She called the cops.

We were both downstairs panting like dogs, glaring at each other, when the police arrived. They looked us over—another domestic violence spat. "If she calls again, pal, you're going to jail."

"Don't worry, officers, I'm packing a bag and leaving right now," I replied.

I went upstairs, threw some clothes in a bag, and walked out, never to spend another night at 229 Monroe. I went to my neighbor, Steve Waterman, now living with Melanie Mayerson, my lawyer's ex-wife, and asked if I could crash. They weren't surprised at what happened, nor was I, other than how my rage had taken me into such a dark place, so hidden from who I thought I was. I was a brawler, just like Cathi; we were two animals who had been caged together for too long. I had lanced the boil of the marriage. I wished it hadn't come to a fight, but I had yet to figure out how to leave a relationship.

Kristen heard the news. Our feelings for each other hadn't changed, except that I could now be open with her. It wasn't as if her life had been smooth. She had been dumped recently and had actually come to my house that first day looking for Ichabod, the lean, lanky carpenter-artist, as a possible romantic interest. We agreed to see each other but go slow.

Cathi and I communicated through our lawyers, the situation far too volatile to be able to talk directly to each other. I pushed to get the Bainbridge house ready to live in. Anything to get my mind off the divorce proceedings.

Curt and I worked at a furious tempo, making sure the roof was completed before winter weather really hit. Now that my house had a bubble turret window installed in the prow of the third floor, a cathedral arched roof in the rear, why not go whole hog and sculpt a bathtub, a California-style spa tub large enough to hold four, to anchor the bathroom, which at this point was nonexistent?

The tub was inspired folly. I hired Ichabod, who, after all, had been the inspiration for Kristen's visit to me that fateful day. It seemed only right that we work together on this ambitious but doable project. With Ichabod as lead carpenter, we sculpted and laminated fiberglass the way you would a boat's hull. We built the frame, cut foam, glued and sanded it to a curvy, comfy feel, and laid down fiberglass mesh and strong bonding agent, followed by endless hours of sanding razor-sharp fiberglass to a smooth sheen so that Pacific-blue marine paint could be applied. The tub would hold four adults and a passel of kids and took a half hour to fill, drawing water from three floors below. As you floated in it, you looked at the Mylar-covered ceiling and saw a reflection of yourself in the tub. Yes, 407 Bainbridge had potential to become a fun house.

On January 6, 1974, I was working in the bubble room at the house by myself when Kristen dropped by. We had been seeing each other for a month but had not been intimate. I had a thermos of coffee and poured her a cup, and we looked in each other's eyes and toasted—drank each other in. Nothing was said, nor needed to be. We hung in that moment, and as the winter sun entered the bubble and warmed our bodies, we surrendered to the other. There was absolutely no doubt Kristen was the woman I was going to spend my life with.

Six weeks later, Kristen gave me the news that she was pregnant. As her last two love affairs had ended badly, she had sworn off men by the time she met me and had stopped using birth control, so when she saw that we were heading toward making love, she had prayed—she told me later—knowing she wasn't protected, and had received a clear response: "Everything will be all right," which she had assumed meant "You won't get pregnant." Oops.

She thought she was not ready to have children; she didn't know if she could trust me, for, after all, I was married and she was also embarrassed by what her parents, relatives, and the neighborhood would think of her. "It's your decision, Kristen. I'd love to have a child with you, but you're carrying the baby." She agreed that it was up to her. She'd have to think and pray about it. Although I did not know it at the time, Kristen studied Christian Science, which her sister Cheryl and her mother followed, the practice of which strongly affirmed the healing power of prayer.

Kristen also consulted her sister and her friend and mentor, Carole Rozewski, who was the wife of the man who would replace Ira as best man at our wedding. Neither told her what to do or even so much as hinted which way they might be leaning and simply said that they trusted Kristen to do the right thing.

Several weeks passed. Kristen told me later that she went to the small room she rented next to the Rozewski household, sat on the floor, and meditated with the thought of finding an answer. After clearing her mind and emotions, she asked, "What if I have an abortion?" She had an immediate visceral reaction, as though something had been taken from her. Then she asked, "What if I have this baby?" She felt whole. Not knowing how our relationship would transpire, she decided to keep the baby.

I hadn't thought far enough into the future to think about marrying Kristen, especially since I still was married, but there was no doubt I was ready to share in the birth of a child. Elated, actually.

As Kristen's belly began to swell, it was time to meet her parents. We drove to Hartsdale, up the Hudson River from New York City, mulling over how we were going to break the news. I was nervous, but I trusted Kristen. She hadn't mentioned her pregnancy, had only said she was bringing her boyfriend with her. I wasn't dressed flamboyantly, although I was bearded and had something of a Jewfro—nothing too scary. I was hoping to make a good impression.

We were greeted warmly. After lunch, we sat on the patio. It was a lovely spring day, yellows and greens shining in the sunlight, everything budding, just like Kristen, although she wasn't showing, at least to the unsuspecting eye. There was no graceful way to say, "Hey! Guess who's going to be a grandparent?"

"A couple of things I have to tell you, Mr. and Mrs. Cutler." I paused.

"Call me Enid," Enid said. "Please. And Howard."

"Well," I plunged in, hoping I wouldn't destroy this newly bestowed intimacy, "Kristen's pregnant."

Without the loss of a beat, Enid exclaimed with complete delight, "Oh, how wonderful!"

Howard looked like a pie had hit him—or worse.

"I love Kristen, and we really want this baby, but there is one thing more." A long pause. Here dropped the other shoe. "I'm married, but I'm getting divorced." Whew! There. Done.

"Wonderful!" exclaimed Enid.

Howard nodded grimly. No doubt his worst fears had been realized.

Kristen smiled and held my hand. I avowed that I loved her madly and that even if I was ten years older than Kristen, I had no interest in anything or anyone but her. This was it. I had found my life partner. Kristen's radiant beauty, her calm joy in her pregnancy, was more eloquent than anything I could have said.

To this day, I marvel at how well Howard played his cards. There wasn't one harsh word, not one malevolent look implying all the things that a father could be thinking; I was grateful for his self-restraint. He had no reason to trust me, but I guess he trusted his daughter, and we spent the night at their house, and by the end of the visit, I felt accepted by the parents.

Kristen and I moved into 407 Bainbridge Street. The third floor was partially finished, livable, if not furnished—a mattress and rug. The second floor was our construction zone, a lumber and tool storage area, and a beginning kitchen with hooked-up stove and sink. The first floor was not even on our radar. Twice a week, we took Lamaze classes and met our midwife, Betsy Tramm, who would help deliver the baby at home.

I had to go easy getting my things out of 229 Monroe. The lawyers agreed Cathi would absent herself when I came over. We couldn't extricate ourselves from his-story and her-story; we had accumulated a lot of past. There were too many masks demanding to be fed. In September, we were divorced, and for the first time, I felt remorse as well as relief for my part in this mismatch. I was the older one; I should have known better, but "shouldas and wouldas" didn't count.

As Kristen and I settled into our new home, the cast of characters who lived adjacent to us revealed themselves. Across the street, in a tenement house similar to ours, dwelled two brothers and two sisters, wizened old Jews from distant ancestral soil, who occupied four rooms on the top floor. A tide had moved out in the sixties, leaving the elderly who had nowhere to go. Their rooms were dingy, cluttered, and smelled of cabbage soup.

Dave, the older brother, his bony hands projecting like sticks out of a short cuffed Shabbos suit and sweater-vest, shuffled morning and night to the synagogue; Alex, who avoided your eye, was a mutterer, with a weirdly smiling, upturned mouth and deep, haunting eyes resembling a commedia dell'arte mask. He rocked back and forth like an ancient metronome.

Belle was the matriarch, the one who managed the siblings, kept the accounts, and had a position at Pennsylvania Hospital. She kept a kosher kitchen and heated her apartment by turning on the gas stove and opening the oven door. Her sister, Mary, was a madwoman, a fluttery piece of thin paper, lovely in her dementia, the hair on her childish face a white fluff, her glasses hanging askew off her nose.

Had Belle and her brood any children, relatives at all? None were seen. But there was a quiet majesty in their daily comings and goings; they were the last of their era, perhaps seeing in the nascent renewal of their neighborhood something hopeful, amazing, and yet slightly out of tune.

On the second floor was Big Grin Harry, a Willy Loman sales rep who hustled little plastic trinkets. A natty dresser, Harry had bulgy eyes, smoked a stogie, lugged a briefcase, and oozed the loneliness of a failed confidence man. He'd hail you, flutter his cigar, and be on his way.

Down the street was stuttering, sweet Barney, a stiff-legged old guy who was curious about whatever I was doing. He'd come over, smiling, saying, "Wha-wha-wha'cha doin' now, Tom?" as I'd be working outside or hoisting the bubble window into place with Curt and Ichabod. "Ain't that some-some-somethin'? Doh-doh-don't climb so high. You'll get hurt!"

In the adjoining tenement lived an African American family: Ms. Alice; her sister, Lil; and Lil's daughter, Yvonne, as well as the gentleman boarder, Al the liquor store clerk. Second floor front was Jitterbug the bartender, Jitterbug cool in his undershirt, leaning out the window, flashing a gold-tooth smile. In his room were a bed, chest of drawers, a revolver, a chair, and a lamp. To someone as afraid of the black community as I was, or certain elements of it, it was good to be friends with Bugs.

Teddy and Rose Milan ran the local hardware on the corner of Bainbridge and Fourth. Each rack, shelf, and counter was stacked in a fashion that only Ted could decipher; his aisles were only big enough for Ted and Rose to squeeze through. Ted looked on life with an ironic, slightly suspicious attitude. He'd be sitting, arms folded, looking at the door. No way you could find anything yourself. He'd shoo you away if you tried. Conversations went like this:

Ted: (looking me over) "So?"

Me: "Hello, Ted. How ya doing?"

Ted: "No use complaining, right?"

Me: "It's a beautiful day."

Ted: "Who said it wasn't? What d'ya need? Don't touch that. I'll get it."

Mysteriously, mounds would be moved, and my item, uncovered.

Across the street, at the Famous Deli, imperturbable deli men had sliced enough lox to pave a highway while the owner Sam Auspitz confessed Zen-like, "You get a bargain, but I charge top dollar."

September found us preparing for the home delivery. I had already witnessed one home birth. You might call it a hippie birth, eight friends of the couple sitting on the floor of a bedroom, smoking hash, waiting, passing the time. The mattress was on the floor too, and I was sitting at the end of the bed with a bird's-eye view of the proceedings, way too up close and personal. I tried to contain my nausea as young Elijah emerged from Melanie's uterus. I wasn't sure how I'd be with Kristen's labor.

On a glorious, clear fall day, Kristen's labor began. Kristen got in the tub to relax. The baby didn't want to come. We chanted "Breathe, breathe, pant, pant" through the night. At first it was exciting then tedious, irritating, and endless; no wonder they called it labor. At nine in the morning, the doctor arrived and broke her waters and shortly, whoa! Wow! Kristen delivered a son: Zachary Cosmos Bissinger emerged. We wept. We laughed. We snuggled. We had become a family. I knew, holding this little essence bundle, that having this child was the greatest thing that had ever happened to Kristen and me.

Chapter Fourteen

The 407 Bainbridge house was nowhere near being finished, nowhere near getting to the point of erasing the tenement-house vibe and turning it into the fun house. The bathtub was fun to slosh around in; it was almost a badge of honor for friends to come over and take a dip, but I felt I was floating, and not just in the tub. The Monroe Street house felt anchored in the ground, but we were third-floor dwellers. We used the second floor to cook and ignored the first floor, which left me feeling vulnerable to the street, especially to the gangs in the Southwark projects towering but a few blocks away. And it was not just the blacks that lived in them who made me uneasy. I observed the Jewish merchants across the street who showed up day after day, a routine set in stone. Max and Dave, father and son, hauled thirty feet of sawhorses and planks out of Famous Deli's cellar each morning at 6:30 am and on them stacked assorted bags, shirts, socks, underwear, and twenty-seven other items. Rain or shine, in the heat of summer and the freeze of winter, up it went, down it went. This ant-like energy left me edgy, guilty, and brooding on my story. If I wasn't as busy as Max and Dave, then what was I? Who was I?

I didn't have the merchant gene. My grandfather, Newton, whose name was my middle name, had it; he had lived and breathed business. My father did not manifest the same enthusiasm. His eyes did not light up talking about hides, wool, and tallow as they did when he was working on a show. And no disrespect to Max and Dave, they were working to make an honorable living, but what I saw was mind-numbing, repetitive selling of things. But wasn't I a seller of theatrical dreams?

My dream focused on the upcoming bicentennial celebration that the city of Philadelphia was doing its best to sabotage by their insistence on the idea of spending millions to build an enclosed, well-guarded historical theme park. They had dithered so long that fortunately little had been built. WPCP, along with the South Street Renaissance, decided to put on a pre-bicentennial bash in May of 1975, hoping to plant the seeds of a libertarian celebration. We had been holding meetings and rehearsals in WPCP during the winter and spring of '75 for a show we called *Fundees Foolies*. Over the years, we had presented a series of "fooleries" around town, consisting of a potpourri of live music, dance, inflatable structures, and puppetry, "hands-on" activities for kids that my one-time housemate, Peggy Waterman, had organized. *Fundees Foolies* was meant to encompass all that.

We erected bleachers in WPCP. The cast was drawn from the neighborhood. Kristen performed a belly dance and a scarf dance and recited Lewis Carroll's *Jabberwocky*. "Tom and the Triplikates," consisting of Kristen and two girlfriends and myself on piano, sang old-time songs. Poets proclaimed, satirists spoofed, ethnic dancers and musicians jammed. Our two shows on Friday and Saturday were sold out; Sunday featured a chess match (contested by two locals for a trophy whose bowl was filled with marijuana) and a twenty-lap bike race around the two-block plaza of Bainbridge Street, now called Bainbridge Gardens. There weren't thousands or even hundreds lining the street, but the street was closed, the bands were jamming, and we danced all afternoon. We had had a fun-house weekend.

I experienced that weekend as the beginning of the end of the happy-go-lucky way of life in the neighborhood. The Crosstown Expressway was headed for defeat, and South Street would be the next big thing: Philly's answer to the Atlantic City Boardwalk. The merchants and realtors would make out fine. What would happen to the artists, outlaws, and dreamers? Who would survive, and who would leave? The neighborhood was saved, gentrification was on its way, but you could feel that the spontaneous way of life was disappearing and, with it, the tolerance for that way of life. Money was replacing magic.

So I figured that it was time WPCP made money. I suggested we turn WPCP into a cabaret, complete with liquor license, food, and entertainment. Curt was on board and enthusiastically drew up architectural plans. Even though I'd been paying him and Walt a stipend, Curt was looking for a way to make real money. Walt was against the idea. "Guys, we've been doing stuff for free all these years. Now we're going to try to make money off it? It's a foolish idea. It'll never work."

We argued with Walt, but he was not persuaded, nor was Kristen. "I don't get it, Tom. I'll support you, but why do you want to go into the bar business? That's not where your heart is." True, I didn't like smoky bars—had mopped enough beer off the floor at WPCP to know that sucked—but Curt said he'd handle the bar and Georgie Stewart and others could book bands while I dreamt up a thirteenth reincarnation of the fun house: *theater, revues, rock 'n' roll, lights, action!* What was I thinking? That I could reincarnate Humphrey Bogart in *Casablanca?* "Play it again, Sam?"

I ignored the doubters, hired Ichabod to build a stage in one corner of WPCP, and bought a liquor license for twenty thousand dollars. I was pouring a lot of cash into making WPCP a fully licensed public bar and theater. Curt, Walt, and I formed a corporation, WPCP Inc. We each had 33 percent of the stock; I was fronting the cash, Curt drew up plans and would run the bar, and Walt was going to handle sound and lights. It sounded good on paper; somehow we'd make it all work, but as costs escalated, I wanted something for my financial investment. I didn't ask my partners to put in money they didn't have, but I thought they could give back a certain percentage of stock, in the eventuality that if one day we did make money or sell the business, I would be remunerated. Boy! Was I wrong! I asked Curt and Walt to have a business meeting with me at our lawyer's, Hy Mayerson's, office.

I told them I wanted to renegotiate the corporate agreement to lower each of their shares from 33 1/3 percent to 30 percent. It wasn't costing them anything, and from my point of view, it was only fair. I couldn't have been more wrong. The shit hit the fan, and a volcano of expletives exploded out of Curt's mouth. He called Hy and me every anti-Semitic name you could think of, beginning with class-exploiting mother-fucking Jew bastards. His fury was unstoppable. Hy and I sat there in stunned silence as Curt kicked over the wastepaper basket, swept papers off Hy's desk, tore up the agreement, and stormed out, saying, "Fuck it, and fuck you! I'm done." I looked at Walt. He quietly got up, said, "I agree with Curt," and left.

I sat in the shards of my dream, traumatized. Was I the villain in all this? I had taken Curt to be my best friend. He had crossed over as great a line as I apparently had; I couldn't see how we'd ever get back together again. Curt's tirade restimulated the meltdown I had experienced with my ex-wife. Was I truly all the things he accused me of? And if so, what else was going on? Was there a "right" in any of this? I returned home to Kristen and Zak, devastated. Only many years later did I appreciate that Curt's explosion, unpremeditated as it was, prevented me from going through with this folly.

I was wracked with anger, betrayal, and guilt. When the husband of Kristen's sister, Cheryl, heard about the breakup of WPCP, he suggested I try reevaluation cocounseling, a method of peer counseling where two people listened to each other in turn and helped one another to "discharge" their feelings or traumas. The thought was that this method of counseling could heal emotional hurts and increase rational thinking so as to prevent ancient traumas from being restimulated. I found a local group, and RC did help.

With the bicentennial looming, Kristen and I decided to try a business venture out of our house. Our first floor, largely unused, had once been a food stand. The front had sliding windows and a plywood cover that could be raised. We decided to sell fresh lemonade and pretzels. Surely, the thousands of tourists passing through the neighborhood would love fresh-squeezed lemonade! Kristen ingeniously fabricated a giant yellow lemon made out of oilskin and stuffed with kapok, which we hung out our second floor balcony as our sign.

In June, we opened for business, eager for the expected throngs. Those few folk who stopped out of curiosity would say, "Got any coffee? Hotdogs? Burgers?"

"No," we answered.

"Oh, well, whad'ya got?"

"Lemonade."

"No, thanks."

I wasn't willing to concede that the customer is always right. It also dawned on us that Mayor Rizzo's paranoia about hordes descending on Philadelphia and especially his ex-cop's mentality that any gathering over a few people represented civil disorder had effectively squelched what could have been a joyous and well-attended national celebration.

WPCP was deserted, the lemonade stand closed, and in September, the final blow was struck.

Chapter Fifteen

The night was stifling hot. We dragged our mattress into the spa room, where the ceiling was high and we could get more air. At midnight a flashlight shining in our eyes awakened us; we made out a black figure holding a baseball bat in his hands. We weren't sure what he wanted, but he wanted something, and we were naked under a sheet.

Immediately we thought about Zak, who was asleep in the bubble room. We had to protect him, so we started to talk to the guy. He smacked me in the leg with the bat and demanded money. Kristen coolly wrapped the sheet around her and proceeded to the next room. When she returned with the money, he began to unbuckle his belt. She later said that at that moment she suddenly awakened from a stupor of fear to the thought, *This is not right. Good is more powerful than evil.*

She ran down the stairs to escape. He ran after her as I ineffectively threw a heavy stone sculpture down the stairs at him. Kristen turned to him. "You don't know what you're doing." The intruder stopped with a sudden look of fear in his eyes, and Kristen thought she had him, but at that moment, he slammed her in the cheek with the bat and fled the house. Her cheekbone was fractured. We bundled up Zak and drove to Einstein Hospital, where Kristen, in great pain, black and blue and bloody, went in for surgery. Thankfully, Zak had been untouched by the intruder, but my worst fears had come true. A punk wielding a baseball bat had breached our home and harmed my woman; any sense of decency, fairness, and liberal piety I might have had was gone, shredded with shame and rage.

Kristen was swollen and sore and had to be stitched up. It was going to take months to heal, but with the help of a Christian Science practitioner and prayer, she healed quickly and had no permanent damage to her eye or cheek. Emotionally, I didn't know. We went to the police station and looked at line-ups. We couldn't pick anyone out. We needed to address our feelings.

Reevaluation cocounseling helped. We went to group meetings and arranged individual counselors, a woman with Kristen, a man with me.

Slowly, we discharged deeper and deeper feelings, cried and wailed, and expressed gratitude that nothing had happened to Zak. We walled ourselves into 407 Bainbridge, put bars on the glass doors that opened to the front of the building. We rationalized that the assailant was possibly as scared as we were, but that didn't make me want to forgive him. There had already been plenty of incidents in the neighborhood. Why should we, privileged people just up the street from the projects, be any different? I got that; I got it all—I got every fucking thing! Slowly, after months of counseling, the violence of our feelings and the incident itself receded.

I sold WPCP's liquor license and turned the lease over to a theater group. I wanted out.

In the midst of this grieving process, I was sitting one morning in the bubble room, welcoming the warmth of the sun, relaxed and happy holding Zak in my arms and singing to him, when the thought came of a week I spent with Cathi in Negril, Jamaica, renting an A-frame bungalow facing a farmer's field. One day, while we were reading on the front porch, a large handsome Rasta, with dreadlocks down to his waist, approached. Joseph asked if we wanted to visit his special place. "Follow me, mon. No worries." So we followed him until we came to a flat promontory that overlooked the ocean, and as we neared the cliff's edge, Joseph magically began to disappear into the ground. In fact, he was spiraling himself down through an unseen circular opening in the ground, and we followed after him until we stepped onto the rocky floor of a cave, where there was enough room to sit and watch the waves swirl through an opening under the cliff, which extended some thirty feet beyond.

Joseph rolled us a spliff the size of a cigar. We smoked, saying nothing, studying this intense man crouched on a rock ledge smiling at us while we toked. The only sounds were the waves ricocheting against the walls of the cave, throwing spray and mist into the air. Joseph began to sing, not words but melodies, cascading vowel sounds that seemed like an angel was singing to us. So ethereal was his song that I visualized Joseph's notes as iridescent bubbles swirling out of his mouth, enlarging into crescendos, and descending from a wail to a whisper. For hours he sang songs of tears and joy, burning and longing, devotional hymns to Jah, his God; he was channeling sounds, serving his Lord. Joseph was his angel.

Every concept I had about singing or chanting evaporated. You may assume that I was stoned (true) and therefore exaggerated. But every day after that at dawn, Joseph worked his crops in front of our cabin, and the sound was the same, breathtakingly pure and angelic, and we weren't stoned. His songs burst into flowers of sounds. I didn't need to comprehend it, any more than in the years ahead I would be able to literally understand Sufi or Native American chants. It was all vibration.

And that's what I wanted for Kristen and Zak and myself—a vibration of love and healing and warm, warm water. I wanted to get out of the City of Brotherly Love. I asked Kristen what we might do that we might never do again in our lifetime. One of the nomads who had breezed through South Street had told us that for $2,000 a ticket, Pan American Airlines would fly you anywhere around the world with no time limit as long as you traveled in a forward direction.

But where? Which way? Traveling with a two-year-old child to Europe in the winter, with its cities and museums, would be frustrating, but the Southern Hemisphere would be warm, and we could travel lightly and efficiently. We pulled out maps and atlases and scanned the globe. With a few broad strokes, picking a country here and there, we enthusiastically mapped our way around the world.

We'd rent the house for a year and leave around February 1977 with a rough itinerary that we would fill in as we went.

One morning before embarking on our trip, Kristen and I were lying in bed. She studied me. "I just had this thought, Tom. You're the man for me. I'm not looking for anyone else. We should get married."

I blanched. "You really think it's a good idea? I haven't been very successful with marriage."

She tried a different tact. "What if something should happen in, say, Iran? Countries with different customs and they look at our passports, and we have different names? They might not understand or approve of our relationship. Sure, we feel married, but it's not on paper, and I don't want there to be any confusion."

Truthfully, I wasn't thrilled with the idea but saw the logic of her position and, several days later, unenthusiastically agreed that we should get married. But if we were going to do it, it had to be a regular ceremony, neither a Quaker self-marrying service nor a civil ceremony.

We thought of Reverend Bill Pindar, a practicing clown as well as minister at Old Pine Street Presbyterian Church, a lovely eighteenth-century Protestant church full of history and only three blocks away. We set the date for January 8, 1977. We figured on a small wedding at the church, lunch at our house, and then an open house for the neighborhood with food, drink, and dancing. In a sense, the party would be a cathartic reblessing of the house after the break-in. The wedding would be the sacred side.

That morning, Kristen and I and Zak walked on newly fallen snow to the church for our 11:00 am ceremony. It was sunny and cold, and I remember how elated we felt. My best man was nonexistent; fortunately, Ron Rozewski took his place. The wedding was a homespun affair: Kristen's parents and sister, my mother and my sister, Peggy, and her family, as well as a few South Street families and their kids. After a sermon, music, and shared blessings by family and friends, I stepped on the wine glass, we slipped on our rings, said our vows, had a reception in the basement of Old Pine, and then all trooped back to our house for a catered lunch.

Zak was two years and four months when we embarked on our world around. Freckled-faced, cheerful, still in nighttime diapers, curious about everything, he turned out to be the essence of the trip, the key that opened doors. As a family with a toddler, we were unique in the world of travelers. A blue-eyed two-year-old white child was definitely going to be a contrast to the darker-skinned world where we were headed. We wanted to recognize the similarities rather than the disparities. We wanted to experience how people lived close to the earth, ruled more by the rhythms of nature than the bustle of city life.

In the months of travel, we evolved the rules of paranoia: the first day (week) you were paranoid about everything; everybody was out to hustle you. The second day (week) you scanned the scene without freaking out. Suspicion, caution, and confusion lessened as you saw most locals were simply trying to get by. The third day (week) you blended in, engaged, and played. And who wanted to play more than anyone? Mr. Zachary Cosmos Bissinger.

We would be a crew: I was captain, overall planner, reader of maps, and director of things to do and places to go; Kristen was first mate, the nester, the homemaker, center of gravity, able to whip a room or a deck of a boat into a little home and immediately create a sense of security. Happily, our instincts coincided in that we trusted each other deeply, knew when it was time to move on, and where we wanted to loiter. We had a deep sense of purpose, which was that we had chosen to make this trip to experience people in countries we might never visit again by dint of their distance from Philadelphia or the United States. We wanted the adventure; we just didn't know what it was going to be or how it was going to turn out.

Top: 407 Bainbridge St before
I bought it. On hot summer
days, folks were grateful for
the shade it provided.

Left:Rock n' Roll on Bainbridge
Street during Fundees Foolies

Isaiah Zagar
Left: Miss Alice and
Miss Lil

Top: DJ,Carl and Ann Duckworth lived next to WPCP.

Big Grin Harry, my neighbor across the street.

Millie, the effervescent waitress at Famous Deli

Left: Jack and Jean Sternbach

Al, Carolee, Shima Jitterbug.and friend.

Mary from across the street.

Ted and Spike.

Barney. The elders kept an eye on the neighborhood.

Our house was on the corner of Bainbridge and Leithgow Sts.

The annual Seder was held in the Bubble on Leithgow St.

Abie

Corner of South & Passyunk Sts.

Bainbridge Garden before and after.
Allan Levitsky lining up for lemonade.

Harvey Finkle took this photo of us shortly after Zak's birth.
We're sitting on the edge of our tub in the not quite finished bathroom.

Kristen and I enjoying the birth of Zak.

To day Oct 4 ZACHARY
COSMOS
BISSINGER

was welcomed
at Abe's party into the neighborhood

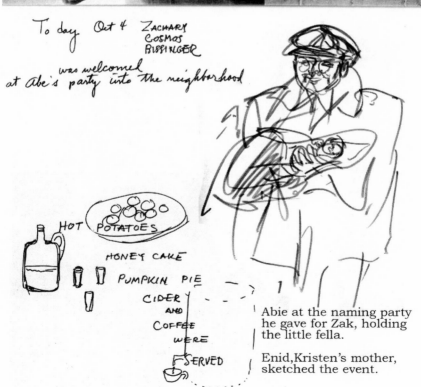

HOT POTATOES

HONEY CAKE

PUMPKIN PIE

CIDER
AND
COFFEE
WERE
SERVED

Abie at the naming party
he gave for Zak, holding
the little fella.

Enid, Kristen's mother,
sketched the event.

Enjoying the bathtub

My Mother and Zak.

Wedding photos by Harvey Finkle

On the way to Old Pine Street Church.

Howard and Enid   Marjorie

Best man and Maid of Honor   Ron and Carole Rozewski

Fiji: The Stella Maris, a fifty foot Trimaran

Zak, Kristen, the skipper Pat Morgan, and
Narayan holding Pat and Marie's son, Brian

Zak with calf in the courtyard of the Pendawa Inn

We bought a lot of masks in Ubud, Bali.
Our friends at Pendawa Inn trying them on.

Zak with Balinese offerings.

Atop a mountain in Sri Lanka
Bawa mortaring a floor

Bawa singing.

In a Paris café, at the end of our around the world trip.

"The spirit don't die.
It's just translated."

Chapter Sixteen

On February 12, 1977, after a brief visit to San Francisco, we were on our way to Hawaii. Packed in our suitcases, among the clothing, was a Sony pocket recorder, minicassettes, a Minox "spy" camera, a Kodak Instamatic, two flutes, one kalimba, and a set of Legos.

I added the *I Ching*, figuring that change and chance were going to be our guides; *The Way of Chuang Tzu*, to keep things in perspective; and Gurdjieff's *Meetings with Remarkable Men*, to stay alert for encountering the remarkable and to remind me that the journey's subplot was a spiritual seeking. Kristen took the Bible and *Science and Health with Key to the Scriptures* by Mary Baker Eddy. For Zak we brought *Dr. Seuss's Sleep Book* and *Hello Bunny*. In addition, we carried basic information books: hostel guides, Golden Guides to oceanography, herbs and spices, seashores, and hallucinogenic plants. A collapsible stroller (good for either child or suitcase) completed the ingredients of our portable fun house.

My impressions of the tropics had been shaped by movies I had seen, paintings by Gauguin, and novels by R. L. Stevenson and Somerset Maugham. The bustle of the streets of Honolulu did not fit that profile, and after a short visit with Kristen's brother, Thor, we flew to Hawaii, the Big Island, with its two mammoth volcanoes, Mauna Kea and Mauna Loa, each of which if measured from the ocean floor, rose higher than Mount Everest. Wherever we were on the Big Island, we were aware that not only were we ants hugging the sides of giants, those giants had frequently exploded and buried people and villages in lava, and what the volcanoes hadn't accomplished, the Pacific Ocean, with its tidal waves and hurricanes, had. You could feel those forces in your bones. It was a high unto itself.

Our little family began to encounter an international network of travelers: pilgrims bearing advice, warnings, shared food, drink, and drugs. We shared meals and maps in campgrounds and hostels, made music, and moved on, looking to find a traveling rhythm—hard enough for one person, much less three. We took in rolling surf whose waves were too great to ride, a special sanctuary where ancient tribes could take refuge, mango-laden trees, and the view of the summit of Mauna Loa. All these impressions fed us but also gave us the first inklings of the difficulties of travel: that it was harder to give back and generate than it was to take and absorb. Although we were actively sightseeing, we were also restrained by our very rootlessness. Because of this paradox, travel became a moving meditation. Without the familiar anchors, one needed to be in the moment; because there were no anchors, one looked for the familiar. How to dance this dance with each other and a two-year-old and do it with skill, ease, and humor—especially humor—became our form of yoga.

Kristen and I felt we needed to leave the yoke of the omnipresent American culture if we were going to have the adventure we had declared for ourselves. It was on the plane going to American Samoa that we met two families: Pat and Marie Morgan and their seventeen-month-old son, Brian, and Greg and Holly Reed with their five-year-old son. Pat had just bought a fifty-foot trimaran anchored in Fiji, and the two families were going to live on the boat and fix it up. "If you're going to Fiji, come by and see us," they offered. The nonlogical connections between events in this world, which Jung called synchronicity, began to manifest. The script began writing itself.

When we landed in Pago Pago, we found, to our dismay, an American welfare state in the middle of the South Pacific, stuck in lassitude, nothing lush about it. What did impress us was how in our small hotel the owner's wife and children ritualistically prepared leis for an evening dance performance, patiently threading the heavily scented flowers, while in the streets, campy, openly gay young men with flowers in their hair and eye makeup preened and posed while the more masculine men played soccer in their T-shirts and lavalavas (wraparound skirts also known as a *sulu*). After one night, we opted to go to Western Samoa.

We booked the six o'clock nighttime mail boat for an eighty-mile trip to Apia, the capital of Upolu in Western Samoa. As we waited in the crowd to board the boat, we felt a tingling, like this was it: the adventure was truly beginning. The boat had a hold for luggage and food and room for a couple of cars, which were parked on the deck, one at the bow and one at the stern. The passengers spread blankets and mats on the deck. We made space where we could sleep under the stars, touched by warm breezes, which at that latitude hovered around eighty degrees. Everybody brought food, including us, and as the night wore on, with the aid of shifting seas and sliding mats, the hundred-or-so bodies heaped on the deck, clumped together.

Zak was sleeping in our arms when out of the darkness, a Samoan man appeared. I looked up into his dark face, and he smiled gently and asked us where we were going to stay. We told him we had no plans, and he asked if we would like to stay with his family. We told him we'd think it over. He retreated as we discussed his offer, and although we thought he could be a hustler, hadn't we travelled for exactly this kind of experience? We looked at Zak, sleeping peacefully. "Let's do it."

I went over to the Samoan and took him up on his offer. His name was Palomia; he drove a taxi, and after clearing customs, he'd take us to his family's house.

The boat docked at three in the morning. We sleepily disembarked and cleared customs, but there was no taxi, no Palomia. I began to wonder what was happening. Didn't he say he was a taxi driver? Palomia eventually appeared and led us to a pickup truck with six guys in the back playing guitars and singing—a cheery bunch of guys for three in the morning. We piled in with our bags and drove into the darkness. Zak, although sleepy, was excited to be traveling in the back of a pickup, serenaded by six singing Samoans. "We're going to my sister's," Palomia shouted from the window of the cab of the truck.

At the house, Palomia knocked hard; a girl opened the door and let us in. There were children sleeping on the floor—many of them. A middle-aged woman was asked to vacate her room, and we were ushered in and told to sleep well. "See you in the morning," Palomia said as he shut our door, and just like that, three souls from Philadelphia, Pennsylvania—a bearded man, a woman with long braids, and a chubby little boy—were standing in a ten-by-ten room in someone's house somewhere in Apia, Western Samoa. We looked at each other, made a space for Zak on the floor, and squeezed onto the single bed. It was both hilarious and bewildering. There was nothing to do but go to sleep.

In the morning, we met Palomia's sister, Loimata, and her husband, Ailupo Petelo. We later learned that *ailupo* was his title, for he was the chief, or *matai*, of the Aiga (pronounced *ainga*), his extended family. Not only was Ailupo the matai of this family, he was also ailupo of a village elsewhere. Loimata taught fourth grade at the Marist Brothers Catholic School, and Ailupo was employed by the Public Works Department of Samoa. They, as well as everybody in the household, spoke English. Children flitted in and out, some related by blood, others by kinship.

As time passed, we learned more about the kinship system. About a quarter of the males on the island were matais, and only they could vote. There was a parliament with forty-three members, who were all chiefs with a title. Above the chiefs were the talking chiefs, and some combination of chiefs elected a prime minister. (This is how it was in 1977; it may have changed since then.) Supposedly anyone could get a title, but not many did. If you wanted a title name, it seemed you needed a decent job and enough funds to cover the requests of your extended family. One of Ailupo's duties was as masseur. We witnessed nightly occurrences when the locals with their sprains or aches came to Ailupo and he massaged them.

Ailupo and Loimata got up at five thirty every morning to go to the Catholic Church for choir practice. The head of the household in their absence was Corinna, a tall, burly sixteen-year-old niece with curly black hair and a sympathetic smile. She shopped for food; she cooked, ironed the clothes, and cared for the kids. She prepared the meals squatting in the yard over a wood fire; a thatch of banana trees gave her a modicum of shelter from sun and rain.

Mid-March was the rainy season. It rained and rained and rained some more. The skies were overcast, and then you noticed a drop or two, and suddenly, from out of nowhere, boom! A giant sky tarp full of water burst, torrents of rain thundered on tin roofs, and rivers immediately flowed over the ground. We sat, doing nothing, as we waited out the deluge. No plans, because sooner or later after this rain stopped, the next downpour would begin. Welcome to wet—to instant mold. We bought lavalavas, two and a half yards of wraparound skirt, which both men and women wore and which dried easily. What you weren't wearing was drying—or not, mostly not. Zak splashed in the puddles a lot.

During a brief dry spell, we got our bearings. The house sat in a clearing of palms and banana trees in a neighborhood of one-story houses. Ours was virtually empty of anything except a few chairs and mats spread around the edge of a linoleum floor. Solemnly posed wedding photographs hung on the wall along with tapa weavings. Possessions were locked in a trunk because, as I was told, "Locks are for honest people."

Often nude or just in shorts, Zak ran around and played with the other children, the pigs, and the chickens. Older children made makeshift games with handmade checkerboards and shells or stones as checkers, and Zak looked on. He loved tumbling with the kids, but we also provided a small space in our room he could call his own.

We travelled in a pre-Pampers era, so Kristen spent a good deal of time with Woolite soap washing Zak's diapers and plastic pants. At night Kristen and I sang songs we knew, and the Samoans sang their songs to us.

It was quite lovely to see the skirted Samoan population hoisting umbrellas to march off to market or work, although marching doesn't describe the Samoan gait—swaying or sashaying would be more like it. These were big-bodied people, enormously fleshy but graceful on their feet, which were huge from walking barefoot.

Our family was eager to join the daily activities of food shopping. We accompanied Corinna to the market and bought baskets of taro and coconuts, green bananas, tomatoes, green beans, and lots of meat and fish. We loved watching the food being prepared, helping out when we could. The taro and bananas were cooked in coconut cream; a special wooden seat with a metal scraper attached got hours of use as the coconut flesh was scraped from the shells and pounded and cooked into a cream sauce prepared daily. The meat and potatoes and beans were cooked in soy sauce or curry sauce over an open fire in the backyard.

It felt good to gather together as one family to eat, although the order of eating was strictly regulated: Loimata, Ailupo, Kristen, Zak, and I ate first, the little children and the girls ate second, and the young men and boys ate last. When we had our fill, the others came to the table. Zak was the wild card because sometimes he sat on the floor and ate with the kids and sometimes with us.

With this family, with its own rituals and rhythms, and the two-year-old Zak, we flowed, we sat, we became bored, we read, we shopped daily with Corinna buying the family's food, we lived.

One day, after the rains stopped, Palomia came by and proposed an excursion to a special cave. We traveled via his taxi (he did have one!) on the ocean road, the sea and sky a paradise-blue, until we came to a Methodist mission. Palomia guided us to a hidden stone pool fifty feet from the beach. One of us sat with Zak as the other entered a cave with Palomia. We dove into one pool, swam into dark waters that concealed a narrow underwater opening, which we nervously squeezed through to find ourselves in a sparkling turquoise-colored cavern, where we sang to each other and listened to the reverberations of our echoes. Shades of Joseph's cave in Jamaica!

Upon returning, we snorkeled in the ocean, where we picked slugs and spiny animals off the sea floor. Palomia showed us how to eat them raw. They had a salty sweetness. "Crudité de mer," he said, winking. As we sat on the beach, white and fluffy like snow, Palomia told us the romantic film *Return to Paradise*, starring Gary Cooper, was shot here. Gary Cooper on a beach? I was a *From Here to Eternity* Burt Lancaster guy, but no matter, all was good, romantic, and best of all, Zak liked it.

Evenings in the household were hot. We sat around while the kids played ball; sometimes Ailupo, Loimata, Kristen, and I played cards. We shared songs and dances. The Samoans were taken by Kristen's dancing ability and her large vocabulary of fluid movement. Loimata and her children performed Samoan dancing, which was somewhat similar to Indian kathakali dance, featuring hand movements and eyes that moved with the hands in a coquettish fashion. The women made soft flowing steps with bent elbows and knees. They kneeled and enacted a traditional kava dance (kava is a pepper root known for its mildly narcotic effect) in which they made the motions of squeezing kava root through banana plant fibers and then threw the fibers over their shoulders to tattooed men (in this case, the boys) who stood behind the women, flapping their hands, feet, and knees.

After we put Zak to sleep at night, Kristen and I strolled through the neighborhood, holding hands, just another couple taking the night air. We were doing well, both as a family and a couple. We knew intuitively what had to happen next—or not. It was mostly a matter of patience, digging what was happening now, knowing that we were rock solid and could fully trust each other. And Zak was our adventure within the adventure.

The rains had stopped, the air was soft, and only a barking dog broke the heavy silence. The sky blazed with stars. Light pollution was nonexistent. We saw the Big Dipper pointing to the North Star, but the North Star was on the other side of the bulging girdle of the equator, so we didn't see it.

After two weeks, Palomia took us on a picnic to Savai'i, Upolu's sacred sister island, where Palomia had relatives. Upon arriving, and after many phone calls, he secured a pickup truck from a Latter-day Saints church, and off we went into the jungle in search of his relatives. It appeared Savai'i was undeveloped, except by the Japanese, who were harvesting timber from the island. The trees were old, thick with vines and enormous leaves, uniformly green. Few flowers or wildlife were seen; there were no soaring mountains or waterfalls or rushing rivers to set your heart pounding. We drove for hours.

Eventually, deep in the jungle, we came into a clearing; a family with many children received us graciously, even though we had arrived unannounced. A series of thatched buildings, some quite elegant, formed their house. We were shown to a small pavillion detached from the house under which sat a canopied, elegantly carved, four-poster double bed. The entire space was draped with mosquito netting. The wife brought out her best linen sheets and made the bed. A feast was prepared.

This family, hidden deep in the forest, treated us, who had just shown up out of the blue, like royalty. At dinner, we were brought masses of food. We knew by now that the swarm of children who surrounded us would eat what remained only when we were finished—and there was no question—but that we should and must eat as much as we wanted. At bedtime, as we got under our linen sheets in the four-poster bed, the jungle was alive with insects and birdcalls. It had to be one of the most surrealistically enchanting moments of our trip. I trusted we would not be eaten by something before morning came.

As we lay in our four-poster bed, Zak sleeping between us, Kristen and I observed that wherever we went, the Samoans asked, "But why do you only have one child? We have at least eight or nine! Have more!" But Zak was enough to make the connection as family, to let our hosts know that family was what we valued, even though having seven or eight more kids was not on our radar.

We returned the following day to Apia, and by the weekend, after the presentation of a red and yellow skirt and top outfit to Kristen made by a local seamstress, accompanied by many hugs, *fa'fe'tais*, and *alofas* (peace/love/goodwill/good-bye), we flew to Fiji.

Chapter Seventeen

Easter 1977. Upon landing in Fiji, we rented a car to drive to Suva, on the other side of the island, where Pat and Marie Morgan's trimaran would be anchored.

Sweltering in the noonday sun, we drove up a narrow road running through forested mountains and farmed fields. Suddenly we noticed a large bus bearing down on us. It was clearly not going to slow down, so with a good deal of cursing, I pulled us off the road into what turned out to be a deep ditch filled with water. One side of the car gently sank into mud, covering the wheels. Fucked.

Kristen's positivity at this moment cheered me. We extricated ourselves from the car, Kristen hoisted Zak onto her back, and we started walking, hoping to find a farmhouse. After a time, we noticed enormous oxen with large horns grazing behind a fence. We found a barefoot farmer working in a field a hundred yards farther and got his attention, and through pantomime (car-bus-oops-ditch-you-oxen), he understood. He chained and yoked two bulls, which he controlled by two rings running through their noses. We were awed by the size of these animals, probably twice the size of the mini we were driving. They effortlessly dragged the car out of the mud amidst lots of giggling from the native children and adults. An hour later, we were gratefully on our way.

We decided to look in on the Morgans before locating a hotel in Suva. We found the yacht harbor, which was full of sailboats and powerboats, but fortunately only one trimaran, its three pontoons bobbing gently in the fiery heat of a Fijian afternoon.

Marie spied us. "Hey! Look who's here! Patrick! It's Tom and Kristen and Zak! Welcome aboard!"

"Where are Greg and Holly?"

"Oh, we had an argument with them yesterday, and they've left. They're living up the hill somewhere. Do you want to stay on the boat?"

That's how synchronicity works, and that's how we came to make our home on the *Stella Maris* for two months. Imagine three plywood fiberglass pontoons, fifty feet long, joined by a cabin with a deck and a cockpit above it. Three steps down into the belly of the right pontoon was a little space for Zak's bed with a walkway beside. Fore of that was a larger bunk just big enough for Kristen and myself to crawl into. The pontoons framed the central galley, where we cooked our food and ate at a table and benches.

In the stern was a cabin for Pat and Marie and seventeen-month-old Brian. In the left pontoon bunked Narayan, a Fijian of Indian descent, and on occasion, Bill, a grizzled old salt who drifted from boat to boat, looking for work, or Van, a young Fijian who took people out on scuba dives.

Stella Maris was anchored to one of the docks of the yacht club, near the highway. Daily, we rowed to the main dock to fill two five-gallon water jugs that served our cooking and drinking needs. We surreptitiously used the showers at the yacht club to bathe and occasionally had drinks at the bar. Nightly we heard drums beating from a church on the hill, followed by a choir's soft, sweet songs.

Patrick, half-owner and skipper of the *Stella Maris*, was a tall, good-looking Australian in his late twenties with curly black hair and a full beard, a swaggering charm, and a brusque, energetic intelligence that smacked of arrogance. His wife, Marie, was from New Zealand, a warm, petite woman who was mostly occupied with her child, Brian. She was the reasonable one when Patrick went on one of his rants. We retreated to our bunks when breakdowns occurred, but the two families generally got on well together.

We were fortunate to have the gentle, easygoing Narayan, who was a great cook, in addition to being a sailor, whipping up Indian delicacies such as pumpkin curries, potato curries, rotis, and one delicious dish of sea urchins with onions and chili peppers. It seemed to be the custom, as we gathered for meals, that one either ate or drank but did not mix the two at the same time. Our family and Marie and Brian ate dinner, but the Fijians and Patrick did not touch food until all the booze was consumed, by which time the meal was long gone or forgotten in a drunken haze. Drink brought out the music, however, and flutes, kalimba, and guitars accompanied a medley of Fijian, Aussie, and American songs into the night. John Denver's *Country Roads*, our gold standard, was frequently howled into the night air.

There are maxims about sailing, received wisdom: you sail a boat one-fifth of the time; the rest of the time, you're repairing her. True. The *Stella Maris*, bought sight unseen by Patrick and Kendall Kruger, a logger from Oregon, had been neglected for several years while waiting to be sold. She needed her three hulls scraped of barnacles and her masts, booms, and engine repaired. Nothing in the tropics happened quickly or without money, which was always anticipated, presumably being sent by Kendall. So the days spun out leisurely under baking skies. It was here in Fiji, sitting on a boat, that we appreciated the expression a "grateful" breeze.

The kids adapted well. Kristen played with Marie and the boys under the sheet that provided some shade on the deck, or sometimes the boys were rolled around on top of the sheet, accompanied by gleeful laughter. Everyday cloth diapers and plastic pants were washed and dried. Boat life was not glamorous but had a regular, mostly uneventful rhythm.

There were always plans to find an electrician, buy supplies, and fix this or that. Each piece of the plan took days or even weeks to accomplish. The aim was to get the boat ready to cross the Pacific and sail to Australia. That was the big plan.

During the weeks at the dock repairing the boat, I fell ill with a high fever and became delirious, hallucinating creatures walking on the ceiling of my narrow pontoon. Kristen got out her Bible and *Science and Health* and spent hours praying as I lay listless on my bed or on the deck, drenched in sweat. Within three days, the fever passed, to our great relief. It was the only serious illness our family experienced on the entire trip.

Zak picked up impetigo from yacht pollution and sewage runoff from the hills above. We rowed our dinghy across the bay to an island where we could swim in clean water, spread a blanket under shady trees, read, and nap. Fijians came to the water's edge carrying their captive green turtles tethered to long leashes; their back legs were pinned so they couldn't break free of the leash when their owners put them in the water to swim.

We started scraping barnacles off the three hulls and removed and replaced damaged lengths of dry rot. The propeller shaft bearing we ordered arrived. The engine was lifted out and repaired. It began to dawn on us that sailing the *Stella Maris* was going to happen.

Finally, the financier behind the boat purchase, Kendall Kruger, a husky guitar-toting lumberjack from Oregon, showed up. We wondered how he and Pat were going to get along. Kendell was laid back, unlike the tempestuous Patrick, and though Kendall had never been on a boat before, he was eager to try out his investment, just like the rest of us. We learned about sails: mizzens, jibs, spinnakers, the main, and cleats and shackles. Which got attached to what? How to read a compass and maps so that we wouldn't ground on a reef, and what to do when the boat was actually sailing? Our fallback position was "No worries, mate!" Highly optimistic.

Trimarans were built for speed. To my way of thinking, three hulls were more stable than a single hull; at least I hoped so, especially if we were crossing seventeen hundred miles of ocean to Australia. With two kids under three years on board, Kristen and I were feeling cautious. Narayan and Bill had experience sailing, Pat said he had, but I was thinking it was, at best, limited. Kristen, Marie, Kendall, and I were landlubbers.

Kristen wrote in her journal, "Pat is very stubborn and argumentative, and he and Marie go at it at times, as well as he and everyone else. Tensions are great, so sailing for a long time [i.e., to Australia] has lost some of its luster. We haven't even sailed yet, so who can say what the future holds?"

After five weeks of restoration, the time arrived. For this preliminary run, the idea was to set out for the island of Kadavu, about a hundred miles south of Suva and along the southern edge of Fiji, and sail to small islands near a barrier reef full of fish and, finally, up the western coast to Lautoka, Fiji's second-largest city, where we could purchase materials to repair things that needed repairing. It would be an easy run, a few hundred nautical miles in all, in preparation for the longer voyage across the Pacific to Australia.

We hoisted anchor on Memorial Day 1977—two families plus Kendall, Narayan, and Bill. Coral reefs concealed by crashing waves make it dicey to ease the boat through a small outlet to the ocean, but aided by maps and a spotter stationed on the prow of the center pontoon, we found the opening and sailed through. The winds picked up, and the voyage became an exhilarating tropical adventure. We passed uninhabited islands fringed with coconut palm trees and empty sandy beaches then skirted an island with Fijians singing songs as they paddled small homemade canoes to another island.

The ocean looked the same as far as the eye could see, yet there was nothing familiar about it. There were no props; the stage was bare, just that menacing vastness, leaving you prey to fear and trembling before an indifferent god. Paradoxically, we were elated, one with the elements.

One glorious day, *Stella Maris* anchored off an unknown island, and Patrick and Narayan rowed ashore to give a gift (a bag of kava, or pepper root) to the chief and gained permission to anchor. After Pat returned with permission, we all rowed to the beach in the dinghy and lolled on the beach. As the afternoon passed, the wind picked up, and the seas started to pitch and roll. Everyone else decided to return to the *Stella Maris,* but Kristen, Zak, and I chose to wait it out on shore. Even though the seas were getting rough, it was still sunny. Why sit on the boat all afternoon? As we played on the beach, blissfully enjoying ourselves, the sky darkened, the seas and wind grew wilder, heaving immense waves onto the beach, and we realized we had a storm on our hands. As the *Stella Maris* was being tossed on the waves, we saw the dinghy ripped away from the trimaran, floating downwind. Kristen and I were able to run down the beach, grab it and pull it to shore, but there was no way the two of us could row the dinghy in these heavy seas, so all we could do was secure it on the beach.

We needed to find shelter for the night on the island. We three *kai valagi* (white foreigners) trudged into the bush, where we found the village. With our best sign language and pidgin English-Fijian-Samoan, we found the chief's hut where the chief was sitting on the floor with his wife, his child, and a few others preparing dinner. Zak, Kristen, and I, clad only in bathing suits and towels, communicated our dilemma, and the chief, with typical Fijian hospitality, invited to us to sit down.

One of the beauties of cross-cultural Pacific Island hospitality was that there was no need to converse. It was more than enough to be present, relax, and let the fire warm us.

After a toddler was bathed in a tub, her body rubbed with coconut oil, the meal arrived: *bimbo* bread (a bland white bread) smeared with peanut butter and served with slices of raw sea cucumber (a seven-inch-long sea slug), salted and limed. The cucumber felt and tasted like what I might charitably call raw pork fat, and I managed a few grimaces of pleasure before easing it to the side.

Dinner ended; the chief got up and motioned for us to follow. We went into a *fala*, a large thatched enclosure where mosquito nets were hung. He lay down on a mat in one net and motioned us to do the same in another. *How sweet, how strange, how surreal—the chief's going to sleep with us tonight*. Nope, a half hour later, he got up and left. Soon after, we heard the men drinking kava in another hut, singing, drumming, and talking for hours. But that night was a milestone for Zak, age two years, eight months: out of necessity, he had to sleep on a mat with no nighttime bottle and no diaper; in the morning, there was no pee on the mat. Such is how a small event becomes a big breakthrough. We were elated. Already free of daytime diapers, that night marked the end of nighttime diapers.

Dawn came early, a touch of green light before a red explosion. We repeatedly thanked the chief, especially as we were unable to offer him the traditional gift of kava, made our way to the beach, and with the seas now calm, rowed back to the *Stella Maris*.

A day or so later we anchored the *Stella Maris* off the island of Ono in the Kadavu island group, where we met a group of Fijians who were swimming on the beach. We walked around the edge of the island to their village, and this time, we had a package of kava for the chief. He brought out an enormous bowl and proceeded to strain the kava through a cloth sieve, squeezing and resqueezing it until it was the color, consistency, and taste of watery mud. The ritual went as follows: Everybody sat in a circle, and the headman dipped a small bowl into the larger one and drank, and we all said, "*Manuia.*" Then he dipped the bowl and passed it to the next one in the circle, and so the ceremony went, round and round, over and over. It was said that kava had a narcotic effect. At best, my gums got a little numb, and I had to pee a lot. It was a social occasion; guitars and ukuleles and cigarettes came out, and the hours amiably passed. The chief insisted that Zak, Kristen, and I spend the night in the village because the path back to the boat was a narrow one on the edge of a hill and, in the dark, it would be difficult to traverse, even with Zak on my shoulders.

We were taken to a house where we were given a beautifully decorated room with mosquito netting and two single beds separated by a cloth-covered table. After we put Zak to sleep, we joined a little "sock hop" dance party made up of Fijian teenagers. Ukuleles and a guitar were furiously strummed, and we all, with a degree of hilarity, jumped, bumped, and shook to the approving smiles of the teens. Kristen made it a point to dance with each of the boys.

Later, as we lay in our beds, I looked at the table between us and realized this was not a table, it was a coffin. The Fijian layaway plan at work.

When we returned to the *Stella Maris* the next day, it was apparent that a showdown was looming between Patrick and Kendall. Kendall was not comfortable on a boat. He was a logger, rooted in the lumberman way of life. He measured, cut, and dropped trees, solid things onto solid earth. The sea was wavy gravy. I never found out how or why he was seduced into buying a boat with Patrick. Pat and Kendall had begun to spar about who the "real" captain was. Evidently, Kendall had put up the money, or most of it, but had no experience sailing. Sailing may have seemed glamorous from afar, but it wasn't. It was cramped, hot, wet, and smelly with diesel fumes. And that was before we sailed! Pat had "found" the boat; he had some experience sailing and wasn't shy about insisting on his authority. After we sailed, it was clear to us that Patrick didn't always know what he was doing, but he was too bullheaded to admit it. But there was nothing we could do but wait for the storm to break out.

Nonetheless, on the seas, we were becoming a team—those who handled the tiller, those who handled the sails, some of us hauling, others sheeting, taking turns cleating and uncleating the sails as they were changed depending on the wind. We felt the speed of *Stella's* three pontoons surfing across the waters, yelling "Coming about!" (meaning, "Duck!") as the boom and sails luffed and swung then snapped to the other side. There were many hours of calm seas under a bright sun, the sails picking up just enough wind to float us across the waters toward a distant lagoon.

Then the fateful day arrived. The partnership imploded as the trimaran pitched and yawed as skies, once sunny, grew dark then blackened as rain and wind tore into the boat with a fury. *Stella Maris* humped and smacked through the surging waves. The rest of us watched as Captain Bligh and Captain Queeg went at each other in the lashing rain.

Kendall: I'm ordering you. Take this fucking boat into harbor!
Pat: Fuck you! You don't know shit!
Kendall: I own this fucking boat!
Pat: So do I!
Kendall: I paid for it. It's my boat. You'll do what I tell you!
Pat: I'm the fucking captain! Go fuck yourself! I'm in charge!
Kendall: You're out of here, Morgan, as soon as we get back to land!
Pat: It's my boat! I found it, I own it. It's mine!

Neither gave an inch. Kendall was too terrified to take the wheel. With Narayan's help at the tiller, the *Stella Maris* ploughed through the maelstrom, bouncing up and down, water pouring over the deck while the two of them stood there, insanely screaming into the gale. Bill and I were holding on to the mainsail ropes with all our might, the women and children were huddled in the cabin as pots and pans spilled and clattered across the galley floor. The boat slipped and slid through the seas like a slinky going down a stair, except we were surfing the down waves and then riding them back up, at times uncontrollably plunging through them.

If it weren't so scary, it would have been comical. When the boat tipped and one of its pontoons lifted off the ocean, water surged over the low-side hull, and we held on for dear life.

Eventually, the storm subsided, the seas calmed, and we were spent, soaked, and shaken. We had been tested and survived—perversely numb and exhilarated. No one talked about the blowup—nothing to say. We sailed back to Suva under sullen skies, reflecting the mood on board the *Stella Maris*. Marie made us tea, but the damage was done. There was to be no Fiji-to-Australia sail for us. Kendall was not a seafarer, and Patrick was too despotic a captain for the risk. Where your heart is, there is your treasure; ours was our family. We had fulfilled a dream: to live on a boat and sail it. We had had enough of cramped quarters and quarrels. Kristen and I had acquitted ourselves; our relationship was stronger than ever, and Zak had enjoyed the stability of being in one place for two months.

We had created the game of "around the world" with Zak. It was time to play elsewhere.

Pat told us to look up his brother, Chip, if we got to Alice Springs in the central desert area of Australia. He lived somewhere outside Alice on an Aboriginal settlement called Papunya.

Chapter Eighteen

We spent a few agreeable days in Sydney, our feet back on the ground, so to speak, since the best way to visit Sydney's neighborhoods was by ferryboat. We were amused by Aussie baby talk—"breaky" for breakfast, "coli" for cauliflower, and "beaky" for biscuit—and impressed by the beach-tanned, sculpted Aussies of both sexes striding godlike through sand and into surf, massively well-built people with rippling pecs, twisting their torsos as they propelled balls over nets or effortlessly flung their surfboards into the sea. After the confines of the *Stella Maris*, Australia was an Olympics of physical exuberance.

We headed to Alice Springs, the red heart of the country, to see if we could find Pat's brother, Chip Morgan, and his Papunya reserve. We liked the sounds of the few Aboriginal words we had picked up: Kristen was a *nungari*; Zak, a *jambajimba*, and I was *jungla*. The word *reserve* wasn't encouraging; I was to find out there were many parallels of exploitation and mass murder among the Aborigines and the American Indian. Like the Native Americans, the Aborigines were the "original" people of this huge continent

Alice Springs was in the middle of the Simpson Desert in the Northern Territory. Our first evening in the town, we pushed Zak in his stroller on a path that followed a dry riverbed. A group of well-inebriated Aborigines dressed in an amalgam of odd-fitting clothes and hats hailed us. One of them leaned into me. "Is that your jambajimba, mate? 'E's a cute lil' bugger. Not me, man. Look at me!" He pulled me closer to look into his bloodshot eyes. "Ya'r lookin' at what the white man did. We friended him, and he poisoned us." He waved his bottle at me. "Now look at me!" He wobbled unsteadily. "Dat's what the man done." He scratched circles in the sand with a stick and drew *x*'s, turned back to his companions, and continued drinking.

The next day, we were sitting in the Melanka Hotel, on edge and feeling foolish, realizing that we hadn't established a meeting time or place with Chip

Morgan. We had written saying we were coming but nothing specific. What the hell were we thinking? *Papunya* was a word—nothing more. How would Chip find us, or we, him?

At that moment, we spied a young blond-haired guy leaning up against the bar, quaffing a beer. He looked like a younger Pat Morgan. We eyeballed each other. Synchronicity! Chip just happened to be in town for some downtime. We breathed a sigh of gratitude. Chip took us to the Department of Aboriginal Affairs, where a welfare officer issued us a permit for the "authority to enter and be upon a reserve for the purposes of visiting friends." We each received a chest x-ray, and then, with permit in hand, we jumped in Chip's Toyota Land Cruiser and headed out to Papunya, ninety miles distant.

Chip was a far different soul than Patrick: younger, gentler, funnier, and far less authoritarian. He served as the reservation's director of the YMCA and was eager for us to see Papunya, although he warned us that if we had expectations, we had to lower them.

The desert was orangey-red sand, and the road that crunched our tires as we went over it appeared to exist merely by the fact that we were driving on it. We bypassed abandoned cars, scruffy bushes, and "humpies" (Aboriginal tents) with people sitting by their fires. Dusk was blotting the sky red and pink as we entered Papunya. The reserve was a collection of corrugated Quonset huts and individual cinderblock "houses" with metal awnings over them, all spattered with graffiti. Chip told us that these cinderblock structures, which were closer to the size of privies, were meant to be homes for the Aboriginals, but they refused to live in them, preferring to camp on the perimeter of the reservation, not in these sterile abominations.

The settlement resembled an urban slum plopped down on baked red dirt. In the far distance, you could see the MacDonnell mountain range, but here everything was tagged with graffiti and trashed, except for a row of neat trailer homes where the Australian administrators, including Chip, lived. A few men, dark and ancient looking, stood and gravely greeted Chip when we drove in. Nothing appeared to be happening. Children were raggedly dressed; their hair was sun-bleached orange or blond. Their eyes and noses ran heavily. That they were surviving in this sterile environment seemed remarkable, but then who were we to know, as privileged outsiders, exactly what they had and hadn't endured?

Chip put us in the spare bedroom and introduced us to his sixteen-year-old Aboriginal girlfriend, who, being extremely shy, sat with a blanket over her head for over two hours during our first meeting.

The government established Papunya ten years earlier when a segment of the Pitjantjatjara tribe came out of the desert because of a drought. To our eyes, it appeared to be a stunning failure. To their credit, Chip and his mates were idealistic activists challenging the Australian government's paternalistic treatment of the Aborigines.

To demonstrate his solidarity with the tribe, Chip had been initiated into the Papunya Pitjantjatjaras by a ritual called subincision. Chip and a dozen teenage boys were taken to a secret encampment where tribal elders, through exhausting ceremonies, deprived them of sleep for several days, primarily to disorient them. Initiates had a mentor who prepared them for the ceremony. The day of the subincision, the young males, in altered state and terrified, were held down on the ground. The subinciser came along with a sharp rock, held the penis, and incised its underside from tip to scrotum. Immediately thereafter, another man came and placed a burning coal onto the incision, cauterizing the wound. Chip said he fainted from the pain at that point. Yikes! I was glad I was eight days old when I had my bris.

The initiates returned to the tribe, where the women had prepared an elaborate feast. Chip's willingness to make this sacrifice might have been foolhardy, but it was also heroic. By taking on the initiation, Chip was bound to the tribe for life. They could call on him at any time for anything, and he would be obligated to respond.

One bright, cloudless morning, Chip told us that members of the tribe were returning from a "business" party, and he had to meet them at their chartered bus and drive them to their humpies, spread out in various locations miles from Papunya. Would I like to come along?

"What kind of business, Chip?"

"They enforced the law on another tribe that hadn't been observing the proper rituals. Those guys needed to be talked to."

It was an impressive-looking group of businessmen. Most wore loincloths, a few wore trousers, and all had red and black ochre smeared around their eyes and cheeks. They were armed with spears and rifles. Chip explained that no villager could look them in the eye as long as they were in their "business" paint. Chip and I were "invisible" outsiders, and other than serving as their ride to the humpies, we were of no account in their world.

As we set out through the bush, I stood on the bed of the Toyota Land Cruiser studying eleven armed men who could have suddenly shown up from ten thousand years ago, as if they had decided to take a break from a past aeon—nothing changed except for their rifles. They muttered harshly among themselves, and once in their humpy villages, anyone who saw them immediately looked away, or down, not daring to confront the men. I stood mutely, fascinated, listening to the eerie growling of the men in the truck, watching the bowed figures frozen on the ground.

Eventually, the last businessman was dropped off at his humpy. His entire possessions consisted of a cook pot, a blanket, and a transistor radio, reminding me of the description of the stage setting for Beckett's *Waiting for Godot*: A country road. A tree. Evening.

I got in front with Chip and Peg Nose, an older scarred man with, indeed, a peg through his nose and a rifle in his hand. We drove in silence until Peg Nose spotted a kangaroo. "Chase it," he commanded. Chip tore through the scrub brush after the animal, which zigzagged, trying to avoid us. Finally, Peg Nose signaled Chip to stop. We watched from the Toyota as Peg Nose quietly stalked the kangaroo, took aim, and shot it. Inside her pouch was a joey, a baby kangaroo. He extracted the squirming joey, heaved the dead kangaroo into the bed of the truck, and handed the baby to me. "Don't let go!"

We sped toward his village, the joey shivering with fright on my lap. As we drove up, a bunch of kids surrounded the vehicle; he took the joey and gave it to kids who were milling around.

Neat. A pet for the kids. But they had no interest in pets. This was lunch. The kids let the kangaroo loose, and when the joey took off, the kids followed as a pack, yelling and hurling rocks at it, definitely trying to kill it.

As we drove back to Papunya, Chip said, "You could live here a hundred years, and every day would surprise you. Aboriginals have lived here maybe thirty-five thousand years in a harsh-as-hell climate. They've song lines that connect them with their dreamtime, which connects them to their myths. They know every creature that lives on the land, flies in the air, swims in the river. It's sacred to them. Check out their woodbark paintings. All the dots and circles and spirals symbolically represent their stories and songs."

Papunya had a modest art gallery, and we did buy a few bark paintings. We were near the beginning of Australia's recognition of its Aborigine population, but in 1977, the posters we saw in Alice Springs featured an Aborigine in chains and the words "Where is justice, land, compensation, dignity? Discriminatory acts still exist."

After spending ten days at Papunya, we moved on, but at the Alice Springs airport, a funny thing happened. I couldn't leave. That is to say, I was literally rooted to the tarmac. I couldn't take a step toward the airplane although we were ready to board. "I'm not done, Kristen," I confessed. "Please. We have to see Uluru." I had romanticized the desert; it was magical to me. I was drawn to it as if magnetized. The landscape was emblematic of Carlos Castaneda's Don Juan stories, each stone formation or gully full of portent, mysterious with hidden life. I was sure I could live here, but Kristen's response was far different. To her, in the middle of the desert, under a full sky of stars, she felt small and insignificant.

"This is the only thing I'll ask of you. Let's fly to Ayers Rock, climb it, spend a day or two, and then we'll get on with our trip." Kristen agreed. We immediately flew to Uluru, known as the Earth Mother to the Aborigines.

Today you aren't allowed to climb it, but then, it was permitted. I climbed first, as the ascent was too steep and long to carry Zak, and then Kristen climbed, while Zak and I looked at the rock paintings at Uluru's base.

In a way, the Red Center of Australia was like the ocean: vast, brooding, seemingly all of a piece but, at every turn, different. The desert made Kristen feel small; I felt expanded. This was a landscape that produced visions. It reminded me of Old Testament prophets and tribes. I sensed that this landscape promised me something. What or where or when this something might show up I didn't know, but the land had spoken, and I was glad of it.

Chapter Nineteen

We made plane reservations for Bali. Perhaps it was hearing Rodgers and Hammerstein's lushly romantic ballad from *South Pacific*, "Bali Ha'i," at the Geary Theater in San Francisco when I was a child that imprinted a longing to visit this island, for, after all, it is a song of longing. Certainly, Bali was an object of desire, the one place everyone we had shared our travel plans with had raved about. It was known for ceremonies, ritual, dance, and drama and that her population integrated all of it seamlessly into daily life. And the beaches were great.

We arrived in Bali with no destination and no reservations, waiting for Ms. Synchronicity to show up. We stood uncertainly at the airport amid a bustle of Australian tourists and motorbikes as evening descended. And then, as if ordained, a young Balinese man approached. "Need a place to stay?" He handed us his card: Pendawa Inn. "I'll take you." His smile was convincing.

Ketut assured us in decent English that we were going to love where he was going to take us. He put Kristen and Zak and our bags in the back of a *bemo*, a shared public pickup truck with a bench nailed to each side of the bed. It was understood that you would be packed and stacked. We soon observed that the Balinese made packing and stacking an art form, such as the intricately arranged multicolored towers of fruit, rice cakes, and flowers placed on pedestals on top of women's heads as the women paraded to temples for their ritual offerings.

I hopped on the back of Ketut's motorbike, and off we went, following the bemo. We wound our way through palm trees until we arrived at Pendawa Loesman (a *loesman* resembles a small family-run motel.) It nestled in a palm grove, minutes from Kuta Beach, known as the hippie beach to the initiated. Each of the three sides of the courtyard contained two units, each composed of a main room with tiled red floors and a separate gravity-fed shower/bathroom.

All the buildings were painted yellow. Our room had a small bed for Kristen and myself, and we arranged a bed on the floor for Zak. Our toilet consisted of a cement hole in the floor, with a pull cord that brought water to wash it through. We got good at squatting but were reminded by Kristen to look for scorpions, not always easy to spot, crawling on the damp dark cement floor. The rooms cost two dollars a night, and this included a breakfast of toast, bananas, and cocoa for all of us. This price meant we could take trips and keep our room while we traveled. We stayed at this tropical hideaway for two months.

In the dense heat of Bali, I realized how much I liked wearing skirts. I was comfortable with the lavalava in Samoa, mostly wore a bathing suit in Fiji, but in Bali, I wore a sulu like all the rest of the men. This did not make the men less masculine but gave the men (and women) a supple, graceful quality. Bottom line, the simple, wraparound sulu kept you far cooler than trousers or shorts.

Pendawa's central courtyard was an oasis of palm trees, flowering plants, and a monkey chained to a tree. Zak played on the porch, in the sand and the yard, and watched the chained monkey, although we had to be careful. This male monkey was dangerous, especially to women. We were told he would become frenzied and attack a woman if she was "on her moon" (menstruating). One day he was loose and a pack of dogs entered the compound, chasing him. We all sat on the porch cracking up as the monkey made, well, monkeys of the poor dogs, tormenting these animals, who hadn't a prayer of keeping up with his comical antics. He bounced, leapt into trees, swung through them, and came down next to an unsuspecting and totally frustrated dog, chattering at him before gleefully dancing on.

Three teenage boys managed Pendawa: Nyoman, Wayan, and Made, cousins of Ketut. Everyone in Bali had one of those four names: they meant one, two, three, four, and if you were a fifth child, you were one again. Simple. The Balinese had formal names, but everyone was referred to by number.

It turned out Ketut had brought us into a quasi-dope lair. How did he know, or was it obvious? The Aussies across the way smuggled Thai weed to Australia inside surfboards. Buddha stick it was called, and the surfers preferred to smoke it à la bong, which, when I smoked with them, I found overpowering. "Come on, mate, smoke the bowl! One inhalation. You can do it!" But I couldn't and, after a toke or two, would fade into the background, just like those Aborigine blokes in Alice Springs: blotto. The teenagers' mother, who came to water the plants and perform prayers each morning, notified the boys when a government inspection was planned so the dopers could hide their stash.

We soaked in a lot of new impressions, which we hoped wouldn't be overwhelming to Zak. Kristen and I did our best to keep routines, eating and napping at more or less regular hours. When those rules were stretched, we surfed through them, much helped by Kristen's awareness of his moods and her ability to shift them.

There always seemed to be rehearsals of dance dramas going on; you could hear the music floating over the rice paddies. We'd *jalan-jalan* (walk) over to hang out, and as we walked, the Balinese invariably raised their eyebrows and wiggled them in greeting. Eye-to-eye contact! Nowhere in the world that we had visited or were to visit had the people looked us directly in the eye like the Balinese did, not only acknowledging but also welcoming us. This was our experience in 1977.

We wondered how Zak was absorbing the many dance dramas we attended that depicted tales from the Hindu epics, the Mahabharata and the Ramayana, and featured intense portrayals of kings, ministers, gods and goddesses, and demons and monsters. The fierce drumming and hypnotic gamelans swept us into a Balinese fun house, an ecstasy of colorful figures dancing, posing, and posturing, each dancer's fingers and feet indicating a specific gestural meaning. We didn't grasp the meanings, but it didn't matter.

We traveled into Denpasar, the capital, to watch the Wayang Kulit, the shadow puppet plays. They were performed at night behind a sheet so that the drama was heightened by the puppets' shadows dancing across the stage while illuminated by flickering torches. A single puppet master masterfully narrated the tale, employing many puppets and different voices, salting his narrative with song and topical humor as a flutist played eerie melodies in the background.

Zak loved playing with the six colorfully painted masks we bought in Ubud. On occasion, clusters of kids, relentlessly curious, would gather around our little boy. Once Zak discovered he could defend himself by wearing one of the powerful character masks, he had the situation licked. He'd put on a mask, and the mob of kids would jump back, laughing, cautious of who exactly this imp was.

If we were traveling on a given day, we were on the road by eight; any later and the day would be too hot. Once, as we crammed into a bemo, we counted fifteen Balinese, two goats, one pig, and multiple woven baskets bulging with vegetables and squawking chickens. Each passenger squeezed gracefully in, while a brace of other travelers hung off the back. Everyone smiled, eyebrows dancing in gentle greeting.

Whatever we were doing, by noon we needed a food break and, not too long after, a nap somewhere. Then we'd be back to base by dinner. Plenty could be accomplished or seen in those hours without having a miserable kid on our hands.

One morning we were waiting for a bus when a group of local village children surrounded us. Fifty kids pressed around Zak, laughing and teasing in their language. "Be cool, Zak. Nothing we can do here," we said as the children came for a close look at our little blue-eyed white boy. Zak stayed remarkably cool. I growled, the kids shrank back; I smiled, they advanced. Kristen and I improvised with much gesture and eye movement. "Hello, little kiddies of beautiful Bali, greetings from America. *Bienvenue. Guten Morgen. Ciao.* We bring goodwill and seasonal greetings sprinkled with love and much respect for your great country, and please don't push, prod, poke, or molest the baby." (Growl!) "Much appreciated, *terima kasih.*" (Thank you very much.) As an aside, "Zak, you're doing a good job. Stay with it, buddy." We figured as long as we kept talking, we kept the respect flowing. It worked.

There was only one time when goodwill evaporated. We visited Tenganan, an ancient traditional village, more a historical treasure than a living community. We walked a mile—jalan-jalan—from where the bus dropped us, passing a school on the way to the village. Few people were visiting. We wandered the decaying thatched houses overgrown with moss and vines surrounding ceremonial grounds, treaded lightly, and began walking back to the bus.

As we passed the school, well beyond the boundaries of the village, the schoolchildren and teachers gathered on the veranda to watch us. As we walked, I began to feel little pebbles hitting us. Soon, bigger rocks starting coming our way. Since we were still in easy range of the missile throwers, I had to do something. Damned if I was going to run. Assuming my best John Wayne stance and a voice I had never aspired to and wasn't sure was there, I turned on our firing squad while telling Kristen and Zak to keep walking. The teachers stood there watching their pupils throw the rocks.

"Listen, you blankety-blank son of blanks! [I knew they wouldn't understand.] Stop what you are doing now! Desist! Now!" All this bellowed out in a roar, in as loud and threatening a voice as John Wayne could muster. They stopped. I turned, and we quickly walked to the bus.

Why were the kids doing this? We were not the first tourists they had seen. Were they just having fun? It perplexed us because it was the only time we experienced violence in any shape or form. The Balinese ritualized their violence; they performed it with dance and puppetry. But not this time. We were not dressed improperly, for we had seen this sign earlier in our travels:

attention: you must be well dressed on the road.
violating this rule, you will be seized and confiscated.

police

A day later, we went to check out the north side of the island. We were staying in Lovina, a small fishing village, lying in bed reading, when an earthquake struck. The bed shook for half a minute, and it took me half that time to realize that Kristen wasn't rocking the bed. The owner of the loesman hurried in and told us to leave our room, even though it was made of bamboo thatch. We later heard that on the neighboring island of Sumbawa, the tide rushed out as the earthquake occurred. Villagers ventured out, as there were tons of fish floundering in the suddenly emptied sea basin. Suddenly, thirty-foot waves poured in and wiped out the villagers and village.

Gede, the young manager of the loesman, invited me to an unadvertised nighttime dance taking place in a forest. We jalan-jalaned down a moonlit road, sounds of Indonesian pop music emanating through the trees, until we arrived at a clearing illuminated by torches. *Warings* (little food stalls) dotted the periphery, offering sweets, *sates* (meats), and *nasi* (rice). In the next inner circle, there was gambling: lots of blankets on the ground with dice numbers painted on them, roulette wheels, and even cloths with painted animals for children to roll their dice and bet. In the center of the clearing was the dance ground.

Three Legong girls, prepubescent lovelies, were being made up in a small bamboo pen around which everybody crowded, watching as the mothers massaged white pancake onto the girls' arms, bodies, and faces. Finally, the gamelan orchestra began to play.

The crowd became an audience and drew close. I never got over how tuned in and comfortable the Balinese were with each other. Wherever we went, Balinese liked to be touching, arms draped around one another. Behind us, the stall merchants hawked food and soda, and the gamblers rolled dice. Ignoring the commerce, the youthful girls flirtatiously danced, their eyes rolling back and forth, expressing various emotions as the tinkling sounds and rhythms of the gamelan disappeared into the forest.

When the dance had concluded, the girls drew names out of a hat, and one man at a time tied a green scarf around his waist and danced with a Legong girl. Audience participation was new to me: each man had his own style; each played to the audience, strutting, flirting, swirling around the girl.

Hours later, the crowd silently trooped out of the forest to their homes. Kristen had stayed at "home" with Zak, as it was too late a night for him. In all our travels, due to the need to care for Zak, she regretted missing this event most of all.

We loved how the Balinese wove together their ceremonies and their society. It seemed every week of the year, the Balinese had a holy day to observe, each of these days tied into a complex calendar based on a caste system, a priestly system, a lunar system, a rice-planting-and-paddy system, a water-distribution system, and a gambling system. Games of chance were played by young and old alike outside the temples on ceremony days, and cockfights were packed by hollering bettors furiously passing money back and forth while the squatting cock handlers calmly stroked their cocks before releasing them to fight, hoping their bird, razor attached to its claw, would kill the other.

We noticed how the Balinese used everything in their buildings. Shells and coral from the beach and sea were gathered, ground up, fired, and made into mortar. Coconut palm leaves served as plates, containers, building materials, string, and hats. There was no end to Balinese inventiveness. On the holidays, Balinese made intricate woven leaf ladders hung on poles over the street; they nailed chickens, spread-eagled and plucked, to their doorways. Towers of food and flowers were brought to the temples as offerings, blessed, and later returned to their home to be eaten.

Even the madness of the French tourist invasion in August didn't disturb the Balinese. Suddenly, one morning, it seemed one hundred thousand Frenchies were roaming Kuta Beach. Strutting around in their bikinis or less, they quickly replaced the ugly American. They didn't have a lot of time, and they wanted what they wanted. Now! Some showed up at the temple festivals walking around in their underwear or something like it, ignoring any signage or respect for culture, while the Balinese were elaborately dressed.

Still, there were plenty of elderly Balinese ladies who wandered about bare-breasted, unconcerned, spitting out red blobs of betel nut. Betel supposedly numbed your gums. It certainly numbed men and women's teeth to the point of extinction so that their smiles revealed a gaping red maw where teeth had once resided. I never tried it, preferring the Buddha stick. My appetite was also whetted by rumors of a magic mushroom. The adventure of travel was enough for Kristen, but I couldn't resist my curiosity.

A restaurant in Kuta called Juniors offered omelets or soup made with blue meanies: little blue psychedelic mushrooms that grew in pastures nurtured by cow patties. The mushrooms floated appealingly in the soup and were just as good in an omelet. They weren't promoted; they were just one among many items on the menu, but their effect was like a full-blown LSD trip.

My Pendawa neighbor, John, and I tripped together three times. The first time, we lay on the beach, soaring through the atmosphere, a blissfully sensual experience. During our second blue-meanie session, we strolled down the beach and lay on a veranda where our energies attracted a kid whom we couldn't shake. He glued himself to us, and rather than be bummed out by his persistence, we took it as a lesson in remaining conscious and grounded while tripping. We chatted with him, we nodded off into psychedelic realms, and he eventually disappeared. Returning to Pendawa, I found Zak was playing in the dirt just like Pendawa's chained monkey. He had been imitating the monkey for weeks, but I hadn't noticed it.

I didn't like this aspect of his animal nature—raw, unformed. I scooped him up and dragged him into the shower where we both sat as the water poured over us. It wasn't that I objected to him playing in the dirt; where else was he going to play? Had I projected my own fear of my coarsening behavior on Zak? Was he a mirror of me? Didn't matter. He and I were under that shower for twenty minutes, he struggling, me subduing him. We emerged very clean.

It wasn't until my third blue-meanie session that I saw the handwriting on the wall. The Aussie dope dealer surfers were smoking and drinking beers on the veranda at Pendawa with their lady friend from Sumatra, whom I saw as an exotic, gorgeous Mata Hari, no doubt the queen of the outlaws. As I peered through my window, the mushroom madly mashing my brain, listening to what I thought to be evil laughter from across the way, the queen began to morph into a dragon lady. This was no longer magical Bali but something dark, scary, and dangerous. Someone was plotting something, and I was threatened. Dylan's lyric, transformed, bounced through my head: *"Something must be happening, and you don't know what it is, do you, Mr. Tom?"* I was streaking through paranoia, and it came to me in a flash, an unambiguous edict from God: *Time to go home. Party over!*

Although still feeling the effects of the blue meanie, I shared my insight with Kristen; she too was ready to return home. We had envisioned a year of travel, but after eight months, we were ready to resume our life in the States and make a stable environment and friendships for Zak.

We had been in Bali for two months. Much of our joy was due to our two-year-old, through whom we encountered in a unique way the sweetest and most hospitable people in one of the most paradisiacal places we'd ever been or hoped to be. It was in Bali that Kristen decided to have her IUD removed. Asked why by the bemused doctor in the clinic in Denpasar, Kristen replied that the beauty of the people and families in Bali inspired her and that she knew we wanted more than one child, although probably not the four to eight children typical of a Balinese family. She told me, and I agreed. We were ready for more family.

Within days, we said our farewells to the friends we had made at Pendawa, including the Aussie dopers and their queen who were unthreatening in the light of day. Bali had been everything we hoped for, and more.

We flew, via Singapore, to Sri Lanka, intending to find some spiritual wisdom with Guru Bawa, the Sufi mystic, in his Colombo ashram.

Chapter Twenty

Sri Lanka cranked at a far higher voltage than we had experienced elsewhere. Based on the pushing, shoving, crowding, and frantic pace that we saw in Colombo, we realized we did not have the physical, emotional, or mental resources to handle traveling to India as we had planned. We would meet Bawa and then make our way to Europe. America seemed farther away than ever. But Bawa was not in residence in Colombo, so after three days of visiting Buddhist sites with a hired car and driver, we took the train to Jaffna, a Tamil city at the northern end of the island.

The family Bissinger had been on the road since February. It was now the end of September 1977. We were well traveled and desiring spiritual food. The last blue-meanie trip had really brought that home to me.

The Serendib Sufi Center was a handsome two-story square building sitting on a nondescript dusty block in a poor area of Jaffna. A family of four ate and slept on an open concrete landing across the street. The only potable water for the neighborhood was fetched from a communal well two blocks distant. Smells of cooked food, manure, and smoke permeated the air.

We announced ourselves and asked if we could stay with Bawa. A Sri Lankan lady in a sari sweetly looked at Zak, now almost three years old, chucked him under the chin, and ushered us in.

Kristen and I had met Guru Bawa while he was visiting the Philadelphia Sufi Center, and we were both deeply impressed by him and his teachings. Kristen vividly remembered that until she met Bawa, she felt she had expressed and experienced unselfish love, but on one of her visits, she had a profound realization that Bawa expressed a love for all far beyond what she had ever witnessed, free of expectations of reciprocity, acknowledgment, or kindness in return.

We were finally summoned to greet Bawa, who was wearing a white sarong and a white T-shirt. A knit cap covered his smoothly shaved head. His skin was silky smooth, his oval face lit by piercing black eyes and a full white beard. He didn't know us, and we weren't his devotees or acolytes, merely travelers who thirsted for his wisdom, his blessing, his love—any of it, if he would have us. As the translator translated, he welcomed us to his ashram. We were served tea and asked to recount what led us to him. His eyes sparkling, Bawa enjoyed hearing our tale.

There were thirteen Americans and a good number of Sri Lankans, coming and going, who lived in the two-story building. The Americans occupied the airy, light-filled second floor where Bawa had his room. The Sri Lankans were on the first floor, gathered in several rooms adjoining a kitchen and the showers. Because Kristen and I were married, we were allowed to lie on mats together with Zak; otherwise, men and women slept separately.

The next morning, I saw Bawa listening intently to another man who was reading something. Undoubtedly, I thought, they were perusing the Koran. On the contrary, it was a newspaper; I was told. "Bawa likes to know what's going on."

As we sat with him the first morning, Bawa told me, "Beards are for the older man." He suggested I shave, which gave me an opportunity to explore the central part of town to find a barber. Having dispensed with razors, I became a faithful customer of the local barber, enjoying an hour or so on my own, wandering the markets each morning before my shave, which cost but a few cents. Bawa clearly stated that with the current political unrest, women were not to go out of the ashram. Kristen and Zak were happy to stay within its peaceful atmosphere.

Daily, we got up at 4:00 am to pray and recite dhikr (the remembrance and praising of God [Allah] in verse). After breakfast of tea and cakes, followed by whatever chores had to be done, we would troop into Bawa's room. He might sing for an hour or ask for questions. His songs were all recorded and translated as he sang.

Opening the eye to wisdom, faith, determination, and certitude were the keys to finding God. Based on what I was hearing from Bawa, my eye was not opening. My dreams indicated as much. On the first night at the ashram, I dreamt of two naked chicks frolicking in the water. Second night: one slice of bacon and one bottle of beer in an icebox. Third night: discussion of sneaking in some Balinese grass. Fourth night: craziness of Kristen dashing about, abandonment of Zachary, love of building a house on the water ruined by sitting with tedious accountants! My mind, or at least my dreams, was a mess.

The ashram was self-contained. When not eating (lots of rice, veggies, and dal), resting, or reading, we were in Bawa's room for his discourses. (We never saw Bawa eat or drink the entire three weeks we stayed at the ashram, although he often cooked food for everyone else and was always in full view.) In Philadelphia, the room had always been jam-packed, forty to eighty people. Here, we had the gift of literally sitting at his feet.

He spoke of us seekers as his "funny family." One American woman he called Lone Ranger, since she swaddled herself in robes and wore a scarf over her nose and mouth like a bandit, in sweltering heat.

When I suggested to him that it was difficult for us householders—that is, those who practiced a regular family life—to follow the disciplined path he was suggesting, he said, "What about me, Tambi?" (Little brother.) "Look at the family I have to maintain! Play your trumpet." What Bawa was asking, and from which he derived never-ending amusement, was that I put my lips together and puff my cheeks and blow an imaginary trumpet, riffing on songs like "Body and Soul" or "When the Saints Go Marching In." I was happy to oblige; it was the one thing I could do well.

Then he would sing. Perhaps the following discourse was directed to me. If you had ears to hear, you could take what landed for you. Bawa's voice was high, reedy, his songs sinuous vocalizations. One could imagine Hafiz or Kabir, the great Sufi poets, chanting similar love songs. Bawa's songs cautioned about the perils and pitfalls that awaited those who wouldn't awaken to the call of God. Islam, after all, meant surrender. Here is a taste of his song:

> This world is a stage.
> Here there is singing and dancing; here there are gatherings—
> Here there are games. But tomorrow, all these will desert us.
> Oh, no one has understood that this world is a stage.
> Who will realize what will happen tomorrow?
> Without understanding this, without understanding
> The One Treasure that has no end, that has no adulteration, that
> cannot be seen, that is a most Mysterious Treasure,
> Without opening their hearts completely,
> And observing through that open heart,
> These men have been born as actors in the world.
> This is the world where they are dancing; this is a stage—this is a stage.
> They do not understand that Treasure which is intimately mixed
> with Love.
> They do not realize or understand their birth or their death or the
> two sections belonging to birth and death.
> They do not analyze and see
> What these two different things are.

The song hit close to home. Wasn't I was an actor on a stage, wanting to look good, looking for approval, attentive enough but holding to my ego? I had too much going on in my head to surrender; I didn't really know if I could surrender, actually give up control, yield to the sheikh (i.e., Bawa). The path to self-realization or God realization appeared endless and exhausting to follow. Let me surrender to Bawa's musicality and love, I reasoned. To grasp an iota of that love would be something.

Kristen and I had talked about having another child. She asked Bawa what guidance he would give for conceiving a child. "First, wash and pray for the child to be dedicated to God. Second, prepare a bed that is not your sleeping bed. That is where you will conceive the child. Then wash and pray and sleep in your regular sleeping bed."

He spoke to us of Zak, who was the only child in the ashram. "Keep Zak in a place with good conduct and good love, and then he'll reflect these qualities of good speech, good action, and good wisdom. Little children have empty cameras. They take the original pictures with empty cameras and new film reels. It's easy to take pictures, and he takes in everything. As he gets older, the pictures won't make as strong an impression on him. We have to show him really good actions, behaviors of truth, wisdom, and patience. Do not expose him to animals because he will take on an animal nature." *Oi vey, the monkey in Bali!* "Expose him to the highest expression of human nature. And then he'll take those pictures. In a child, the magnet is still working."

Bawa told us this about Zak's namesake. Zachariah came from the family of Abraham. Zachariah's wife and Mary were cousins. Zachariah meant "witnessing the word of the truth of God" or "remembered of God." Zachariah's son, given by God, was John the Baptist.

We celebrated Zak's third birthday at the center. We had been there three weeks, absorbed a lot of teaching, and had been embraced warmly by Bawa and the ashram. It was early morning when we said our good-byes on the veranda; I kissed Bawa's hand and looked in his eyes and wham! I became faint, dizzy, and had to look away. I couldn't handle the energy coming from his eyes. Call it ego, fear—whatever was blocking the light—I could only absorb so much. I carried that realization into the taxi, and we took the train back to Colombo.

The next day as we awaited our flight in the Colombo airport, the lights went out, and the airport was plunged into darkness for ten minutes. It seemed an apt metaphor for the country—brilliant light enveloped by darkness, deep poverty and an aura of animalistic spirits coupled with the diamond-like wisdom of Bawa and the Buddha.

Zurich was a culture shock. It was October—cold, an onslaught of new impressions and fast tempi. Wealth gleamed from storefront windows—piles of gold and diamonds, electronics, furs, pastries, and automobiles. We had been lying on mats, tiny bunks, shitting in a hole in the floor, and now, we were in the heart of the empire. We bought a little sweater for Zak and some warm clothes for ourselves, enjoyed elegant pastries and hot cocoa in big white cups, and then rented a car and drove out of the city, across Switzerland to France, where we stopped en route to Paris to visit the Jacobs, two artists who had formerly lived on South Street and now lived in the country near Tours.

Berenice and Harold gave us a chance to decompress and somewhat reacquire a Western appetite, although our digestive systems were hardly prepared for what awaited us. Harold and Berenice had just completed helping their neighbor bring in the grape harvest. We were graciously included in an elaborate seven-course celebratory meal with multiple wines, champagnes, pâtés, and cheeses preceding and following many main courses. The feast was emblematic of our nine-month excursion around the world: a cornucopia of sights, sounds, and tastes, filling us to the brim and beyond.

We dropped the car off in Paris, and we took a few days so that I could show Kristen and Zak my Paris haunts. We paid a visit to Mitzo, now married, went to the cinema, and saw the first *Star Wars*. It was enough. We had spent the good part of a year exploring the fun houses of other people—the more unlike American houses, the better.

Our last night, as we pushed Zak in his stroller over the Pont Neuf, one of Paris's fabled bridges, I looked down to the Seine flowing past and saw my life being carried in the current. Sixteen years earlier, I was a raw youth recently graduated from Stanford, living in the City of Lights, frequently walking over this very bridge. I had witnessed some mind-blowing theater, whose images were still fresh in my mind and which had spurred on my career in New York. Many, many fun houses had been constructed and deconstructed in the sixties, and I had been privileged to be a player and witness.

As the water swirled under the bridge and the tourist boats slid by with their sparkly lights, I thought of Philadelphia's South Street days and nights. What a great party that had been. The times had been revolutionary. We saved and rebuilt a city neighborhood and introduced new fashions, new cuisine, and new ways of being with each other. Who knew how long any of it would last? All would flow away at some point, but we had had a great party, and wasn't the point of a great party to bring people together who might not know each other and break down the barriers of suspicion and fear with the possibilities of trust, fun, and love?

And hadn't I married someone who was truly a mate, who was walking next to me at this very moment, whose eyes were as fresh and open as the first time we met, and with whom we had had Zak and very probably would have another child? We had been around the world and seen places most people would never see. At that moment, ready as we were to return to Pennsylvania, we were filled to satisfaction; our cup had run over, spilling our memories into the Seine.

I shivered.

After nine months, we were going home.

Acknowledgments

I am deeply indebted to my editor, Walter Bode, for his skill and gentle counsel in helping make the book a joyful education and to Bill Reese for suggesting Walt to me. Many thanks to Peggy Hartzell for her layouts and collages of the photographic sections as well as providing some of the photos of South Street life. I am grateful for the use of photographs taken by Harvey Finkle, Suzanne Sennhenn, Bill Wingell, Ron Rozewski, and Anne Jackson (for her facilitation with some of the images).

I am also grateful to my sister, Peggy Pressman, and my brother, Paul Bissinger Jr., who gave me early encouragement. Mick Stern, Philip Beitchman, and Patricia Adler were readers who helped me with their perceptive observations. Other readers who supported me with their suggestions were Chris Lindstrom, Don Consul, Elon Gilbert, and George Keegan. Christiana Acree lovingly urged me to "tell it like it was" no matter where it might lead me.

The New York and South Street days were filled with many friends whom I have not mentioned but who made my life richer for their having been part of it.

Most of all, I thank and give my love to my wife, Kristen, without whose help I could not have written this book. She has been on and by my side for almost forty years. I am deeply grateful for her and our two children, Zachary and Esther, and their families.